Books by Sheldon Marcus

CONFLICTS IN URBAN EDUCATION
(with Harry N. Rivlin)

URBAN EDUCATION: CRISIS OR OPPORTUNITY
(with Philip D. Vairo)

FATHER COUGHLIN

FATHER
COUGHLIN

FATHER COUGHLIN

The Tumultuous Life
of the Priest of the Little Flower

Sheldon Marcus

with illustrations

LITTLE, BROWN AND COMPANY — BOSTON — TORONTO

Library of Congress Cataloging in Publication Data

Marcus, Sheldon.
    Father Coughlin; the tumultuous life of the priest
of the Little Flower.

    Bibliography: p.
    1. Coughlin, Charles Edward, 1891–   I. Title.
BX4705.C7795M37   271'.79 [B]   73-186969
ISBN 0-316-54596-1

Published simultaneously in Canada
by Little, Brown & Company (Canada) Limited
PRINTED IN THE UNITED STATES OF AMERICA

To Joyce
my wife, my companion, my love —
for bringing meaning to my life.

Father Coughlin was a man ahead of his time . . .
the giant of his generation among the committed
priests of America.

> Richard Cardinal Cushing of the Massachusetts
> Archdiocese, June 8, 1966

He was unscrupulous . . . rarely told the truth . . .
completely without conscience . . . amoral. His only
interest in people was in using them.

> Morris Steinberg, president of the corporation
> which initially printed *Social Justice*, May 4, 1970

. . . I was anti-Semitic too, but never like that (like
Coughlin).

> Philip C. Johnson, architect, October 21, 1970

There was always a great fear among us about
Father Coughlin because of his tremendous following . . . we were afraid.

> Philip Slomovitz, editor, *The Detroit Jewish
> News*, April 17, 1970

He was the greatest man who ever lived.

> John Constable, employee at the Shrine of the
> Little Flower Church for over thirty-five years,
> April 15, 1970

Contents

Illustrations

Acknowledgments

This study was greatly facilitated by the fact that I was able to secure the cooperation of Father Coughlin, who for the first time since 1933 agreed to assist a biographer. I was also fortunate in gaining access to such primary source materials as personal letters of Father Coughlin and financial data related to his activities, little of which had been utilized by earlier biographers.

In addition to Father Coughlin, I owe many thanks to individuals who, familiar with events discussed in this study, agreed to assist me in the gathering of information. Especially helpful were John L. Spivak, who provided me with leads for finding primary source material; Brother Andrew T. Codyre of Manhattan College, who placed a complete set of *Social Justice* at my disposal; and Morton Kass, who gave me access to Anti-Defamation League material on Father Coughlin. I owe a sincere thanks to Harry Sions, my editor, for the hours he devoted to this manuscript. I am indebted to Fordham University for its assistance in the financing of my research. I am also indebted to Dr. Simeon Guterman and Dr. Solomon Simonson of Yeshiva University, Dr. Joseph F. X. McCarthy of Fordham University, and Dr. Philip D. Vairo of the University of Tennessee for their suggestions and editorial comments.

My wife, Joyce, and my two children, Beth and Jonathan, displayed immense patience and forbearance while I devoted the better part of five years to this study. My wife played an additional role in the completion of this manuscript because without her encouragement, suggestions, editing and typing assistance, this book would not have been possible. She was also of great help in assisting me in my research in Detroit in 1970 and 1971 and in Toronto in 1971.

Because of the controversies that have occurred over the years as to what Father Coughlin said or did not say, much documentation has been included in the chapter notes. I ask the reader's indulgence for it.

S. M.

FATHER
COUGHLIN

1

Introduction

It was a sad, low period in history. All over the world it appeared that democracy was buckling under its problems and challenges. In Europe many people, embittered either by the frustrations of World War I or by the conditions wrought by depression, looked to dictatorship to alleviate their discontent.

The rulers of Nazi Germany and Fascist Italy successfully utilized propaganda to convince their citizenry of their racial and cultural superiority. The Soviet Union was torn by the savage political purges ordered by Josef Stalin. The failure of the League of Nations to stop Japan's aggression in Manchuria and Italy's rape of Ethiopia coincided with the reemergence of nationalistic forces throughout a world dominated by the clash of fascist and communist ideologies.

The United States reacted to these developments by seeking safety behind an isolationist wall, which it believed would prevent communism from reaching American shores, while punishing its former World War I allies for welshing on their war debts payments. Americans were disillusioned by the exposures of the Nye committee investigations in the United States Senate, which made it appear that America's entry into World War I was dictated purely by the profit motives of munitions makers. It seemed to many that this capitalistic greed had created the conditions which had led to the Great Depression of the 1930s.

3

Millions of Americans no longer believed that tomorrow would be a better day. There were too many yesterdays of hardships, too many promises unfulfilled. Jobs were scarce and hundreds of mortgages were being foreclosed daily, blotting out generations of hard work and throwing thousands of families out on the street. Many Americans were living in primitive conditions, constantly haunted by starvation. *Iron Age* reported that steel plants were operating at 12 percent of capacity. Industrial construction had dropped from $949 million in 1929 to $74 million in 1932. On October 28, 1929, the industrial average of the stock market, as published by the *New York Times*, stood at 350. On July 8, 1932, it was at 58. In the same period, retail trade had declined by one-third.[1]

And the voices of prophets were heard in the land. In the United States the extremist groups flourishing on the Right and Left were similar to the Know-Nothing and Nativist movements of the 1840s and 1850s and to the populism of Thomas Watson at the turn of the twentieth century. They represented nothing new on the American scene. What was different, however, was that by the late 1930s the most important and influential figure on the extreme Right was a charismatic Catholic priest, Father Charles E. Coughlin, whose Sunday afternoon broadcasts gave sustenance and inspiration to millions of listeners. Just how many millions is impossible to determine, but estimates range up to thirty million each week.[2] With this vast radio audience as his foundation, Father Coughlin became one of the most powerful figures in America. His influence was one of the outgrowths of the Great Depression which by 1932 had resulted in more than thirteen million workers being unemployed in the United States. This was a time when men who offered new visions of hope and salvation were heard and accepted by the populace. One of these men, Franklin D. Roosevelt, was elected President of the United States on his promise to reestablish a viable political, economic and social structure. Father Coughlin, too, promised hope and salvation.

Wernersville, Pennsylvania, was a small mining town eight miles from Reading. By 1932, most of the mines were closed and the miners unemployed. Sunday afternoon, however, was a time when they could forget their troubles. For this was Father Coughlin time. After lunch, having no radios of their own, entire families, Protestants and Catholics alike, dressed in their Sunday best, would congregate outside the local Ford auto agency to hear Father Coughlin on the agency radio.

At the seminary outside Wernersville, the novice priests hurried through their morning prayers and chores and set out on the seven mile walk to mingle with the townspeople outside the auto agency and hear Father Coughlin. One of the young seminarians who made that regular Sunday trek was Father Edward Clark, who would one day be chaplain of Fordham University. The Coughlin broadcasts are as vivid to him now as they were almost forty years ago; the magnetic voice with its Irish brogue, the simple, clear message it delivered, and the exhilarating effect on the listeners who had finally found someone who cared about them.

The large crowd became silent as three o'clock approached. The people seemed almost to stop breathing. Even the children were quiet. Everyone looked at the loudspeaker. It was time. The voice was heard — and in his mind's eye each weary listener saw his advocate standing ten feet tall and carrying the burden of truth and justice on his shoulders.[3]

Manny Makufka was a simple Jewish immigrant who came to this country from Poland to search for a better life. He did not find gold in the streets of America. He found something better — a home.

By 1935, he had settled in the Bronx, but Sunday was customarily devoted to taking his wife and son downtown to the Lower East Side to visit with his mother-in-law. The Third Avenue El was not the fastest way to the East Side, but it was cheaper than paying an additional bus fare to the IND subway.

From the East 180th Street Station the El moved southward past Crotona Park to 174th Street and then to Claremont Parkway. From the train Makufka could look into the dreary shadow-encased tenements surrounding the elevated tracks. It seemed as if the people living on Third Avenue were condemned to their own sort of noisy hell. As the train moved further south, it entered the

Irish section of the Bronx: 156th Street, 149th Street, and finally the last stop in the borough, 138th Street.

Radios were heard blaring all along Third Avenue whenever the train stopped at any of the stations. On a warm Sunday Makufka could hear the voice that told people how to end the depression — the voice of hope. The closeness of the buildings to the elevated tracks near 138th Street gave the El rider the feeling that the buildings were embracing the train. Here, in this Irish area, a Coughlin stronghold, it seemed that the radio was next to the rider's ear. Often it was. The shrill *r*'s, the call to action — the voice golden and unmistakable carried out the open tenement windows to the open windows of the train, and to the sky above.

Manny Makufka was atypical, for although he knew who Father Coughlin was, he had no interest in his radio program. But many of his Jewish friends did listen to Coughlin. They had told him that the priest was a stimulating speaker and that he was not anti-Semitic. Makufka was not interested. After all, what could a priest say to an East European immigrant Jew that would be meaningful? His years in Poland had taught him that priests simply did not say things that would be helpful to Jews — America or no America.[4]

Syracuse, New York, had never experienced such excitement. On this hot summer day in 1936, Father Coughlin was going to appear in the city's outdoor stadium, and hours before his scheduled 3:00 P.M. appearance it was packed to capacity. Thousands of farmers and small-town residents from the northwestern part of the state had made the trek. Many of the faculty members and students from surrounding colleges had also turned out for the event. Some people came out of a feeling of curiosity, but most came because they wanted to see and hear in person the man whose radio broadcasts had made such a profound impression on them.

As three o'clock approached, the master of ceremonies kept up a running commentary on Father Coughlin's progress toward the stadium: "Father Coughlin's train is arriving at the station." Ten minutes later he announced, "Father Coughlin's train has arrived."

The spectators cheered as they were told, "He's in the car and on the way." The "warm-up" speakers on the podium were still addressing the crowd, but no one was listening. "He's two miles away!" "He's ten blocks away!" It was now a few minutes before three. Necks strained. "He's five blocks away!" Fathers lifted their children high so that they could see over the heads of the people in front of them. "He's three blocks away!" All eyes were focused on the open end of the stadium. Suddenly there was a burst of activity as state troopers entered the stadium. "There he is!" "I see him! Look!"

The priest entered the stadium and it erupted in a tumultuous welcome. He smiled, looked up at the mass of people, and waved. Then, shaking hands and waving, he made his way through the surging crowds toward the podium. People tried to touch him. It took him a full ten minutes to reach the podium, and when he did, the foot-stomping, yelling and applause continued for several minutes more. When the noise abated, he began tearing into Roosevelt and the international bankers. His powerful voice could be clearly heard as he gave the people what they had come to hear.[5]

John Constable has been a staunch follower of Father Coughlin since 1935. Although he was fortunate enough to be employed in an optical plant in Geneva, New York, during the depression, he was unhappy with the chaos in the country and was strongly attracted to socialist doctrines. A number of his friends had told him that listening to Father Coughlin's Sunday broadcasts would be a method of restoring his religious faith. Constable was reluctant to do so, for he felt that a priest's business was to tend to his parish and not to get involved in politics.

One Sunday, strictly by chance, he did tune in the Coughlin broadcast and was impressed with what he heard. Father Coughlin really made sense. The priest's assertion that the international bankers had precipitated the depression was in agreement with his own views on the subject. Just as important as what Father Coughlin said was the way he said it. Constable felt that the priest had the ability to reduce complex problems and solutions to simple terms that could be easily understood by the exploited masses. He thought about Coughlin until he retired that night. It was to be a night he would never forget.

Constable claims that he had a vision in which the Virgin Mary and a priest stood by his bed and Mary told Constable to go to Royal Oak, Michigan, to serve her son — Father Coughlin. The next morning he began to make the plans which would take him to Royal Oak and eventual employment as a maintenance man in Father Coughlin's Shrine of the Little Flower Church. When he saw Father Coughlin for the first time, Constable recognized him as the priest who had appeared in his vision.

Constable believes that Coughlin represents the second coming of Christ. He points out that Coughlin was born in 1891, the same year Leo XIII issued his important papal encyclical *Rerum Novarum*. Constable also remembers that when many of Father Coughlin's followers urged him to run for the presidency in 1936, he refused to do so. To Constable this action was similar to Jesus' refusing the throne when Satan offered it to Him. Just as Jesus was crucified by his enemies, so was Father Coughlin crucified. Coughlin was Christ, returning to redeem a world of sinners. And the sinners remained unrepentant and refused salvation and instead looked "to Roosevelt, the money changers, the English and the Kennedys."

When pressed for further evidence of Coughlin's divinity, Constable said that Archbishop Edward Mooney, who became Coughlin's Church superior in 1937, was the Judas who turned Coughlin over to his enemies. Mooney died on Father Coughlin's birthday, while attending the First Ecumenical Council in Rome. Constable was with the Royal Oak priest when word was received of Mooney's death. Coughlin was silent for a few moments and then said: "My Father has given me a birthday present."[6]

Far from Royal Oak, there lived another well-known priest — a man who was only one step ahead of his creditors. There were so many children to be cared for and operating expenses were high. Few people really seemed to care whether his life's work on behalf of the helpless and innocent continued. In spite of these troubles, he carried on his efforts.

In the midst of his own financial problems he still found time in his busy day to review the needs of others. Thus, he slowly reread the letter requesting financial help for an organization he had assumed was in excellent financial condition. The personal integrity of the letter's author was unquestioned by the good priest and the letter did speak of the organization's dire need for funds in order to carry on its activities. It did not matter that his own financial plight was desperate. He opened the desk drawer and took out the checkbook. As he began to write the check his eyes focused on his bank balance. He paused to ponder how much longer he could carry on his work. He signed and then continued to fill out the check, in the amount of $100.[7] He placed the check in an envelope which he addressed to:

> Father Charles E. Coughlin
> c/o Radio League of the Little Flower
> Royal Oak, Michigan

Slowly, he got up from his desk. "If there were only enough money to support all the worthy causes in the world," he thought. Although Boys' Town was now $100 poorer, Father Edward Flanagan had an abiding faith in God and the goodness of the American people. They would see to it that Boys' Town survived. At the same time he must see to it that Father Coughlin survived.

The boy's voice was clearly audible. It was early October in Minneapolis and the first chilly winds of winter were blowing through the streets. The boy was selling copies of *Social Justice* and distributing handbills which contained a photograph of Father Coughlin standing in front of a microphone, looking directly at the viewer, his eyes penetrating, his mouth serious. In his left hand Coughlin held his sermon, while clenching his right fist as if to bust America's un-American enemies in the face.

The handbills publicized a Minnesota Christian Front Rally at the St. Paul Auditorium on Saturday, October 21, 1939. "In honor of Our Teacher's Birthday — the Reverend Charles E. Coughlin." Father Edward Lodge Curran of Brooklyn, who was president of the International Catholic Truth Society and Coughlin's good friend and eastern representative, would speak. Father Coughlin, too, would be heard at the rally, speaking directly from Royal Oak to scores of similar birthday celebrants throughout the country. All proceeds, after the program expenses, were to go to Father Coughlin for use in defraying the costs of his weekly broadcasts. In order to insure a large turnout, the rally's sponsors were raffling a 1939 sedan as well as giving away a hundred one-year subscriptions to *Social Justice*. The forty-piece St. Luke's Symphonic Band under the direction of Eugene A. Trowbridge was to provide entertainment. The names and addresses of many citizens of Minneapolis and St. Paul appeared as sponsors of the rally or as members of various committees devoted to making the rally a success.

The newsboy shouted, "Come hear Father Coughlin! For God and country. Come help Father Coughlin fight communists and atheists. Come hear Father Coughlin! Come hear Father Coughlin! For God and country!" But people seemed more intent on getting home than in taking a handbill. Remembering his instructions from his Christian Front group leader, the boy threw half his handbills to the wind, fell to the pavement, and started to scream and cry. Immediately a crowd gathered around him. When asked why he was crying, the boy replied: "A big Jew kicked me." It was not long till his papers were sold and his handbills distributed.

It was a chilly autumn day in 1965. Father Coughlin was supervising the lunch recess in the yard of the elementary school. The children flocked around him, nearly engulfing him. Their smiles and laughter testified to their affection. Their feelings were reciprocated, for his face reflected pure enjoyment as he smiled at one boy of seven and tousled the hair of another.

The lunch recess over, he gestured with his right hand to call the children back to class. They trudged into the building. He walked around the play area, gently prodding the tardy few who were desperately trying to finish the last inning of a punchball game.

His figure was straight. His head, topped by a black homburg which covered his once-famous curly hair, was held high. He wore the rimless eyeglasses that had been his trademark. His face was rounder now and the flesh about his chin was showing signs of flabbiness. Yet he appeared as physically fit as the day, thirty years earlier, when he had prevented a group of his followers from annihilating a would-be assailant.

When the school yard was empty, he walked slowly towards the church tower, his head down, his hands in the pockets of his light gray trench coat.

This lonely, solitary figure was once the most revered, the most loved, the most hated and the most feared American of his time. He was Christ; he was Hitler; he was savior; he was destroyer; he was patriot; he was demagogue — he was Father Coughlin.

2

Early Life

CHARLES Edward Coughlin's great-grandfather and grandfather had been laborers. The former had helped dig the Erie Canal. The latter had followed his brother John, an army captain, to LeGros, Indiana. It was here that Thomas Coughlin, one of twelve brothers and sisters, was born.

Poorly educated and frequently victimized by the strong anti–Irish Catholic sentiment of many midwesterners, Thomas, like many other Irish, turned to the sea for a livelihood. At the age of sixteen he became a sailor on a Great Lakes steamer. He shoveled coal, stoked wood, and endured the heat, filth and grime of sea life until, contracting typhoid fever, he was hospitalized in St. Catherines, Ontario. The illness was diagnosed in its early stages and he recovered, determined not to return to the back-breaking duties of a stoker. Instead, he settled in Hamilton, Ontario, where he found a job as sexton at St. Mary's Church.

It was here that Thomas met Amelia Mahoney, a young seamstress whose family had moved to Hamilton from Strabane to seek work. Amelia was a devout Catholic and frequently prayed at St. Mary's, where she met and eventually married Thomas Coughlin.

Thomas did well for himself. He became foreman of the Harris Bakery and owner of a comfortable four-room home at 60 Cannon Street, in the heart of a middle-class Irish neighborhood. It was in this house that Amelia gave birth to a son, christened Charles

Charles E. Coughlin at the age of seven (United Press International Photo)

Edward, on October 25, 1891. Five months after Charles' birth, the Coughlin family moved around the corner to a five-room house at 179 McNabb Street, two houses away from the home of Amelia's sister. The back yard of the new home bordered the grounds of St. Mary's Church, where Amelia attended mass every day. Fifteen months after Charles' birth, she bore a daughter, Agnes, who died at the age of three months. Charles often heard his parents speak of the "little darling angel, whom God had taken to His bosom."[1]

From infancy Charles was exposed to the Church. He served as an altar boy at St. Mary's and attended the parish school. He was a good student, particularly in mathematics, a subject in which he tutored his classmates. He was also an athletic boy who enjoyed swimming and playing marbles, baseball, handball and rugby.

Charles was particularly close to his older cousin Millie, whom he came to regard as a sister. Millie recalled that when she came down with the measles, her mother told Mrs. Coughlin that she should keep Charles away from the house. Charles overheard the sisters talking about Millie's illness and immediately went to the living room of his aunt's home, where he tearfully embraced Millie, who was lying on the sofa. Shortly after, Charles came down with the measles.[2]

As an only child, Charles monopolized the love of his parents. For his part, he was a devoted son and remained so till his parents died, each at the age of eighty-six, ten years apart.

From his early youth, Charles had the companionship of dogs. His first was a collie puppy; he spent so much of his free time with his collie that he neglected his piano lessons, much to his mother's displeasure. But he usually could get whatever he wished from his parents, even breakfast in bed, by feigning sickness. One sickness he did not feign, however, was typhoid fever, which he contracted at the age of nine and which incapacitated him for several months.

Upon his graduation from St. Mary's in June, 1903, at the age of thirteen, Charles entered the high school at St. Michael's College in Toronto, forty miles from Hamilton. Its primary purpose was to train priests for the archdiocese of Toronto.

It was a sorrowful moment for the Coughlin family when Charles entered St. Michael's. Although his parents wished Charles to become a priest, they suddenly realized that his training would result in their seeing less and less of him. In Toronto, when the Coughlins said their farewells, all three cried. Finally, Mrs. Coughlin embraced her son and kissed him good-bye in the proud knowledge that she was giving a son to the Church. What better way was there to serve God? What better way to climb the social ladder and avoid discrimination? Yet in seven days of soul-searching following her return from St. Michael's, Amelia Coughlin knew only one thing — she missed her son and she wanted him back home. She wrote to Charles asking him to resign from the school and return home. But Charles never received the letter. The school authorities, aware that there were many parents who felt as Mrs. Coughlin did, had appointed a censor to check the mail of all freshman students. Mrs. Coughlin's letter was intercepted and destroyed.

After three months of school, Charles was allowed to receive visitors every weekend, and Mrs. Coughlin took full advantage of this privilege. It was indeed a rare weekend when she did not make the eighty-mile round trip to see Charles. Worried about her son's loss of weight, she brought homemade cookies, cakes, pastries and candies with her. Charles usually had more than he could eat and would share the delicacies with his rapidly multiplying number of friends.

The grading system at St. Michael's was rigorous and school standards exceedingly high, but Charles' grades were generally good although he had difficulty in economics. In June, 1907, Charles was graduated from the high school, and in the fall entered St. Michael's College. There he played fullback for the school team that won the Junior Canadian Rugby championship. He was also a counselor for the Blessed Virgin Mary Sodality and second vice-president of the Dramatic Society. It was customary for the college seniors with good grades to serve as faculty members, and so he taught the preparatory course for students in grades six through eight. In 1911 Coughlin was president of the first graduating class to receive a University of Toronto degree

"Chuck" Coughlin at St. Michael's College, Toronto, 1910 (United Press International Photo)

Rev. Charles E. Coughlin with his parents in their home at Royal Oak, Michigan (United Press International Photo)

signed by the chancellor, the president of the university, and the president of the newly federated St. Michael's College.

As a graduation present, Coughlin's parents sent him to Europe. There he had the time to think through the problem of what vocation he would follow. He knew his parents wanted him to become a priest, but he was consumed by an ambition to be a politician. He loved the feel of power and the give-and-take of debate. By the time he returned from Europe he had decided that he would try to do what few other priests had ever attempted in North America — combine priestly duties with political leadership.[3]

He now began the arduous preparatory work for the priesthood at St. Basil's Seminary, which was adjacent to St. Michael's and was run by the Basilian Order. He had his moments of doubt and even succeeded in presenting his church superiors with problems which made them question whether he would — or should — become a priest. One year Coughlin was cut off from all social contacts. Another year was devoted to prayer and performing such manual labor as washing floors, digging latrines and plowing fields. At one point Coughlin became so fed up with this routine that, without permission, he left the seminary to see his parents. They were happy to see him but they urged him to return to the seminary immediately. He did so and his punishment was mild; he was deprived of his semiprivate quarters and was ordered to sleep in the high school dormitory.

St. Basil's was not a totally negative experience for Charles. It was here that he became drawn to the writings of Pope Leo XIII, and particularly to his encyclical *Rerum Novarum*, which was the Vatican's response to the changes wrought by the Industrial Revolution.

In 1914 Coughlin and two other seminarians, Jack Spratt and Walter Gonter, were sent to St. Basil's College in Waco, Texas. There Coughlin continued his study of theology while teaching philosophy.[4] Life was pleasant, and with the warm Texas weather the three faculty men found time to play baseball as illegal members of the college team. Spratt, a pitcher, and Gonter, a catcher, were both excellent athletes. Along with Coughlin at second base, they provided St. Basil's with the nucleus of a fine baseball team.

St. Basil's won its first two games of the season and then was scheduled to play its powerful cross-town rival, Baylor, which happened to be a Baptist school. Baylor had never lost to St. Basil's and it had little reason to believe that it would do so now. Although Baylor partisans did not really think his presence necessary to beat St. Basil's, the famed Tris Speaker was in the Baylor lineup, under an assumed name, trying to work himself into shape for the coming baseball season. But the approximately fifty spectators, most of them Baylor students, became more perturbed as the score mounted against them and the defeat of their team seemed likely. They cursed and taunted the St. Basil's players, and when the game was over, they rushed onto the field and, aided by some of the Baylor players, started to pummel the St. Basil's team. Coughlin recalls this event as "the worst physical beating of my life. But it was worth it. We showed them that Catholics could beat Baptists."[5]

When St. Basil's school year ended, Coughlin left Texas and returned to Toronto, where he continued his studies for the priesthood. By the spring of 1916, Coughlin's oratorical abilities had created enough interest to result in his being selected to preach the Easter Sunday sermon in the seminary chapel at St. Basil's. This was a privilege rarely extended a novice.

On June 29, 1916, Charles Edward Coughlin was one of three young men ordained as priests in St. Basil's Church in Toronto. The next day he celebrated his first mass at St. Joseph's Convent in Hamilton. The mass was a private one for the nuns and priests and for his proud parents. His first public mass was celebrated the following Sunday at St. Mary's Church. It was a memorable day for the entire Coughlin family. Parents, relatives and friends crowded into the church, whose shadows embraced the house in which Charles had grown up.

In the fall of 1916, Father Coughlin was assigned to Assumption College, in Sandwich, Ontario, on the Canadian border near Detroit. He taught psychology, English and logic, and directed the Dramatic Society. His specialty was the production of Shakespearean plays. Because of the rapidly increasing numbers of

Catholics finding employment in Detroit plants there was a shortage of priests, and Coughlin was assigned to St. Agnes' Church in Detroit every Saturday and Sunday. At first he heard confessions and performed minor duties within the church, but after two months he was told that he would be given the opportunity to preach a sermon.

Carefully, he planned that sermon. He wrote it and rewrote it. He practiced delivering it. He tried different facial expressions and experimented with methods of utilizing his arms and hands to give more emphasis to his words. The sermon was preached and was warmly received. Even so, Coughlin was still not sure of his effectiveness. In the months that followed he would often ask fellow clergymen from Assumption to accompany him to Detroit and on the way back to school he would ask them to criticize his sermons.[6] In a short time he was delivering sermons regularly and church attendance increased sharply. He was well on his way to mastering the oratorical skills that in a few years would make him a weekly visitor in millions of homes.

While teaching at Assumption College and preaching at St. Agnes' Church, Father Coughlin found time to arrange for his parents to leave Hamilton and move to Sandwich. The major stumbling block had been finding Thomas Coughlin a job that paid as much as the high salaried one he held in Hamilton as the chief examiner of steel for the Imperial Munitions Board. Fortunately for the elder Coughlin, the war had created a surplus of jobs and a scarcity of men to fill them. Through a personal contact, Father Coughlin was able to secure a position for his father in Windsor, supervising laborers for a steel construction company. The Coughlins then sold their home in Hamilton and purchased a comfortable house on Campbell Avenue, close to Assumption College and only a few miles from Windsor. It was an arrangement that enabled Father Coughlin to have the company of his parents and to enjoy his mother's cooking.

In 1918, the Basilian Order, of which Coughlin was a member, underwent a change. It had originally been brought to Canada by French missionaries in the seventeenth century and continued to be dominated by Basilian superiors in France. At this time Father

Frank Forster, the English-speaking superior general of the Basilian Order in Canada, established a separate clerical entity stressing the concept of a Basilian community in conformity with canon law as observed by other such clerical communities in Canada. Such action resulted in an end of the domination of the order by Basilian superiors in France. This new community required that its members take a vow of poverty.

Priests already in the Basilian Order in Canada were given three alternatives. First, they could comply with the new regulations and remain in the Basilian Order, sharing all material belongings with their fellow Basilians as well as sharing in the government of the community. Second, the priests could refrain from taking the vow of poverty and remain in the Basilian Order with no voice in its affairs. The final choice offered the opportunity to leave the order entirely and continue priestly duties as secular clergy. Father Coughlin and five other priests opted for the last choice, which would allow them to be more externally oriented. Initially, however, there was little change in his life. He remained at Assumption while continuing his duties at St. Agnes' Church in Detroit.

As a secular priest, Father Coughlin was subject to the control of the local bishop, John Foley. When Foley died he was replaced by Michael Gallagher, who had been titular bishop of Grand Rapids. Monsignor John Doyle, chancellor of the diocese and a friend of Coughlin's, asked the young priest if he wished to accompany him to welcome Bishop Gallagher to Detroit. Coughlin recalls:

We met Gallagher and Archbishop Schrembs of Cleveland, who was accompanying him, at Ypsilanti and we got on the electric train for the ride back to Detroit. Gallagher shook hands with Doyle and said, "Who's this young boy?" "Coughlin." "Glad to know you, Father. Sit down. Sit down." I took an immediate liking to Gallagher and he to me. I was close to him ever since that day. And next to my own father, I think he was the most beloved man in my life.[8]

On February 26, 1923, Father Coughlin was incardinated into the Detroit diocese, and was assigned as assistant pastor to St.

Augustine's parish in Kalamazoo, a factory and agricultural center, halfway between Detroit and Chicago.

But Coughlin was too impatient, too ambitious and too talented to remain in Kalamazoo. After only three months, with the help of Monsignor John Doyle, he was able to arrange a transfer to St. Leo's Church in Detroit. St. Leo's had a congregation of approximately ten thousand; enough to have several assistants in addition to a pastor. Father Coughlin's duties consisted of stimulating church attendance, increasing the amount of money in the building fund, and periodically conducting mass. The popularity of his sermons following mass helped to increase donations. In all these duties he did an outstanding job. This, coupled with his friendship with Monsignor Doyle and the liking Bishop Gallagher had taken to him, resulted in Coughlin's being assigned his own parish in North Branch, Michigan, after only eighteen months at St. Leo's.

In early 1926, Bishop Gallagher returned from Rome, where he had attended the canonization rites of St. Thérèse, the Little Flower of Jesus. Once back in Detroit, Gallagher decided to erect a church in her honor in the Detroit suburb of Royal Oak, twelve miles north of the city. Although there were only twenty-eight Catholic families in Royal Oak, Gallagher believed that many of the increasingly large number of Catholics attracted to Detroit by the booming auto industry would decide to settle there. At the moment, however, establishing a parish posed many problems. In addition to having a paucity of Catholic families, Royal Oak was a stronghold of the Ku Klux Klan, which in the 1920s had attracted many followers in the Middle West. In Royal Oak they formed a sullen, aggressive, hostile barrier to the settlement of Catholics in the area.

Gallagher knew that the pastor of the new church would have to be a young, aggressive priest who would be able to overcome the threat posed by the Ku Klux Klan. He sent for Father Coughlin and commanded him:

Build a church at the crossroads of faith and religious persecution — at the intersection of Woodward Avenue and Twelve Mile Road in Royal Oak — in the midst of the fiery hatred of Ku Klux Klanism.

Build your church there in the wilderness. Name it the Shrine of the Little Flower. Make it a missionary oasis in the desert of religious bigotry.[9]

The Shrine of the Little Flower Church was a hastily constructed, russet-brown wooden building of simple design located at the intersection of two dirt roads in an area which lacked sewers and was infested with mosquitoes. It could seat six hundred worshippers, which many clergymen in the chancery office thought an optimistic folly. Bishop Gallagher had advanced $79,000 to build the church, but actual building costs totaled $101,000, despite the fact that a rectory was not constructed.[10] Father Coughlin lived in a small room in the back of the church and relied on parishioners for food. This situation changed when Father Coughlin's parents moved to Detroit. They occupied a spacious eight-room house at 3262 Hogarts Avenue, thus giving him a more comfortable place in which to spend his spare time.

Father Coughlin knew that to a large extent his success would be determined by the financial situation of his church. He also knew that, at the moment, there were so few worshippers in the parish that the normal use of a collection box would be futile.

But even before he could deal with the financial problems of his parish, he was presented with a more immediate threat. Barely two weeks after the completion of the church, the Ku Klux Klan burned a cross on the lawn of the church, along with a sign that read, "Move from Royal Oak." Never a man to be easily frightened, Coughlin resolved that one day a monument to his fortitude and devotion to Christ would be built on the very spot where the Ku Klux Klan had burned the cross. "Some day we will build a church and raise its cross so high to the sky that neither man nor beast can burn it down."[11] But that would have to wait. First his concern must center on putting his parish on a sound financial basis.

Now he showed his flair for making headlines. Always a rabid baseball fan, Coughlin had become friendly with Wish Egan, a scout for the Detroit Tigers. Coughlin asked Egan if he would bring some Tiger players to the Shrine as a publicity gimmick. Egan not only obliged, but also made arrangements for Babe Ruth and a number of other Yankees to appear at the Shrine when they came to Detroit in midsummer. The news of the visit spread throughout the Detroit metropolitan area and on the day that Ruth and the other ballplayers made their appearance, the streets outside the church were mobbed. Ruth immediately took charge and told Coughlin, "Listen, Father, you say mass and do the preaching and leave the collection to us." Coughlin replied, "I can't do that." Ruth, irrepressible as ever, took Coughlin by the arm and, as Coughlin recalls, "gently but firmly, assisted me to the altar and told me to keep the hell out of the way."

The thousands of people gathered outside waited impatiently to enter. When the doors opened, ballplayers, stationed at each entrance holding either cardboard boxes or large hats, greeted them. Ruth's thundering voice could be heard, "You can't get in without your money!" As the people filed in they put their bills in the hats and the cardboard boxes. Some waited for change, but Ruth, although never a businessman where his own interests were involved, shouted, "No change today! No change today! Keep moving! Don't block the door."[12] After the church was filled to capacity, loudspeakers were utilized to enable the masses of people who could not crowd into the church to hear the proceedings. When the total receipts were counted, Father Coughlin had raked in $10,000, and convinced himself that only by employing flamboyant methods could a priest rise above the crowd.

Although the money raised by the appearance of the Yankee and Tiger ballplayers alleviated some of the church's financial problems and helped to let people in the Detroit area know that an enterprising young priest was in their midst, the financial woes persisted. The interest payments on loans utilized to build the church totaled $100 per week. Father Coughlin even had to wonder how he would be able to pay for the coal to heat the church in the winter. He knew that he must act.

Adversity had a great deal to do with what you term my "success and fame" which has been to me simply service. I believe now, as I did then, that adversity, as well as necessity, is very often the reason for action. If I had had a comfortable parish and a comfortable rectory —

pleasant escorts to religious duty — and if my Bishop had not been the inspiration he was and still is, all this probably would never have happened. But there I was sleeping in the vestry, threatened with pneumonia, shivering with the cold, and unwilling to admit defeat. Something had to be done.[13]

Something had to be done, he felt, not only to solve his financial problems, but also to enable him to project his views on a society and an economic system that forced a church — a House of God, a church that disseminated God's word and followed His instructions — to totter on the edge of disaster. Father Coughlin had been impressed with the great potential in radio for reaching masses of people. Many Americans who could not read English tried to compensate for this fact by purchasing radios. Some optimists were even predicting that in a few short years every American home would have a radio. He knew from the remarks of friends and from members of his church that he had a fine voice. His early interest in drama and theatrics had left its mark on him. His voice was clear, his enunciation excellent. His voice conjured up varied images in the minds of his audience. Why not use this voice to reach the thousands, perhaps millions, who listened to their radios? By broadcasting he could bring God into the homes of people who did not enter the House of God and money into His church.

Father Coughlin shared his thoughts with a few of his parishioners, but they were skeptical. Some even objected to a priest talking on the radio. It seemed almost sacrilegious to take God out of the Church and onto the air. Others pointed out that broadcasting would result in considerable expense to the Church. But Father Coughlin was convinced that his idea was a sound one and he was determined to carry it out.

In September of 1926, he discussed his idea with Leo Fitzpatrick, station manager for WJR, Detroit. Fitzpatrick clearly recalls that first meeting with his friend:

I had a small office then. Radio was in its infancy. Its future was then uncertain. Father Coughlin and I met that fall, around the first week in October, I think, introduced by a mutual friend. It was just a few months subsequent to his opening of the Shrine at Royal Oak. He was much younger then, and his face lighted up with the same enthusiasm as it does now when he speaks. He talked about the serious situation he faced, about the activities of the Ku Klux Klan, and recited a story of low finances and no resources. He wanted to do something. I asked him how he would like to go on the air. I had heard something about him as a preacher; I asked him what else he could do. He told me he could play the organ and sing a little.[14]

The very next day, Father Coughlin met with Bishop Gallagher and discussed his plans for a radio broadcast. The bishop was enthusiastic. Father Coughlin then met again with Fitzpatrick to outline plans for the broadcast. Fitzpatrick knew that

there wasn't any Catholic leader, any priest on the air, and I figured it might be worth his trying. So I told him I could arrange to let him have the time free, but that he would have to stand the cost of the lines, and I quoted him the bare figure — $58 a week. If he went over, then we would talk terms and time prices, I told him.[15]

Fitzpatrick then conferred with Dick Richards, owner of the Detroit Lions and radio station WJR, and told him of the plan to put Father Coughlin on the air. Richards, who would eventually become one of Coughlin's biggest financial supporters, was cautious. He wanted to meet the priest before giving his approval. Father Coughlin chuckles as he recalls his first meeting with Richards. "Although Dick was an Anglican, he told me that he would like to hear me preach a sermon. So he came over to the church two or three Sundays and he kept coming after that."[16]

3

Growing Fame

On October 17, 1926, at 2:00 P.M., Father Coughlin conducted his first radio broadcast. Standing in his priestly vestments at the altar of his church, he spoke into a WJR microphone, and delivered a sermon on the importance of religion in man's life.

At its conclusion, he retired to his room to assess his performance. He stood in front of the mirror and repeated many of the lines he had delivered on the air, using facial expressions and gesturing with his hands to increase the impact of his delivery. Looking into the mirror, he could not help but be impressed. He was five feet, ten inches tall. His piercing eyes flashed and the rimless glasses he wore reflected the light's glare. His smile radiated warmth and compassion. He was an aggressive, bright, ambitious and capable man who even now had the ability to charm those with whom he came in contact. In time, he would become quite vain, but as he looked into the mirror after that first broadcast he worried about the audience response.

Three days after the broadcast he wrote answers to the five laudatory notes he had received. The radio station, however, had received many more letters. Fitzpatrick was satisfied that the broadcast was a success and told the priest that, with certain modifications, it would be made a regular feature on WJR. Every Sunday afternoon at 2:00 P.M., Father Coughlin delivered his sermon. The program also featured organ music and a male choir.

Each broadcast resulted in an increasingly positive response to the priest — a response often accompanied by financial contributions. Most of the contributions were small, ranging from one to five dollars, but some listeners sent fifty and one hundred dollars, which were certainly not small amounts for that time.

Father Coughlin's growing popularity was noted by the Detroit press, which began to devote considerable space to his activities. Coughlin was good copy, and the people of the Detroit area seemed fascinated by him. Coughlin knew quite well the religious value of his radio show. He remarks:

When one thinks of the hundreds of miles traveled by St. Paul along the coastal cities of Greece, when one visualizes historically the hundreds of converts which he drew to Christ through his indefatigable labors, he cannot but know the potential good which can be accomplished by his successors who are making use of God's latest gift to man — the radio. . . . The radio is the modern medium of preaching the gospel to all nations.[1]

Father Coughlin attributed his broadcasting appeal to the fact that "we avoid prejudicial subjects, all controversies, and especially all bigotry."[2] If these words expressed his true sentiments at that time, they would be forgotten at a later date. Father Coughlin urged all people who believed in God, not only Catholics, to follow him. At the same time, he displayed a remarkable insensitivity to the religious beliefs of other denominations by talking of the need for his audience to "believe . . . in the three Divine Persons, in the birth of the Saviour in the manger, and in His death on the cross at Calvary."[3]

Despite Father Coughlin's growing prominence, the local chapter of the Ku Klux Klan continued to display its hostility. Eventually, he succeeded in winning them to his side. In May, 1927, a Ku Klux Klan funeral procession moved up Woodward Avenue, past Father Coughlin's church, toward Roseland Park Cemetery. Father Coughlin vividly recalls that day. "It was pouring rain and Woodward Avenue had turned to mud. I went out and walked with them at the head of the procession and helped them conduct their memorial service. After that we got along just fine."[4] Father Coughlin could not recall why the Ku Klux Klan allowed him to lead their funeral procession, nor could he explain why they allowed him to conduct the graveside services for the deceased, since Catholics were not even eligible for membership in that organization.

In the fall of 1927, after a summer respite, Coughlin resumed his radio broadcasting on a hookup which carried his voice across Michigan and into neighboring states. By now people all over the country had heard of the Catholic priest who delivered stimulating sermons and replied to questions submitted by listeners. Prompted by Coughlin's radio invitation, they flocked by the hundreds to the Shrine of the Little Flower Church. Sunday services were conducted before standing-room-only audiences. Many Catholics in the Detroit area, who were prospering primarily from jobs in the automobile plants and could afford new homes, now moved to Royal Oak. Living in Father Coughlin's parish was becoming a status symbol. Building contractors in Royal Oak could not build homes quickly enough to satisfy all the potential buyers. The increased number of people moving into the parish and attending Sunday services contributed significantly to alleviating Coughlin's financial problems. In addition, the contributions sent in by listeners to his radio show created a tremendous surplus of cash. He knew exactly what he would do with this money; he would build a church that would be the showplace of houses of worship in the United States, a church that would be a monument to Christ, to the Virgin Mary — and to himself.

In late 1928, Father Coughlin met with Henry McGill, of the New York architectural firm of Hamlin and McGill, to discuss plans for the construction of a church a few yards behind the original church that would be startlingly different in design from other churches of the day. It was to be octagonal with the altar in the center of the octagon. A tower was to rise above the church — a tower so magnificent that it would inspire the people who saw it. A tower with a crucifix on each side — "a tower that would climb to the sky to the Virgin Mary's bosom."[5] It would be a tower that neither man nor beast could tear down or defile.

The other details for designing the church were left to McGill.

By the fall of 1929, Father Coughlin, Fitzpatrick and Richards succeeded in adding two new outlets for the Sunday broadcasts, Station WMAQ in Chicago and Station WLW in Cincinnati. This added millions of potential new listeners, although weekly program expenses were now up to $1,650. His sermons resulted in a tremendous increase in mail, to some three thousand letters a week.

His appeal grew as the United States fell into the depths of a worldwide depression which was to change the course of history. It certainly affected Royal Oak and Father Coughlin. He recalls that "the depression was horrible. There was no food. . . . My community was starving. People were thrown out in the streets because they couldn't pay rent."[6] Father Coughlin sought to alleviate the suffering by contributing $7,500 to a fund for the distribution of food to the needy people of Royal Oak and by beginning construction of the new church, the purpose of which, he alleged, was solely "to give people work."[7] The Cooper-Little Company was in charge of actual construction. Nonunion labor was employed. Although Father Coughlin promised to pay a minimum wage of fifty cents an hour to workers, somewhat higher than the prevailing nonunion wage in the area, it was still below the level of union wages.

In retrospect, it seems somewhat strange that in the midst of a depression, in a time when money was scarce, Father Coughlin could afford to begin to construct a church that would cost over $800,000. Coughlin has a simple explanation:

Tens of thousands of good Americans were convinced that they were the victims of an international conspiracy aimed at enslaving them. People looked to me and respected me because they knew that I was not frightened by these conspirators. Many of these good people knew that I needed money to win the battle and although they were in desperate need themselves, they sent me their hard-earned money.[8]

Father Coughlin was deeply troubled by the confusion and poverty which had overcome millions of Americans. He was convinced that there was no one in the government who could lead the nation out of its dilemma; so he would have to. He was not frightened. He would tell the people who their enemies were. Would not the Catholic Church thereby receive the gratitude and goodwill of millions of non-Catholics who would regard him as their savior? He was appreciative of his own talents: "Although I don't want to seem immodest, I knew damn well that I had ability. Real ability. I knew that I could help the American people. And what the hell, no one else seemed to be interested in doing a damn thing."[9]

On January 12, 1930, Father Coughlin changed the format of his program. He devoted this broadcast to attacking bolshevism and socialism, without bothering to distinguish between the two. Audience response was very favorable. Fitzpatrick recalled that "Father Coughlin clicked again. There was virility in his sermons — the virility of simplicity. And what a wallop he packed."[10]

On Sunday, January 19, 1930, Coughlin delivered a sermon entitled "Christ or the Red Fog." The following Sunday he attacked Bertrand Russell and Dr. William Leonard, an English professor at the University of Wisconsin, for their communist-socialist leanings. Audience response was overwhelmingly supportive, as evidenced by the thousands of letters praising the broadcasts.

As the intensity of these attacks on the "Red Menace" increased, so did the responses to the attacks. Norman Thomas, leader of the Socialist party, accused Coughlin of having "indulged in serious misrepresentation of the nature of socialism and the Socialist party and hopeless confusion of it with communism." Thomas went on to make a point that would be made with increasing frequency and that finally led to changes in broadcasting codes. Speaking for the Socialist party, Thomas claimed:

It is not enough that we have the right to sue for slander. Radio is a public utility. It is under far greater obligation than a magazine or newspaper to permit reply to attacks that may be made on individuals or organizations because it enjoys the use by public license of wave lengths that cannot be privately owned . . .[11]

Fitzpatrick, replying for Station WJR, denied that either Thomas or the Socialist party had been discriminated against. He did, however, convince Father Coughlin to refrain from mentioning the Socialist party in future broadcasts. Although his own veracity and his knowledge of socialism and communism had been questioned, Coughlin had enjoyed this quarrel. After all, many more people now knew who he was and were talking about him. His broadcasts continued to hit hard at communism and socialism, and he even expanded his criticism to include American capitalists, who, he said, were providing fertile soil for the spread of leftist ideology because of their greed.

The priest devoted so much time to his broadcasting activities that he found it difficult to tend to his rapidly growing parish. With the consent of Bishop Gallagher, two Franciscan fathers, Father John de Deo and Father Reginald, were assigned to the Shrine of the Little Flower as his assistants. The three priests shared a newly constructed house situated only a few yards from the church.

In July, 1930, a congressional committee, under the chairmanship of Hamilton Fish, Jr., of New York, an ardent isolationist, visited Detroit as part of its investigation of communist activities in the United States. The Royal Oak priest was invited to testify before the Fish committee; he was now considered an "expert" on communism. A dozen witnesses, called prior to Coughlin, had viewed with alarm the operation of communist agitators in the Detroit area, but agreed that "the situation was well in hand." Father Coughlin disagreed: "Communism is increasing rapidly and there will be a revolution in the United States by 1933." He went on to tell the committee that the revolution would be a bloodless one and accused Henry Ford of being the man most responsible for the growth of communism in the United States. Startled, Fish asked for a clarification of this accusation. Said Coughlin:

Last winter, on the eve of the automobile show in New York, Mr. Ford issued a statement, which was printed on the first page of every newspaper in America, saying that he needed 30,000 additional workers at his Detroit plants. . . . As a result of that statement many more than the 30,000 flocked to Detroit from Alabama, Mississippi, Tennessee, Kentucky, Indiana, and many other states, and while the weather was at zero they stood in front of his plant trying to get those jobs.

Girls handling fan mail at the Shrine of the Little Flower (United Press International Photo)

There were no jobs for them and the only redress they had was to have the fire hose turned on them.[12]

By the mid-1930s Father Coughlin and Henry Ford would become very close friends. But in July of 1930 Coughlin and many other Americans were furious at Ford for concluding a thirteen-million-dollar deal with the Soviet Union for the construction of truck and tractor factories there.

In the fall of 1930, Father Coughlin negotiated an agreement to broadcast his Sunday show over the CBS network, which was heard by an estimated forty million listeners, and included sixteen stations carried into twenty-three states. He would finally be in a position to tell the American people what was wrong with the country. His broadcasts commenced on October 5, 1930, at 7:00 P.M. for a season lasting twenty-five weeks. He was heard in most of the large cities in the United States — and the shortwave station of WCAU in Philadelphia carried his broadcasts all over the world.

From October through December, 1930, his broadcasts concentrated on bread-and-butter economic issues. He stressed the acceptance of the concept of social justice as stated in *Rerum Novarum*. He spoke of the need for workers to be paid a living wage for the sacred commodity they brought to the economic marketplace — their labor. He also attacked socialism and the international bankers for helping to disseminate communism.

Within three weeks of his first CBS broadcast Father Coughlin had become a national figure. Fifty-five clerks were employed to handle the tremendous inflow of mail from his listeners. By 1935 he was to require one hundred. Letters from listeners were always answered. Reprints of his talks were sent to listeners on request.

His mail was overwhelmingly favorable. It came from Catholics, Protestants and Jews, thousands of whom sent small contributions that attested to the faith they had in him. And it was money that his listeners found increasingly difficult to come by as the depression continued to deepen.

I knew damn well that the little people, the average man, was suffering. I also knew that no one had the courage to tell the truth about why this nation was in such mortal danger. I knew that if anyone was going to inform the American citizenry of the truth it would have to be me. After all, I knew from the letters I was receiving that the people trusted me and would believe me when I spoke.[13]

His schedule was a busy one, but his tremendous energy and restlessness provided him with ample strength, and his two assistant pastors assumed much of the burden of running the parish. He did, however, find time for parish activities on Mondays, Tuesdays and Wednesdays. Thursdays and Fridays were devoted to preparing his radio talks, which also included a "Children's Catechism" that was broadcast on Sundays over WJR in Detroit, from 3:00 to 4:00 P.M. Sometimes even Saturdays were devoted to preparing his radio speech; by Saturday night the text had to be in the hands of Bishop Gallagher for his approval.[14] But on occasion, after Bishop Gallagher returned the script, Father Coughlin would spend Sunday mornings writing the final version. Thus, the bishop did not always see the text that Father Coughlin delivered, "because it wasn't necessary. This good man had wonderful confidence in me."[15]

A major controversy in Father Coughlin's public career occurred as a result of his broadcast of January 4, 1931. His friend Congressman Louis McFadden of Pennsylvania had supplied Coughlin with what he said were "incontrovertible statistics" proving that the Treaty of Versailles had precipitated the depression and that only a complete revision of the economic provisions of the treaty and the termination of power in the hands of the international bankers could bring the world out of the slough. Father Coughlin claimed that CBS learned of the controversial nature of his broadcast and that on the Saturday prior to his broadcast, CBS vice-president Edward Klauber telephoned requesting him to delete any inflammatory remarks from his text. According to Coughlin, he told Klauber that rather than omit any part of his text he would deliver a discourse on a totally different subject having nothing to do with the depression, the Treaty of Versailles or the international bankers. True to his word, the priest delivered a totally different talk from the one he had origi-

nally prepared. But it was one that took CBS by surprise. Coughlin devoted his entire talk to denouncing CBS and detailing to his
audience the alleged attempts by CBS to censor his material. He
received a deluge of mail following this broadcast which overwhelmingly supported his efforts to combat what he said was
censorship.[16] The following Sunday, Father Coughlin delivered
his originally planned talk.

In the weeks that followed, he continued to deliver savage attacks on international bankers, who, he claimed, ran a suprana-
tional organization which controlled the world.

> Ladies and gentlemen, as we listen to the siren song which floats to our
> ears from the pulpits of capitalism, we begin to wonder whether or not
> there is depression. We are lulled into the belief that the evils of mass-
> production, of stock gambling, of unemployment, of starvation, of
> discontent are nothing more than wicked concoctions devised by dis-
> eased minds and propagated by rebellious voices of soap-box orators.
> Attune your ears long enough, and you will be persuaded that our
> economic evils have been foisted upon us by the witchery of some
> preternatural agency over which good government has no control.[17]

CBS was so upset by the priest's accusations of censorship that
when he concluded his broadcasting season in April, despite his tremendous following, it did not renew his contract. Coughlin then
attempted to buy time on NBC, but was refused by that network
on the advice of its Religious Advisory Committee. Franklin Dun-
ham, an NBC executive, stated that NBC did not sell radio time to
individual members of religious groups, although it did supply a
half hour per week of free time to the National Council of Catholic
Men.[18]

Undaunted by denial of radio time by CBS and NBC, Father
Coughlin, working with Leo Fitzpatrick and Dick Richards and
Alfred McCosker of WOR, New York, organized an independent
chain of stations covering an area from St. Louis, Missouri, to
Portland, Maine. By 1932 this chain of networks was expanded
from eleven stations to twenty-seven stations and covered an area
from Kansas City to Bangor. By the middle 1930s Coughlin could
be heard weekly from Maine to California. His popularity con-

tinued to increase; contributions from listeners enabled him to pay
the cost of his weekly broadcast — $14,000.[19]

Among the lower and lower-middle classes — both rural and
urban — Coughlin succeeded in galvanizing a feeling of class discrimination, which evolved into class and eventually religious
hatred. His followers had become fed up with big business and its
tool, the federal government. They wanted scapegoats for the
depression and solutions to bring them out of it, and many were
convinced that Father Coughlin was providing these solutions.
Regardless of prior ideological commitment, on the Left or on the
Right, they were attracted by Coughlin's slashing attacks against
the concentration of power in the hands of big business and the
federal government's passivity in the face of crisis.

One factor is often omitted when people discuss the causes for
Coughlin's appeal. Certainly, there was a depression. Certainly,
there were widespread frustration, fear and unhappiness among
the American people. Certainly, there was a power vacuum created by the absence of an effective response to the depression by
the Hoover administration. But he possessed an important characteristic that made people look to him as their leader. He had
charisma — and he had it in abundance. Charisma inspires blind
loyalty, and faith. It was a quality possessed by only a few other
figures in the 1930s — Franklin Delano Roosevelt, Hitler and Mussolini. All were strong figures. They seemed to know the answers
to the ills of their societies. They acted with decisiveness — they
acted as if they really *knew* the answers. Father Coughlin acted
that way too. His crisp voice with its shrill *r*'s, his vibrant personality and his message were wonderfully suited to the time in
which he lived and to the new medium which was sweeping the
country. His access to the radio, coupled with his charisma, catapulted him into the limelight. Even today, one cannot sit in a
room with Father Coughlin, discussing the past, without being
keenly aware of the force of personality, of charisma. One can
understand why millions of Americans were enthralled by him.

And, in the 1930s, there were very few topics he was reluctant
to discuss. For example, he devoted considerable broadcasting time
to attacking prohibition. He stated that the issue of prohibition

was merely a clever smoke screen employed by the capitalists to divert the attention of the American people from the really pressing problems on hand. In his broadcasts of October 25, November 8 and November 15, 1931, he espoused this view, and also urged that temperance rather than abstinence govern the drinking habits of Americans. Dr. Clarence True Wilson, executive secretary of the Methodist Episcopal Board of Temperance, Prohibition and Public Morals, charged that American Legion conventions were "planned ahead of time as drunken orgies." In response, Coughlin said that Wilson's remarks had defamed the American dead of World War I. In a low-key radio address, the priest accused Wilson of having sneered at the "children and wives and gray-haired mothers when on this Armistice Day they are mindful of their loved ones."[20]

His next target in the 1931–1932 broadcasting series was the President of the United States, Herbert Hoover. The priest belabored the President and his associates for their repeated remarks that the country had turned the corner and that the depression would soon be over. "It appears to have been a circular corner to which they referred; a corner which if we could turn, we would not be willing to negotiate if it foreshadows a repetition of those recent occurrences for the children of generations to come."[21]

He castigated President Hoover for saying that relief for suffering people was best left to local government. He also pointed out that while billions of dollars were loaned to foreign governments, no money was forthcoming when the American people were desperate. As for his own county, Father Coughlin recalls:

there were thousands and thousands of people starving around here. They could not pay rent, buy clothing, buy food. . . . I met with some of the area's most important citizens in an effort to do something for all these poor people . . . Senator Couzens, Fred Fisher, head of Fisher Body Works, B. F. Stevenson, Chairman of the Board of General Motors and Dick Richards. All these men were my close friends. Fisher and Stevenson were both Anglicans. We didn't quite know what to do, but I announced on my radio show that all the people in the area should come to my church the next morning between 10:00 A.M. and 12:00 noon, and I'd take care of them. Later, at my house, Dick Richards told me: "You're a fool. You can't take care of the people that are coming here tomorrow. You will have five thousand people there tomorrow." But those wonderful men I just mentioned helped out. That night they contacted the big store owners and arranged to have over 100 trucks of clothing and food available on Woodward Avenue the next day. Over fifty thousand people turned out that morning, and we took care of every one of them. . . . Stevenson, who owned most of the Hazel Park Housing Development, an area populated by workers who were unemployed, canceled rent payments. Over 1,500 houses stopped paying rent that day as a result of Stevenson's edict. Fisher and Couzens each gave better than a million dollars to buy food, clothing and medicines.[22]

(Late in 1931, Father Coughlin contributed $7,000 to the Southern Oakland County Milk Fund in addition to an earlier contribution of $500.)

The priest continued his attacks on President Hoover, depicting him as a tool of the international bankers who had accumulated their fortunes as the result of "torture more refined than was ever excogitated by the trickery of the Romans or the heartlessness of slave owners."[23] He lashed out at Hoover's attempt to end the depression. In earlier broadcasts, he had been critical of the President for leaving solutions of the depression up to local governments; now he was critical of Hoover for the actions he did take. After Hoover launched the Reconstruction Finance Corporation, Father Coughlin described it as a step down the road to "financial socialism" that would result in increased power being centered in the hands of large financiers.

He went on to describe the Federal Farm Loan Bank, which was created by the Federal Farm Loan Act to ease the plight of farmers, as "an agent of torture and destructive confiscation." He flailed another Hoover measure, the Agricultural Marketing Act, as another step toward "financial socialism" and accused program administrators of wasting hundreds of millions of dollars.[24] The audience responded favorably to these attacks on Hoover. "After all, the American people knew that I was telling the truth."[25]

By 1931 Father Coughlin was regarded by many Americans as an economic expert, particularly in the area of monetary policy. As such, in April, 1932, he was called to Washington, D.C., to testify before the House Ways and Means Committee, which was studying the feasibility of legislation calling for a bonus for soldiers who had served in World War I. Convinced that such a bonus would enable millions of indigent veterans to have the purchasing power to "put $2 billion into the channels of commerce and trade," the priest urged Congress to give precedence to "human rights over financial rights."[26]

When thousands of veterans marched on Washington, D.C., and camped in shantytowns, Father Coughlin showed his sympathy for their plight by contributing $5,000 to a fund to help the marchers. Coughlin was bitter in his criticism of Hoover when the President ordered General Douglas MacArthur to disperse the Bonus Marchers and tear down the shantytowns they had constructed. Coughlin stated: "For the first time in the history of a civilized nation 10,000 of its heroes, who had borne the brunt and hardship of battle while their fellow citizens remained at home to enjoy lucrative positions and immense war profits . . . have been told that there is no bread for them."[27]

Some people thought that Father Coughlin was less concerned with solving the problems of veterans than he was with the desire to create cheap money.

Coughlin's proposal to cheapen money by simply printing and distributing it would have undermined the confidence of the people in the American dollar. Powerful lobby groups could have henceforth pressured Congress to tamper with the value of money with possible destructive results on the mortgage rates, savings, and insurance policies of tens of millions of Americans. There is little doubt, however, that the scarcity of money in circulation was crucial to the whole problem of ending the depression. But Walter Lippman pointed out that Father Coughlin and Senator Elmer Thomas, in citing the absence of adequate amounts of money in circulation as a basic cause of the depression, had "cor-

"I have no intention of interfering with Father Coughlin," said Bishop Michael Gallagher of Detroit, shown here with Father Coughlin (United Press International Photo)

rectly diagnosed what is wrong with the patient. . . . But instead of calling in the best surgeon available to perform the operation, they are proposing to call in a somewhat intoxicated butcher. . . . [the] Bonus Bill . . . is a plan to turn over the management of American money to fluctuating Congressional majorities."[28] For his part, Coughlin predicted that unless the currency were inflated a revolution would occur and result in the removal of control of money from the hands of a few prominent financiers.

But Father Coughlin's attention to monetary reform was distracted when he became embroiled in a series of controversial affairs. His public activities had become a source of interest, concern, dismay, and/or pleasure to various figures and organizations associated with the Catholic Church. Just as he evoked strong, but mixed, emotions among the citizenry as a whole, so he did the same within the Church itself. William Cardinal O'Connell of Boston, the most powerful American churchman of the 1930s, was one of the clerics concerned with the remarks Father Coughlin was making. In April of 1932, Cardinal O'Connell labeled Coughlin's radio broadcasts a series of "hysterical addresses" and pointed out: "The Catholic Church . . . deals in human souls. You can't begin speaking about the rich, or making sensational accusations against banks and bankers, or uttering demagogic stuff to the poor. You can't do it, for the Church is for all."[29] But if O'Connell's criticisms were meant to silence Coughlin, his efforts failed.

Bishop Gallagher said flatly, "I have no intention of interfering with Father Coughlin. Christ was not setting class against class when he rebuked the abuses of wealth."[30] Bolstered by this support, Father Coughlin refused even to reply to O'Connell's criticisms. He merely said, "I am a soldier in the ranks. Bishop Gallagher is my superior, and I shall do what my superior tells me. . . . He is not only my Bishop and my inspiration, but my friend."[31]

But in December, 1934, in the face of additional criticisms by O'Connell, Father Coughlin did strike back at the cardinal on one of his radio broadcasts:

Let it be understood that the Cardinal has no jurisdiction over me: that he has no jurisdiction outside of his own diocese. . . . William Cardinal

O'Connell has no authority to speak for the Catholic Church in America and no more business as a churchman to impose his thoughts on people living outside his jurisdiction. It is high time that this bubble be bursted. . . . William Cardinal O'Connell practically accuses me of misinterpreting the encyclicals of both Leo XIII and Pius XI. Every word that I have written has received the imprimatur of my Right Reverend Bishop. When this is taken into consideration, William Cardinal O'Connell practically accuses a brother bishop who for years has been famed in Michigan for his defense of the poor and for his opposition to the pampered evils which have been so rampant in the textile industries of New England.

Father Coughlin concluded his broadcast by firing a final salvo at O'Connell:

For forty years, William Cardinal O'Connell has been more notorious for his silence on social justice than for any contribution which he may have given either in practice or in doctrine toward the decentralization of wealth and towards the elimination of those glaring injustices which permitted the plutocrats of this nation to wax fat at the expense of the poor.[32]

In 1932, at the beginning of his controversy with Cardinal O'Connell, Father Coughlin became embroiled in the "Jimmy Walker affair." Walker, the flamboyant but injudicious mayor of New York City, was under fire for his incompetence, negligence and laxity in running the city government. On April 26, 1932, Father Coughlin addressed the annual communion breakfast of the New York City Fire Department Holy Name Society at the Hotel Astor. A commotion in the ballroom caused Father Coughlin to stand up to see what was happening. Before he could observe what was taking place, applause and cheers vibrated through the room. Mayor Walker had paid a surprise visit to the affair. When he reached the dais he embraced Father Coughlin to the resounding cheers of the twenty-five hundred assembled firemen.

In his address, carried live by WOR and WHN, Father Coughlin defended Walker and lashed out at such well-known critics of the mayor as the Reverend John Haynes Holmes and Rabbi Stephen Wise. The priest's remarks were greatly appreciated by the firemen and when he had concluded Mayor Walker whispered, "Thanks."[33] Shortly thereafter, an investigation of Walker's activities by Judge Samuel Seabury discredited the dapper mayor.

Whether he was involved in national monetary policies, clashes with cardinals, or siding with a city politician of questionable character, Father Coughlin retained the steadfast support of Bishop Gallagher, who believed that the priest's message was in the tradition of Christ, Pope Leo XIII and Pope Pius XI.[34]

Because of his supportive nationwide audience, it was not surprising that Governor Franklin Delano Roosevelt of New York, a leading Democratic presidential candidate, should invite Coughlin to the Democratic Convention to be held in Chicago that summer of 1932. Father Coughlin was flattered by the invitation and accepted.

I accepted because I had been friendly with him and I liked his philosophy at that time. Roosevelt seemed like the natural person to do something about the crisis our country was in. I didn't understand the predicament Hoover was confronted with. I only found out later that Hoover was the greatest president of America in my lifetime.[35]

4

High Finance

FATHER Coughlin saw Roosevelt as the obvious Democratic party candidate for the presidency, and therefore decided to get in touch with the governor through his cousin, G. Hall Roosevelt, the city comptroller of Detroit, to lay the groundwork for a political alliance.

In the spring of 1931, Coughlin told him of his desire to meet with Franklin Roosevelt. The Detroit comptroller then wrote to his cousin to tell him of the priest's wish:

Father Coughlin is probably known to you by this time and is famous for being the director of fifty-two secretaries, which he has found necessary to handle his mail which gets as high as 250,000 letters a day. He would like to tender his services. From what I can make out his brethren in the Church tolerate him. He would be difficult to handle and might be full of dynamite, but I think you had better prepare to say "yes" or "no". Of course, he has a following just about equal to that of Mr. Gandhi. We would probably enjoy the leadership of a lot of Indians however.[1]

Father Coughlin does not recall any response from Franklin Roosevelt at that time. But by the spring of 1932 the priest, using Frank Murphy, the Democratic mayor of Detroit and a member of his parish, as his liaison man, did make contact with Roosevelt. In a meeting at a New York hotel, the priest and the future

President of the United States met for the first time and ex-
changed views on the issues of the day. Coughlin was greatly
impressed by the governor's advocacy of cheap currency and a
"new deal" for the common man. According to Father Coughlin,
Roosevelt seemed very impressed with his knowledge of economics and the social problems confronting the masses of the
American people. Before they parted, Roosevelt promised Coughlin that he would be his close confidant on economic and social
issues. Coughlin, for his part, promised to throw his support behind Roosevelt's presidential candidacy.[2] How serious Roosevelt
was about his promise to Coughlin is open to question. There can
be little doubt, however, that Roosevelt knew the size of Coughlin's listening audience, and wanted his support during the upcoming campaign.

At the Democratic Convention in the summer of 1932, Coughlin threw all his influence behind Roosevelt's candidacy, a decision which he still maintains was a correct one in view of the facts
then available. "It was Roosevelt or ruin because Roosevelt promised to enact legislation to take care of the poor and to enable us to
get out of our emergency."[3] Both Coughlin and Frank Murphy
played large roles in hammering out the Democratic party platform. They stayed in adjoining hotel suites and spent many long
nights devising suggestions for the platform. Roosevelt was gracious to both men and encouraged them in their efforts.[4] With
Roosevelt's nomination accomplished, the priest asked Roosevelt
to ensure that Jimmy Walker would receive a fair hearing from
the Seabury committee. To show his support for Walker, Coughlin wrangled an invitation from Roosevelt to attend the hearing in
Albany.

I went over to the governor's chambers, where the case for indicting
Walker was being heard. I listened. I sat there and said nothing. Mr.
Roosevelt was there and he was very gracious to me. He smiled at me
and I smiled back. He let everyone know we were friends, which was
all right, because we were.[5]

Upon his return to Royal Oak on August 12, Father Coughlin
wrote to Roosevelt and told him of how he had been thinking of

the deleterious consequences for Roosevelt in the presidential election if Walker were dealt with severely:

Whether it is fortunate or unfortunate, religion does play a prominent part in major political campaigns. I was thinking of the 20 odd million Catholics in this country, among whom are 5,000,000 voters. I was thinking of the tremendous influence which Mr. Walker has upon the majority of these voters. It was possible for clever Republicans and others who feel that they have been victims of circumstances to use this Walker case against your best interests.

The priest went on to label Samuel Seabury a "member of the Klan," and to warn Roosevelt: "You have gone to the extreme limit on the matter of this perilous case. I would not be loyal to you or to the Democratic party unless I spoke fearlessly and truthfully of those pertinent things."[6]

Roosevelt's reply was polite: "It is good to have your letter. . . . I am, as you know, giving the defense every latitude and I am being scrupulously careful not to make up my mind in any way until their case is wholly in. I do hope I shall have the privilege of seeing you again soon."[7] Shortly thereafter, the matter was resolved through Walker's resignation as mayor of New York City.

With the Walker affair out of the way, Father Coughlin once again turned to the monetary problems facing the country. In a letter to Roosevelt a month later, the priest again advocated a soldiers' bonus as a way to get the country off the gold standard. He went on to boast of his influence: "I have twenty-six of the most powerful stations in our network. The east is thoroughly covered as is the middle west and the west as far as Denver."[8] Then he bluntly asked Roosevelt to mention him in a campaign speech as a priest "who spoke for the rights of the common man." There is no record of Roosevelt's having followed this suggestion.

On October 30, 1932, with his broadcasting contract renewed, Father Coughlin began a series emphasizing that Wall Street bankers had manipulated the gold standard to bring on the depression and then to perpetuate it. The country was at the nadir of the depression. Over eleven and a half million workers were unemployed. Almost one million farmers had lost their land. Thousands of banks had failed. The United States Treasury was empty. Father Coughlin told his radio audience that he was convinced that the international bankers were responsible for the nation's pitiful economic condition. He maintained that the nation's economic ills could be overcome if the government revaluated the price of gold, an action that he believed would result in more currency circulating in the economy, and in the reduction of public and private debts, since they could be repaid by cheaper money. "The only two ways out are revaluation of our gold ounce or repudiation of our debts. One way is Christianity. The other is Bolshevism."[9]

The Coughlin prescription called for the price of gold to be raised from $20.67 an ounce to $41.34 an ounce. The priest claimed that the resultant cheapening of money would automatically slash the United States national debt by 50 percent. With Roosevelt's victory in the November election, Father Coughlin was positive that he was now in a position to be the catalyst in the implementation of his financial program.

In January, 1933, shortly before the inauguration, Roosevelt invited Coughlin to visit him at his New York City residence. When the priest arrived, the President-elect was having his portrait painted. Roosevelt was most effusive in conveying his thanks to the priest for his support during the election campaign. Shortly after, the two men retired to talk privately and go over the "shopping list" Coughlin had brought with him.

Father Coughlin recalls that he told Roosevelt of the financial program he wished to see enacted into law, and Roosevelt promised that it would be given careful consideration and that a substantial portion of it would be incorporated into the fiscal policies of the new government. Pleased with Roosevelt's response, Coughlin went on to point out the paucity of Catholics holding ambassadorial rank, even to those governments whose populations were overwhelmingly Catholic. He mentioned South America as a glaring example of this situation, telling Roosevelt, "I'd like to have some Catholic ambassadors down there who would do good for all of us. If I know Catholic psychology that's the way to placate these people." Roosevelt doubted that this could be done, as

his nominee for Secretary of State, Cordell Hull, had already selected the ambassadors. But Roosevelt did have one spot available.
"I'll tell you what I can do. You can have the Philippines if you
want it." Quickly Father Coughlin said, "Frank Murphy would
make a fine ambassador." Roosevelt concurred and Murphy was
summoned to New York City, where on the next day the President-elect told him, "Frank, you are going to the Philippines."[10]
Shortly thereafter Roosevelt announced that he had appointed
Murphy Governor General of the Philippines.

Despite this action there is evidence that Roosevelt was becoming disenchanted with Coughlin and his demands. Roosevelt con-
fided to Rexford Tugwell, a close adviser, "We must tame these
fellows [i.e., Coughlin and Huey Long] and make them useful to
us."[11] Mrs. Roosevelt said later that her husband had always "disliked and distrusted" Father Coughlin.[12]

If that were so in 1932, Father Coughlin was certainly not aware
of Roosevelt's feelings. In fact, the President-elect asked the priest
to prepare a draft for the Inaugural Address. Coughlin understood
that Raymond Moley and Thomas (Tommy the Cork) Cochran,
two of Roosevelt's advisers, had also been asked to prepare texts
for possible use by the incoming President. Father Coughlin maintains that Roosevelt's Inaugural Address was probably a combina-
tion of the three texts, but he is certain that he "wrote quite a bit
of it."[13] His recollections, however, are disputed by James Farley,
Eleanor Roosevelt and Raymond Moley.[14] Farley claims that
there was a suggestion that Coughlin be asked to draft a speech for
Roosevelt's inauguration, but that this suggestion was vetoed by
Moley. How much Father Coughlin actually contributed to
Roosevelt's Inaugural Address is open to question, but there is no
doubt that the priest considered himself an insider in the President's policy-making council. The validity of Father Coughlin's
conviction was not confirmed by the course of events.

On March 4, Roosevelt declared a national bank holiday, and
Coughlin seized this opportunity to charge on his radio show that
holding companies controlling a large number of banks were hide-
out banks, which robbed "the widow and the orphan." He went
on to charge that officers of the First National Bank of Detroit

had advised businessmen with large deposits in the bank to withdraw their funds prior to the bank holiday. The priest said that
$63 million had been withdrawn and that the bank was only
$12\frac{1}{2}$ percent liquid while it proclaimed that it was 80 percent liquid.
When the Union Guardian Trust Company failed, Coughlin
claimed that Detroit bankers were responsible because they had
approved claims to themselves which allowed them to cover financial losses.

Cognizant of the furor raised by these charges, Secretary of the
Treasury William Woodin appointed federal officials to oversee
the assets of the Guardian National Bank of Commerce and the
First National Bank of Detroit. Father Coughlin claims that his
accusations and the government investigation of the Detroit banks
had been worked out beforehand, and that Woodin had led him to
believe that it would be necessary for him to attack the Detroit
bankers in order to provide the wedge for the federal government
to move in.[15] The Roosevelt Papers provide proof that Coughlin
was in touch with Woodin and Marvin McIntyre, Roosevelt's
appointments secretary. McIntyre, himself, wrote of having returned a phone call from Coughlin, noting that "I had him talk
with Woodin."[16]

Father Coughlin's March 26, 1933, broadcast contained many of
the statements and expressions which made him understood and
loved by millions and hated by countless others. He spoke of

the Morgans, the Kuhn-Loebs, the gamblers of Wall Street assisted by
the Mitchells, the Harrimans and their lieutenants in crime attired as
sleek as undertakers and wearing white carnations in their lapels. . . .
Modern banking had degenerated into a crap game where the dice too
often were loaded, a crap game played by the unscrupulous expert with
other people's money.[17]

Claiming to be speaking for the administration, Father Coughlin
was particularly critical of the actions of E. D. Stair, president of
the Detroit Bankers Company and publisher of the *Detroit Free
Press*, a newspaper that was strongly opposed to his activities.
The priest claims that the editorial stand of the *Free Press* had
nothing to do with his criticism of Stair. Rather, Fred Fisher of

Fisher Body, a close friend of his, had told him about the financial manipulations of the Detroit bankers. Stair "took it upon himself to defend the banks. He was talking up a chimney because he didn't have all the facts. Mr. Fisher had more facts than he had."

Coughlin admits that he had never discussed the matter (the Detroit banking situation) with Roosevelt. "But I thought I knew his mind. . . . I just knew that Roosevelt wanted me to do something to rectify these banks."[18] By the following day the White House was well aware of the potential embarrassment it faced. McIntyre wrote to Louis Howe, a trusted Roosevelt adviser, of his phone conversation with Father Coughlin and of his finally referring the priest to Woodin:

Mr. Woodin did talk to him on the telephone but I don't know in detail what he said. Professor Moley can probably throw more light on this matter. Confidentially, I think the Reverend Father took considerable liberties with the facts and most certainly misquoted me and misstated the case in saying that the request for him to go on the radio and to answer the Commissioner came from the Administration. Will take up with you the question of whether we should pass this up or take some action. I told the President at the time just what was said. I believe that the Father asked to talk with the President but am not absolutely sure about that now.[19]

Three days later Attorney General Homer Cummings received a transcript of Father Coughlin's radio talk from Steve Early, Roosevelt's press secretary. Obviously, Father Coughlin was keeping everyone in the White House awake.

On Monday, March 27, 1933, the *Detroit Free Press* led the counterattack against the charges made by Coughlin, labeling them "flamboyant demagoguery." The newspaper denied the veracity of Coughlin's statements and claimed:

The demagogue Coughlin, raving over the radio for two years with his attacks on the banks, did much to bring about the present condition. He robbed the people of confidence in these directors and their banks and was one of the chief causes of withdrawals of funds from them during the past two years to a total of over two hundred million dollars.

And it is ironically true that while a priest of the Church did his best to destroy the First National Bank with his radio bombast, the Church he misrepresents was the largest single debtor to the institution.

In addition to the editorial rebuking Father Coughlin, Stair sent a telegram to President Roosevelt requesting a complete investigation of Coughlin's charges. This telegram was printed in the Tuesday, March 28, edition of the *Free Press:*

Dear Mr. President: A slanderous radio attack has been made against myself and other citizens of this city in connection with the banking situation here by Fr. C. E. Coughlin who presents himself from time to time as the spokesman for your administration. To clarify the situation and to save our city from over inflammatory attacks, to still all false rumors and to vindicate the decency and the dignity of our community I urgently request that you direct your Department of Justice to begin an immediate and thorough and complete investigation. We stand unafraid and eager to cooperate in every way to save our city from slanderous wreckers.

On that same day, the *Free Press* renewed its attack on Father Coughlin, refuting point by point the charges made by the priest in his Sunday broadcast. On Wednesday the *Free Press* accused Coughlin of speculating on the stock market with money gathered from contributions made by tens of thousands of poor Americans who had no idea that their money was being used for the personal accumulation of wealth by the priest. The newspaper accused him of running a radio racket and of having lost $13,955.80 on an investment in 500 shares of stock in Kelsey-Hayes Wheel Corporation at $60 per share.

Only $4,233.72 of the required money to purchase the stock came from his personal account. $9,216.28 came from the account of the League of the Little Flower, a nonprofit, nontaxed corporation controlled by Father Coughlin. An additional $10,587.50 was borrowed on a note from the Guardian National Bank of Commerce, then known as the National Bank of Commerce. The total sum required for the purchase was $30,110.89. Paine, Webber and

Company served as the broker. On June 5, 6 and 9, 1930, the 500 shares, plus 238 additional shares of the stock he had purchased later on, were sold for $23,485.78.[20] During the week of March 27, 1933, this stock was selling for twenty cents a share.

There can be little doubt that Father Coughlin was dealing in large amounts of cash. On March 19, 1931, he purchased $80,-048.04 worth of government bonds. The money for this purchase was withdrawn from the Guardian National Bank. On June 5, 1931, the priest withdrew $30,000 from the account of the League of the Little Flower and on December 16, 1931, he withdrew $27,000 from the same account. On that day Father Coughlin transferred $50,000 from his three bank accounts to the Guardian National Bank to meet a debt incurred in the name of his own St. Thérèse's Parish.

Money came easily to Father Coughlin. On March 4, 1930, for example, Father Coughlin's personal bank account had totaled $10,018.82. By June 10, 1930, his account totaled $55,512.20. His money came from contributions made by listeners from all over the country. "Most of the currency turned in by the priest for exchange came in small bills, which clerks of the banks say frequently amounted to $20,000 in one dollar bills at one time."[21]

In a radio reply to the *Free Press* accusations, Father Coughlin denied that he was guilty of any impropriety. He admitted that listeners sent him a great deal of money, but he said that broadcasting expenses alone for 1932 and 1933 totaled $202,856.75. Coughlin also mentioned that hundreds of thousands of copies of his speeches were mailed to all who requested them. The annual expense for an organization just to perform this service totaled $450,000.

He went on to say that it was necessary to invest or hold in safe places funds that accumulated to him. One such way was to invest in stocks of such companies as Kelsey-Hayes and the Packard Motor Car Company and in United States government bonds. While admitting to a $13,000 loss on $110,000 he had invested, Coughlin claimed that if he had placed the $110,000 in the First National Bank of Detroit, a subsidiary of Stair's Detroit Bankers

Company, his losses would have been $66,000 because that bank was able to pay depositors only forty cents on each dollar withdrawn from an account.[22]

But the *Free Press* continued its offensive. On Friday, March 31, 1933, the paper claimed that "the Reverend Charles E. Coughlin filed no income tax returns for a period of years up to 1931." It further stated that the Detroit office of the Collector of Internal Revenue was conducting an investigation of this charge. When the investigation was completed the government returned $8.61 to Father Coughlin for overpayment on his income tax returns. Fred Cook, the chief field deputy of the Bureau of Internal Revenue, delivered a stinging rebuke to the *Free Press* in a report to Marvin McIntyre:

> The examination disclosed that there was no merit whatever to the statements made by the *Detroit Free Press* and it is my opinion that the *Free Press* having knowledge that the Collector must necessarily investigate any complaint made, entered such complaint with intent to embarrass Father Coughlin, with whom they were in controversy. In fact, their entering a complaint on flimsy evidence amounted to a subsidization of governmental functions to assist them in their private feuds.[23]

Father Coughlin never forgave Stair and his *Free Press* for the nine days of broadside attacks against him. There would be a lull in the battle until the summer of 1933, at which time the ill-will between Coughlin and Stair would rise to the surface once more.

Critics of Coughlin, such as E. D. Stair, and later John L. Spivak, raised questions as to how the priest managed the huge amounts of money he received regularly from his admiring radio audience. Father Coughlin never responded to the queries. The answer is complex. During the course of his career as a public figure from 1928 to 1942, Father Coughlin controlled myriad corporations through which he carried on his activities. On January 10, 1928, he founded the League of the Little Flower, a nonprofit corporation, with himself as president. The League had no real or personal property. The principal place of business for the corporation was Woodward Avenue and Twelve Mile Road, which happened to be the address of his church. The League was created to meet the financial strains caused by the growth of his appeal, although its stated purpose was to obtain funds to build a new church. Father Coughlin was able to exercise close supervision over the corporation through control of its officers, all of whom were clerical workers in his employ. Only the original organizers or their successors could choose officers.[24]

By the time the League was dissolved on July 24, 1930, it had over $40,000 in assets and no liabilities.[25] Included among the assets was $3,904.87 owed to the corporation by Thomas J. Coughlin.[26]

On August 15, 1930, Father Coughlin organized the Radio League of the Little Flower, whose ostensible purpose was to raise money to defray the costs of his radio broadcasts and of publishing printed material. The Radio League was to be financed by donations from his radio listeners and by the sale of periodicals and literature. The priest's control of the corporation was strengthened by the fact that as with the League of the Little Flower, only the original organizers or their successors could choose corporation officers. The three officers were also its original organizers. Father Coughlin was president; Eugenia Burke, vice-president; and Amy Collins, the secretary and treasurer of the Radio League. The 1930 Annual Report of the corporation listed assets of $44,484.38, while liabilities were $5,579.61.

By 1933, Father Coughlin required 106 clerks and 4 personal secretaries to answer the mail resulting from his increased radio audience. An incredibly large number of the letter writers sent dollar bills to support the priest's cause.

The Radio League of the Little Flower was Father Coughlin's largest money-maker — nonprofit, nontaxed, and essentially financed through the donations of listeners who thought that the money would be used for broadcasting and for religious and charitable causes.

In 1935, the Royal Oak Post Office revealed that the Radio League of the Little Flower had cashed four million dollars in money orders in a twenty-month period.[27] By this time, Father Coughlin was broadcasting over twenty-six stations from Maine to

Colorado, although the assets of the Radio League declined. This can be partially attributed to the cost of his radio show, which was between $14,000 and $15,000 a week, and the construction of the new Shrine of the Little Flower Church, costs of which were paid by the Radio League.[28] Furthermore, in 1934, Father Coughlin organized the National Union for Social Justice, which proved to be a drain on funds of the Radio League to the tune of $76,692.17. The Radio League also provided funds to the Social Justice Publishing Company, a privately owned, profit-making corporation which consistently lost money. However, the annual reports of the Radio League from 1936 to 1941 showed a marked increase in corporate assets.

On March 30, 1933, in the midst of the controversy with Stair and the *Free Press*, Father Coughlin's home was bombed. The explosion occurred shortly after 3:00 A.M., breaking four windows in the cellar and filling the house with smoke. No one was injured, but Father Coughlin was greatly agitated and telephoned Mayor Murphy to ensure a prompt investigation of the blast. The police said that the bomb — black powder in a four-inch by ten-inch cardboard box with a short fuse — had been lowered into the basement by tying it to a cord from a child's bathrobe. Father Coughlin believed that the explosion was meant to intimidate rather than kill him. Police were stationed around his home and the church for the next several weeks, but the culprit was never found.

His broadcasts during the remainder of the 1932–1933 broadcasting year concentrated on attacking the money changers and demanding that they be driven from their positions of power. Father Coughlin was doing his best to accomplish this, particularly in his own Detroit area. In June, 1933, he requested a federal investigation of the banking situation in Detroit. This request was made to Jesse Jones, newly appointed chairman of the Reconstruction Finance Corporation, and William Julian, the Treasurer of the United States.[29] Copies of these letters were sent to Marvin McIntyre with a note reinforcing the request for a federal investigation.

I am damnably in earnest about this thing. Perhaps I have a clearer insight into this whole affair because I am on the ground where I enjoy a ringside seat.

I am asking you as a sincere favor to bring this to our beloved President's attention. One word from him will set Homer Cummings in action.[30]

There was no response to the letters.[31] But Coughlin was not to be deterred; his mission had now become a vendetta. His attacks on the Detroit bankers had resulted in an increase in the mail he was receiving. He now had to maintain a truck to pick up from the post office the many sacks of letters sent to him. Some weeks he received over 400,000 letters, most of which supported his attacks against the bankers.

Father Coughlin's constant pleas for an investigation finally culminated in the appointment of Judge Harry B. Keiden to investigate the banking situation in Detroit. On August 23, 1933, Father Coughlin testified before Judge Keiden. The courtroom was jam-packed as the priest sat in the witness stand and claimed that stockbrokers' accounts purportedly showing his stock market dealings were faked by the *Free Press*. Coughlin now admits that he did make the stock transactions in question, but that the *Free Press* had written in his name on the photostatic copy it reproduced on its news pages. An examination of the photostats bears out his contention.

Coughlin soon turned his appearance before Keiden into an effort to publicize his support for President Roosevelt and his fiscal policies:

We have wondered if there is such a thing as slander and calumny, whether it is a function of the press to obstruct the new deal, whether it is the province of certain individuals to load adverse criticism on a man whom I love because he is my friend and whom I revere because he is my President, Franklin Roosevelt.

I know how his heart is anxiously set upon putting into effect the promise he made in his inaugural address, to drive the money changers out of the temple. I know there is no power in this city and no group of editors and publishers who dare to stand and oppose Franklin Roosevelt's new deal. I for one would give my life rather than let them get away with it.

And then, after bringing about the depression, they turned on President Roosevelt — and here I certainly censure them; they turned on the President of the new deal and in this very courtroom got away with murder by blaming Mr. Roosevelt for causing the wreck of our banks.

I hope no newspaper man here will say I am defending Mr. Roosevelt. But I am defending a principle; I am defending Pope Leo XIII: and Pope Pius XI. I am defending a Protestant President who has more courage than 90 percent of the Catholic priests in the country, a President who thinks right, who pleads for the common man, who knows patience and suffering, who knows that men come before bonds, and that human rights are more sacred than financial rights.

Oh I know that millions were pooled to defeat Roosevelt. I know that Catholic Smith said, "Stop Roosevelt," and I know that Protestant Hoover cried "Radical Roosevelt," but, nevertheless, he is a President who wants to give Christian doctrines a chance to make good, who is willing to make the Christian experiment.[32]

This was probably the high point of Father Coughlin's support for Roosevelt. His strong public stance in defense of the President would soon vanish. Speaking to newsmen, Father Coughlin stated with certainty that Stair and other Detroit bankers could not "escape indictment by the Federal court. . . . I don't say they'll be found guilty but they misled the public. . . . The Detroit Bankers Company might better be called the Detroit Looters Company."[33]

Stair's testimony was in sharp contrast to Father Coughlin's. He spoke in a monotone, and he never mentioned the priest by name, although he did characterize him as a man "devoid of truth and honor." Nor did he mention the name of Michigan Senator James Couzens, who had also accused members of the board of directors of the First National Bank of manipulating the bank's assets for their own gain.[34]

No indictments were ever returned against Stair or any other Detroit banker. The results of Father Coughlin's controversy with the bankers and the press are difficult to measure. More mail than usual was sent to Coughlin, most of it supporting his stand. He received a great deal of publicity throughout the nation and became the advocate of millions of common people in the struggle against the rich bankers and businessmen who, they believed, had precipitated the depression.

Roosevelt, however, "was as angry as hell at Coughlin for getting the administration involved in that mess."[35] Roosevelt's anger was, in the long run, the most important consequence of the dispute, and although their relationship remained outwardly friendly for two more years, the freeze had already set in. But Father Coughlin did not know this at the time.

Because of his involvement in the Detroit banking controversy and because of his broadcasts which consistently advocated a restructuring of the nation's monetary system, Father Coughlin's reputation in some circles as an expert on this nation's fiscal problems grew. Millions of his listeners regarded him as such, and in the Congress six senators and fifty-nine congressmen even petitioned President Roosevelt to appoint him to the United States delegation to the London Economic Conference. Included among the senators were Huey Long and Henrik Shipstead of Minnesota, a close friend of Coughlin's who became associated with the American Far Right in the 1930s. Most notable of the representatives who signed this petition was Congressman Emanuel Celler of New York City, who until 1972 remained one of the most influential members of the House.

The London Economic Conference ended in failure. Though not appointed a delegate, Father Coughlin was pleased when Roosevelt refused to make any of the concessions necessary to ensure international monetary reform. The priest believed that the President had acted to minimize the power of the international bankers in the United States. When the conference ended, Father Coughlin sent President Roosevelt a message applauding his actions. The President, criticized in many quarters for his undercutting of the conference, thanked Coughlin for his "nice telegram about my message to the Conference at London. It was good of you to send it and I am grateful for it."[36]

In July, 1933, Father Coughlin sent the President a wire urging him to take action that would result in "real revaluation. In other words, there must be an issue of greenbacks."[37] By now Roosevelt was weary of the priest's telling him how to manage the financial affairs of the nation, but he was not ready to tell him so. Instead, the President instructed Marvin McIntyre to acknowledge the wire by writing a gracious letter, thanking the priest for his concern.[38] McIntyre went a little beyond these instructions by mentioning to Coughlin that the President was looking forward to seeing him soon.[39] Coughlin wired back asking for a specific appointment. Realizing that McIntyre had made a mistake, Roosevelt still politely refused to be tied down to a specific date.[40]

By now Coughlin was beginning to understand that the President was putting him off.

> Listen. I was never stupid. I realized that the President now considered me burdensome. But, he owed me things. After all, I had helped make him President. Besides it wasn't him who was against me. It was the people around him. I was determined that I would win him back over to my side.[41]

Father Coughlin made an attempt to accomplish this by first admonishing Roosevelt for the legislation he was supporting, but then promising to support him in his endeavors. When the National Industrial Relations Act (NIRA) was passed, establishing the National Recovery Administration (NRA), he wrote Roosevelt informing him that

> NIRA alone cannot break the depression. . . . It is true that NIRA shares work but in doing so it shares prosperity along with poverty . . . the laborer is not satisfied with a minimum wage which he fears will become the maximum and which at present does not permit him to pay his debts nor to purchase the conveniences of life.[42]

Publicly, however, Coughlin cited the success of the NRA, claiming that it would prevent the exploitation of labor and unfair competition. He went on to say that the success of the NRA had resulted in Roosevelt's becoming equal in stature to George Washington and Abraham Lincoln. But privately he continued to warn Roosevelt of the failures of the NRA and its unpopularity with his listening audience.[43]

When Congress enacted the Agricultural Administration Act (AAA), which called for crop reduction and livestock and crop destruction, Father Coughlin was displeased. He thought that the solution to the farmers' problems was for the government to issue greenbacks. He described the provisions of the AAA as "foolish proposals aimed at starving us into prosperity."[44] By now Coughlin felt that his two great enemies in the Roosevelt coterie were Raymond Moley and Henry Wallace, the Secretary of Agriculture. He tried to counteract their influence by writing the President to inform him of the evils that these two supporters of the AAA were creating for the nation.[45] There is no record of Roosevelt's reply.

On October 11, 1933, Roosevelt and the AAA and politics were far removed from Coughlin's thoughts. It was a great day in his life. The official dedication of his new Shrine of the Little Flower Church and its beautiful Charity Crucifixion Tower, which was already completed although much work remained to be done on the rest of the church, was to take place. Bishop Gallagher, confined to Providence Hospital, sent words of blessing. In Gallagher's absence, his close friend Archbishop Schrembs of Cleveland was present. Also present were Wilbur Brucker, governor of Michigan, Frank Murphy, and many other important Church, state and municipal figures.

It was a beautiful church. The tower reached 180 feet into the sky. At night, a battery of floodlights illuminated the building. A larger than life figure of Jesus Christ looked down on the intersection of Woodward Avenue and Twelve Mile Road. Circling the base of the tower were sculptured stone carvings of archangels, one of which, St. Michael, wore the face of Michael Gallagher. It was from the tower of the church that Father Coughlin would now make his weekly broadcasts, thanks to a wire run to it from WJR, Detroit. His broadcasting room could be reached only by walking up a dark, narrow spiral staircase to the top floor of the tower. In a corner of the room was the desk at which he sat when delivering his radio speeches. The wiring which once carried his voice throughout the nation is still there today, although his broadcasts have long since become history. The tower also contained offices for his employees who were officers of his corporations as well: Eugenia Burke, Dorothy and Marie Rhodes, Cora Quinlan, Amy Collins and Bernice Marcinkiewicz. In the large basement of the tower as many as one hundred and six of his employees received, catalogued, and responded to the millions of letters he received annually. A small printing office in the tower ran off reprints of his Sunday sermons for distribution to admiring listeners.

The church itself was in the shape of an octagon. It seated 2,600 people and when completely furnished cost over one million dollars. It was constructed of the finest Vermont granite and Indiana limestone. Exterior stones bore the names of the various states from which contributors had donated money to build the church. Inside the church were many beautiful lustrous marble statues from all over the world. By 1970 these statues were insured for over one million dollars. In one section of the church were depicted flags of nations. Included among these were the flags of the Soviet Union and Nazi Germany.

Under a square canopy of stained glass there was an open arena bordered by a communion rail. The ceilings were painted in soft pastel shades. According to Father Joseph Fitzpatrick of Fordham University, the architecture of the edifice, "with its altar in the center of the church, surrounded by the pews, was forty years ahead of its time in terms of conducting religious services."[46]

Unhappily, commercial enterprises would soon surround the church. Motels would multiply along Woodward Avenue to accommodate the tens of thousands of people who would come to visit the church. Neon signs would proclaim their existence a good distance away. The "Shrine Super Service Gas Station," only a few feet from the church, would service the automobiles that brought many of the visitors to Royal Oak. The church itself would cater to visitors by selling pictures of Father Coughlin, Bibles, crucifixes and selected books, some of which, such as *The Mystical Body of Christ* and *The Rulers of Russia* by Reverend Denis Fahey, were anti-Semitic.

With his church dedicated, Father Coughlin resumed his campaign to reform the nation's monetary policies. On November 27,

Father Coughlin holds a meeting in New York Hippodrome, November, 1933. Henry Morgenthau, Sr., father of the Secretary of the Treasury, is speaking (United Press International Photo)

1933, he addressed an overflow crowd of seven thousand in the New York City Hippodrome. He urged his listeners to back the fiscal policies of President Roosevelt, and suggested once again that by edict the government double the value of the four and one half billion dollars worth of gold in its possession. It must be pointed out that Roosevelt did raise the price of gold to $35 an ounce as a result of the passage of the Gold Reserve Act in January, 1934, a few months after Father Coughlin's Hippodrome speech. This does not mean that Coughlin spoke with Roosevelt's approval. To the contrary, when the priest informed McIntyre of the contents of his Hippodrome speech, prior to its delivery, and asked him to secure the President's support for its contents, there was not even an acknowledgment of his request.[47]

By now it should have been obvious to Father Coughlin that the President neither welcomed his aid nor felt kindly disposed toward him. James Farley recalls that in late 1933, "the President was so upset with the constant demands of Coughlin that he said of him, 'He should run for the presidency himself. Who the hell does he think he is?' "[48] That remark would seem almost prophetic by the time the 1936 presidential elections rolled around.

In the midst of his attempts to bring about monetary reform, Father Coughlin became embroiled in a public dispute with another powerful figure, his onetime close friend, Al Smith, a former governor of New York and the 1928 Democratic party presidential candidate. The dispute had its origins in Smith's political break with Roosevelt and his criticism of the President's fiscal policies. Smith strongly supported the maintenance of the price of gold at $20.67 per ounce.

In a telegram to Roosevelt, Father Coughlin told the President not to worry about Smith's criticisms:

In 1929 the good governor sold out to Mr. Morgan, Bishop Gallagher of Detroit and the late Bishop Dunne of New York being seated in the Governor's motor car at the corner of Broad and Wall Street while the sellout took place. The Governor on coming forth from the building boasted to the two bishops that he had received a magnificent loan through the graces of Mr. Morgan and that the Empire State Building could now be saved.[49]

On his November 26, 1933, broadcast, Father Coughlin blasted Smith, accusing him of being a wealthy banker who was on the payroll of the County Bank of New York. Smith declared this charge "absolutely false," and denied that his position on the monetary question was in any way affected by a loan from J. P. Morgan. Monsignor Thomas Carrol, Chancellor of the New York archdiocese, described Father Coughlin's attack on Smith as unwarranted. The Reverend John Belford, pastor of the Church of the Nativity in Brooklyn, described Father Coughlin as an "infernal nuisance" who should be mandated to cease his "wild ranting that is a disgrace to the Church . . . a public enemy; a very dangerous man. . . . He is using his church as a soap box to exploit himself, and he has won an enormous following. His talks are not religious, but political and purely selfish."[50]

John Jacob Raskob, a millionaire friend of Smith's, denied that the former governor of New York had obtained for him the loan needed for the construction of the Empire State Building. Raskob said that he had made an arrangement with the Metropolitan Life Insurance Company of New York to finance the project. The *New York Times* criticized Father Coughlin, but urged that he be allowed to continue to speak out. "Let stormy eloquence roll on like thunder. After it will come again the small voice of reason."[51]

But the priest was not without his supporters, the most important of whom was Bishop Gallagher. On the occasion of the Smith controversy, Gallagher said that Father Coughlin was "justified in his conclusions" about Smith, although he himself did not consider Smith a tool of Wall Street. Gallagher went on to point out: "As in previous controversies I have no intention of interfering. No heresy has been preached. Father Coughlin in his address is advocating the principles set down by Leo XIII and Pius XI. He is perfectly justified in doing that."[52]

It may come as a surprise to many to learn that Father Coughlin also received the backing of Monsignor John Ryan, the well-known social reformer and close friend of President Roosevelt's, who would later become a bitter enemy of Coughlin. Ryan claimed that Father Coughlin was "on the side of the angels." In a letter to Monsignor Belford, Ryan wrote that "Father Charles E.

Coughlin is a messenger of God donated to the American people for the purpose of rectifying the outrageous mistakes they have made in the past."[53] This was a far cry from what the two men would be saying about one another in the middle and late 1930s. Recalling the dispute with Smith, Father Coughlin says that he spoke too hastily in publicly chastising the former governor of New York. "I have great reverence for Mr. Smith. . . . I think he was the finest governor we have had in New York."[54]

By the end of 1933, Father Coughlin had modified his monetary views to favor symmetalism:

I advocate using gold and silver together not separated together in one coin. In this coin, which we call the dollar, there will be 25 cents' worth of gold and 75 cents' worth of silver. Of course, this coin will not be meant for circulation. Paper money will be printed against it, but the paper money will be backed by real gold to the value of 25 cents and by real silver to the value of 75 cents.[55]

Father Coughlin's break with the Roosevelt administration revolved around this advocacy of increased reliance on a silver rather than a gold standard.

James Warburg, vice-chairman of the Bank of Manhattan Company, a friend of Roosevelt's and in the late 1930s a constant target of Father Coughlin's, responded to the priest's plea by saying that there was not enough gold and silver in the world to carry out his proposals.[56] But Father Coughlin renewed his advocacy of monetary reform in an appearance before the House Committee on Coinage, Weights and Measures. He proclaimed that if Congress did not support Roosevelt's plan to revalue money then "there will be a revolution in this country that will make the French Revolution look silly." He said that his listening audience believed that in the current economic crises "it is Roosevelt or ruin . . . our beloved President, inspired by a desire to preserve capitalism while ridding it of its major abuses and a desire to preserve human rights when confronted by property rights, has taken the first essential step toward revaluation of gold." Father Coughlin closed out his remarks by dramatically pointing out that "silver is just as good as gold. Christ was betrayed for thirty pieces of silver."[57]

Two days after his appearance before the congressional committee, Father Coughlin met President Roosevelt privately at the White House. For nearly an hour the two men were alone. Father Coughlin recalls that they spoke about the nation's monetary problems. "The President promised me that the country would go on the silver standard. It turned out that he was lying to me. But he was so damn charming that you couldn't help but like him."[58]

On his February 3, 1934, broadcast, Father Coughlin urged nationwide wage increases and shorter working hours. Commenting that "I should not teach the principles of industrial reform unless I practice them," the priest announced that he was immediately raising by 10 percent the pay of one hundred clerical employees and one hundred construction men in his employ.[59]

In March of 1934, Father Coughlin returned to Washington, D. C., to testify before a House banking subcommittee. Once again he used the opportunity to plead the case for remonitization of silver as essential to halt the decline in agricultural output. On March 11, 1934, Father Coughlin prescribed his own program to solve the economic ills of the country. He called for, among other things, the nationalization and revaluation of all gold, the restoration and nationalization of silver coinage, creation of a central bank to control currency and credit, the extension of credit for consumers as well as producers, and the elimination of all government bonds. In later broadcasts, he elaborated on the details of his program. He urged that a National Depository be created to replace the Federal Reserve System. He believed that a National Depository would serve as a depository for funds of private national banks and also serve as a reservoir of credit for the national government. In this system the federal government would directly control the issuance of money and credit.

Father Coughlin's hectic schedule was soon to have a detrimental effect on his health. Although his blue eyes still blazed and his brown hair was without a trace of gray, his weight had increased to two hundred pounds from constant nervous eating, and he had become a chain smoker. One Saturday evening, while alone in his office in the tower, he was struck with terrific chest pains. "I thought I was having a heart attack and that I would soon meet my Father. This incident hit me hard. I realized now that I was only human and that I could die, too."[60] For eleven hours the priest lay unconscious, until he was finally discovered at 8:00 A.M. on Sunday. His doctor diagnosed the problem as an attack of acute indigestion. The attack, however, did result in his being unable to make his regular Sunday broadcast. Despite this seizure, he soon returned to his normal rigorous schedule.

On his April 9, 1934, broadcast, Father Coughlin warned his listeners that the continuation of his radio show in the 1934–1935 broadcasting season and completion of his recently dedicated church were jeopardized because of a shortage of funds. The announcement of his financial needs must have had a beneficial effect, since construction of the church proceeded and the radio broadcasts continued to be heard in 1934 and 1935.

In his final broadcast of the 1933–1934 season, Father Coughlin was openly critical of President Roosevelt:

On March 4, 1933, we were an optimistic people. We had high hopes that the new day of financial independence had arrived. But something like consternation is beginning to be felt in America as the clouds of suspicion are darkening our hopes. . . . Meanwhile the rumor grows that while he may have been the Moses to lead America out of an Egyptian depression, he is getting lost in his narrow confines of the desert, beyond which there is the promised land of prosperity.[61]

As a result of this public criticism, President Roosevelt may have thought that it was the proper time to discredit Father Coughlin and many of the individuals and organizations that were pushing for unlimited coinage of silver. In late April of 1934, Secretary of the Treasury Henry Morgenthau, Jr., made public the names of individuals and organizations with large silver holdings. One name on that list stunned millions of Americans. Amy Collins, Father Coughlin's secretary, owned 500,000 ounces of silver. Also listed as owning 100,000 ounces of silver was Mrs. Maureen Thomas, the wife of Edward F. Thomas, a Detroit insurance man and a close friend of Father Coughlin's. The 500,000 ounces of silver owned by Miss Collins made her the largest individual owner of silver in the state of Michigan. She was also the secretary and treasurer of Father Coughlin's Radio League of the Little Flower, Inc. In a statement signed by Miss Collins, but written by Father Coughlin,[62] it was admitted that $20,000 of funds of the Radio League of the Little Flower were used to purchase the silver in the hope that it would result in a profit. Miss Collins went on to say that she had made the silver purchases on her own because she thought that a rise in the price of silver was imminent. An increase of one cent an ounce would have resulted in a gross profit of $5,000 on 500,000 ounces of silver. Miss Collins' statement added that Father Coughlin had nothing to do with the finances of the Radio League of the Little Flower.[63] This was an obvious falsehood. The articles of incorporation of the Radio League of the Little Flower gave Coughlin complete control over all aspects of the corporation's activities.

Father Coughlin issued a separate statement in which he attacked Treasury Secretary Morgenthau for releasing the names of people holding silver contracts. The priest stated that Morgenthau had acted to protect "the gold advocates, the Federal Reserve bankers, and the international bankers of ill repute. . . . This silver investigation smells to high heaven in so far as it is a dead herring smeared across the path of monetary reform."[64]

There are many significant aspects to Father Coughlin's involvement in silver speculation. First, the cotton exchange firm of Harriss and Vose, which had handled the purchase of the 500,000 ounces of silver, was an important lobbying agent working with Senator Elmer Thomas of Oklahoma for the passage of legislation revaluing upward the price of silver. Robert Harriss and George Le Blanc, two key members of this brokerage house, were close friends of both Father Coughlin and Senator Thomas and attended many of the former's public appearances in the New York area. While condemning financial speculators and Wall Street bankers, Father Coughlin seemed to be playing the same game he criticized others for playing. He had advocated the policies the government should follow to assist the common man, while standing to profit handsomely from the implementation of these policies. Many thousands of his listeners must now have begun to doubt his motives. If the Dies-Thomas measure on the floor of Congress had been enacted, the price of silver would have been fixed at $1.29 per ounce. Thus, Miss Collins' silver holdings would have brought in a profit of about $425,000. A vast sum of money in any day, but during the depression an amount almost beyond the imagination of most weary Americans. Even in explaining the acquisitions of silver, the priest was less concerned with what he had done than with attacking those he held responsible for divulging the information on the silver purchases. Exposure involving him with silver speculation did not result in his giving up his role as the champion of the common people. He resolved instead to play the role of martyr, the man whom the international bankers had decided to victimize because he was too dangerous to them. Addressing a crowd of 5,000 people on May 3, 1934, at the national convention of the Farmers Holiday Association, he once again raised the cry of "we want human rights to precede financial rights." But never again would Coughlin have the same huge, unquestioning audience he had prior to the disclosure of his involvement in silver speculation. Many people now saw him as a liar and a hypocrite.

Father Coughlin blames Roosevelt for the publication of the record pointing up the silver holdings.

We were supposed to be partners. He said he would rely on me. That I would be an important adviser. But he was a liar. He never took my advice. He just used me and when he was through with me he double-crossed me on that silver business.[65]

Any idea of a partnership with Roosevelt was now gone. Father Coughlin would have to find another way to shape the policies of the United States government, and he devoted his energy to devising new ways to accomplish this. "For the sake of millions of Americans, I knew that I must not fail in this task."[66]

5

Entering Politics: The National Union for Social Justice

FATHER Coughlin's direct involvement in America's political scene was formalized on December 11, 1934, when he created the National Union for Social Justice (NUSJ). The ostensible goals of the NUSJ were to uphold and defend the right of private ownership of property within the United States, with the qualification that this right was to be subordinated to human rights, and to strive to protect the masses of the American people against the greed and domination of powerful vested interests. The National Union stated it would do everything it could within the law to promote the common welfare by securing for all Americans, regardless of their race, creed or social situation, a genuine application of the principles of social justice.

Although the National Union for Social Justice was not legally organized until December 11, Father Coughlin had announced its creation on November 11, 1934, on his regular Sunday broadcast. In this broadcast he urged his listeners "to organize for action if you will: to organize for social united action which will be founded on God-given social truths which belong to Catholic and Protestant, to Jew and Gentile, to Black and white, to rich and poor, industrialist and to laborer."[1]

Father Coughlin presented his listeners his sixteen principles of social justice, and their preamble, which he still regards as being his great legacy to America:

Establishing my principles upon this preamble, namely, that we are creatures of a beneficent God, made to love and to serve Him in this world and enjoy Him forever in the next: that all this world's wealth of field, of forest, of mine and of miner has been bestowed upon us by a kind Father, therefore I believe that wealth, as we know it, originates from natural resources and from the labor which the children of God expend upon these resources. It is all ours except for the harsh, cruel and grasping ways of wicked men who first concentrated wealth into the hands of a few, then dominated states, and finally commenced to pit state against state in the frightful catastrophies of commercial warfare.

Following this preamble, there shall be the principles of social justice towards the realization of which we must strive:

1. I believe in liberty of conscience and liberty of education, not permitting the state to dictate either my worship to my God or my chosen avocation in life.

2. I believe that every citizen willing to work shall receive a just, living, annual wage which will enable him both to maintain and educate his family according to the standards of American decency.

3. I believe in nationalizing the public resources which by their very nature are too important to be held in the control of private individuals.

4. I believe in private ownership of all other property.

5. I believe in upholding the right to private property but in controlling it for the public good.

6. I believe in the abolition of the privately owned Federal Reserve Banking system and the establishment of a government owned Central Bank.

7. I believe in rescuing from the hands of private owners the right to coin and regulate the value of money, which right must be restored to Congress where it belongs.

8. I believe that one of the chief duties of this government owned Central Bank is to maintain the cost of living on an even keel and arrange for the repayment of dollar debts with equal value dollars.

9. I believe in the cost of production plus a fair profit for the farmer.

10. I believe not only in the right of the laboring man to organize in unions but also in the duty of the Government, which that laboring man supports, to protect these organizations against the vested interests of wealth and intellect.

11. I believe in the recall of all non-productive bonds and therefore in the alleviation of taxation.

12. I believe in the abolition of tax exempt bonds.

13. I believe in broadening the base of taxation according to the principles of ownership and the capacity to pay.

14. I believe in the simplification of government and the further lifting of crushing taxation from the slender revenues of the laboring class.

15. I believe that, in the event of a war for the defense of our nation and its liberties, there shall be a conscription of wealth as well as a conscription of men.

16. I believe in preferring the sanctity of property rights; for the chief concern of government shall be for the poor because, as it is witnessed, the rich have ample means of their own to care for themselves.[2]

Father Coughlin believes that the principles of social justice are just as important and just as valid today as they were when he announced them in 1934.

Although I have done some things that I would not repeat and some I am ashamed of, I stand one hundred percent behind the sixteen principles of social justice. I am still confident that long after I am gone, and my disputes with various individuals and groups are forgotten, I will be remembered for my sixteen principles. These principles will one day be enacted into law. They have to be.[3]

Father Coughlin considered his next broadcast so vital that he asked Bishop Gallagher to open it and then introduce him. In his remarks Bishop Gallagher left no doubt that he fully supported Coughlin's project when he said that Father Coughlin "has undertaken to apply Christ's principles to every day problems. May God bless his efforts."[4] Father Coughlin then defined what he meant by "National Union for Social Justice":

The word "national" implies that it is not for Michigan or for New York only. It is for every State in the nation.

The word "union" implies that it is not for Catholic or for Protestant or for Jew alone. Nor is it for laborer or farmer or for industrialist only. It is for all of our citizens irrespective of race, of color, of creed or of profession. It is to be dominated not by Catholic priest or Protestant minister or Jewish rabbi but by American citizens as such.

The words "social justice" point out that it is, first of all, opposed to the absolute injustices which are rampant in our midst, and signify that it stands for a fair and equitable distribution of wealth, of profits and the establishment of those principles which will guarantee us a right to life, liberty and to the pursuit of happiness. Lastly, it is an active organization which will not be contented to talk about these things, but which plans to reduce these things into practice. . . .[5]

In general, the National Union's program followed the guidelines set down by Pope Leo XIII in *Rerum Novarum* and by Pope Pius XI in *Quadragesimo Anno*. Father Coughlin saw the NUSJ and its sixteen principles as his vehicle for interpreting to the American masses, in a simplified manner, the abuses of capitalism which he was convinced had brought on the depression. Through the NUSJ he hoped to be able to present Americans with a viable political alternative for lifting the nation out of its social and economic depths.

On December 2, 1934, Father Coughlin announced seven additional principles that were to be used in combatting the evils of capitalism. They indicated Father Coughlin's growing belief that only increased government regulation could remedy the negative effects of the depression:

1. We maintain that it is not only the prerogative but it is also the duty of the government to limit the amount of profits acquired by any industry.

2. We maintain that it is the function of the government to see that industry is so operated that every laborer engaged therein will secure those goods which will be sufficient to supply all needs for an honest livelihood.

3. We further maintain that it is the duty of government to secure the production of all those industrial goods — food, wearing apparel, homes, drugs, books and all modern conveniences which the wealth of the nation, the natural resources of the land and the technical ability of

our scientists are able to produce until all honest needs within the nation are amply supplied.

This principle is contrary to the theory of capitalism. Capitalism produces for a profit to the individual owner. Social justice advocates the production for use at a profit for the national welfare as well as for the owner.

4. We maintain the principle that there can be no lasting prosperity if free competition exists in any industry. Therefore, it is the business of government not only to legislate for a minimum annual wage and a maximum working schedule to be observed by industry, but also to curtail individualism, that, if necessary, factories shall be licensed and their output shall be limited. For it is not in accordance with social justice that the owner of an industry will so operate his factory as to destroy free competition and thereby use his private property to the detriment of society.

5. It is the aim of the National Union for Social Justice to assist in the re-establishment of vocational groups. By this I mean that the laboring class who practice the same trade or profession should combine in units independent, if they so choose, of the factory where they work or of the industry in which they are employed.

6. It is the aim of the National Union for Social Justice to so work towards a reform in government that the Department of Labor shall not only protect labor but shall counsel and guide it in its negotiations with capital.

7. The National Union for Social Justice contends that strikes and lockouts are absolutely unnecessary. For in the case of disagreement between employer and employee it is the business of the public authority to intervene and settle such disputes which can be settled amicably by the parties involved. For it is our observation that both strikes and lockouts have occasioned more harm to the common good of the nation than any benefit which has been derived. But in the case of the government's neglecting its duty to settle such industrial disputes, always keeping in mind that there is no settlement without a just and living wage for the laborer and an equitable distribution of profits to all, then there is nothing left except for a united labor to refuse to sell its services at a loss just the same as it is unreasonable to expect the farmer to plow his ground and sow his seed at a loss.[6]

Father Coughlin's attack on America's economic system stemmed from his belief that the central government had an obligation to supply work for the labor force and guarantee it a minimum annual wage. He tried to win the support of the working class by emphasizing its contributions to society. He stressed that a man's labor was something sacred. An employer was hiring a man's soul, as well as his muscles and skills. These views emerged at a time when labor unions were involved in legal, political and physical struggles to establish their very existence as meaningful bargaining agents.

While upholding the sanctity of private property, Father Coughlin stated that property owners had been entrusted with a stewardship from God and must not exclude their fellow men from a just wage. But he added that these property owners and international bankers, an invisible group of wealthy individuals who made up a supragovernment, had successfully seen to it that only a fraction of the nation's means of production were being utilized. Only by making a limited supply of commodities available to consumers could the bankers guarantee their enormous profits. If the government failed to rectify these abuses by legislating a profit-sharing plan for workers, then the workers had no recourse but to strike.

Father Coughlin insisted that communism and capitalism were remarkably similar: each sought to concentrate ownership of the means of production — capitalism in the hands of private individuals, communism in the hands of the state. He said that his plan was to multiply private ownership, rather than destroy it, and he believed that this could be accomplished by increasing the money supply.

To this end, he attacked one of the "capitalistic money hoarding dynasties," the Du Ponts. The priest accused them of being unpatriotic in selling industrial machinery to Japan, and said with a characteristic flourish that "they would sell the flag from the top of the Capitol if it would help increase the profits for the Du Ponts."[7] To combat such dynasties Coughlin welcomed support from Catholics, Protestants, Jews, Democrats, Republicans and Socialists.[8]

At various times Father Coughlin's actions contradicted the principles he set down for the National Union for Social Justice.

Father Coughlin talks about inflation before a gathering of senators in Washington in January, 1935. Seated (at table) is Senator Elmer Thomas (D., Okla.). In the background are, left to right, Senator Bronson Cutting (R., N.M.), Senator John Bankhead (D., Ala.), Congressman John E. Rankin (D., Miss.), and Senator Burton K. Wheeler (D., Mont.) (United Press International Photo)

While stating that it was not only the worker's right to unionize, but the government's responsibility to protect such organizations as well, Father Coughlin used nonunion labor to build the Shrine of the Little Flower and would later try to create a company union in the Ford plants, speak out vigorously against United Auto Workers' attempts to unionize General Motors, and oppose the inclusion of his own employees under the provisions of the Social Security Act. Although critical of modern American capitalism because he thought it unable to provide for "a just, a living wage or an equitable price level established for the commodities of the farm and factory,"[9] Father Coughlin, as mentioned before, was heavily involved in silver speculations and in the stock market. Another contradiction can be found between Father Coughlin's prior public utterances and actions and principle eight, which called for the "repayment of dollar debts with equal value dollars." In fact Coughlin had always championed inflationary fiscal policies and had consequently gained support from the tens of thousands of individuals who, as a result of the depression, found themselves in debt.

Nowhere in the sixteen principles can there be found any statement regarding the type of political system that the National Union for Social Justice would support. One can only conclude from this that Father Coughlin believed, at this time, that his principles of social justice could still be achieved within the existing political structure. It was not until the late 1930s that Father Coughlin publicly advocated a restructuring of the American political system along the lines of Mussolini's corporate state, to implement his sixteen principles.

These principles did succeed in embodying many of the real needs of the American masses at a very difficult time in the nation's history. Elements of the NUSJ program were supported by millions. Most people favored a fair profit for the farmer and a living wage for all. Roosevelt's New Deal had promised much of what the NUSJ hoped to achieve. But they differed in the eventual method of achieving these goals. After the NUSJ failure in the 1936 elections Father Coughlin seemingly encouraged hate tactics, propaganda and street terror tactics, similar to those utilized by Europe's dictators, to implement his program.

Response to the NUSJ program was varied. The *New Republic* stated:

It is not quite true that Father Coughlin's agitation is "full of sound and fury, signifying nothing," but that is pretty close to the truth. It is full of sound and fury all right, and its definite content is puny compared with its pretensions. No doubt he is subjectively "sincere," but that does not prevent him from being a dangerous demagogue — dangerous, not because he promises too much, but because he does not know how to fulfill his promises.[10]

But Rabbi Leon Fram of Temple Beth El in Detroit described Coughlin's program of social justice as "surprisingly mild." Rabbi Fram pointed out that Coughlin's program was not radical and that various Protestant, Catholic and Jewish organizations had backed more thorough programs of social justice.[11]

Rabbi Ferdinand M. Isserman of Temple Israel, St. Louis, Missouri, speaking before a meeting of the NUSJ in Detroit, best summed up the feelings of tens of millions of Americans when he stated:

I am not a member of the National Union for Social Justice, but in sympathy with much though not all of its program. . . . If this National Union for Social Justice will rally to maintain democracy, and if it will endeavor to secure social justice for men and women of all creeds, of all denominations, of all races . . . then it may become a great instrument in establishing a new order of social justice in the United States, and thus blaze a trail of hope for the children of men everywhere.[12]

It was a big "if," one that would prove insurmountable.

Father Coughlin's control over the organization was absolute. He and two of his employees, Marie and Dorothy Rhodes, were its board of trustees as well as its incorporators. Only they had the power to make, alter, amend or repeal the corporation's bylaws.

The notary public who witnessed the birth of the corporation was yet another Coughlin employee, Eugenia Burke, a lifelong loyal friend. The corporation was organized on a nonstock basis, listed no assets, and was to be financed solely through voluntary contributions.[13] The offices of the National Union were located at the Shrine of the Little Flower. In the church's large basement there were hundreds of subdivided cabinets, each labeled with the name of a city containing a population of over twenty-five thousand. Every morning clerical workers would make their way to the church to utilize fifty typewriters, to file and sort mail, and to respond to the hundreds of letters that were received daily by the NUSJ.

Operation of the organization from offices in a church was subject to criticism. But Coughlin risked it in the attempt to foster the image that the NUSJ was somehow related to the activities of the Catholic Church. The location for the NUSJ was also determined by his desire to oversee every aspect of the organization's activities. The church was where he lived and worked. What better place could there be for the headquarters of his political organization? Since membership dues or initiation fees were not required, another important consideration was the monetary savings accrued because rent would not have to be paid.

Father Coughlin set a goal of five million members for his NUSJ. He divided the country into sixteen geographical districts. Enrollment of a new member was made by an organizer in the local district, but only after the potential member first forwarded his name and address to Coughlin, who then referred it to the local district. In this way, the priest was able to accumulate a lengthy mailing list of sympathetic individuals, as well as to keep an eye on the organization's growth and to remind local organizers that it was actually he who was recruiting the new members.

In the two weeks following the broadcast announcing the formation of the NUSJ, Father Coughlin claimed that well over two hundred thousand requests for membership had reached him. This was an impressive figure, and, if true, he had a good start toward achieving his goal of five million members. Coughlin was aware of the importance of the legitimacy of the applications. For example, in a letter to John M. Feigh, a NUSJ member, Father Coughlin cautioned:

It will not do for our many enemies to say at a future date that these memberships were obtained out of a telephone directory or that the membership blanks were signed by some person other than the one whose name appears on the blank. I hope you understand this point clearly. It would be disastrous for a Senator or a Representative who is hostile to us to make this charge on the floors of Congress and then to prove it even in a half-dozen cases when Congressional investigators search through our files.[14]

On the reverse side of the membership applications were listed the sixteen principles of social justice and their preamble. The application also required that each member of the NUSJ promise

that independent of political party, race, creed or color I shall spend my efforts to publicize these principles and to work through the agency of the National Union for Social Justice to put these principles into practice.

In January of 1935, Father Coughlin announced that the five million membership goal of the National Union for Social Justice had been attained. A membership goal of ten million members, to be reached within two years, was then established. Father Coughlin candidly admits that even the five-million-member goal was not achieved and that he was merely trying to employ the band-wagon technique to keep up the momentum of the NUSJ.[15]

The annual financial report of the NUSJ filed on December 12, 1935, covering the one-year period ending December 31, 1934, listed no assets and an indebtedness of $8,945.69. The deficits grew, and the financial report filed on April 20, 1936, in accordance with the provisions of the Corrupt Practices Act, revealed that the NUSJ had borrowed $76,692.17 from the Radio League of the Little Flower.[16] In addition, the Radio League had supplied machinery and clerical help to the NUSJ. From the end of 1937 until its dissolution on June 30, 1944, the NUSJ listed no assets and no liabilities.

The propriety of a nonprofit corporation expending funds for reasons other than those stated in appeals for financial assistance is open to question. This is particularly true when money is utilized to finance a political organization. Even the Shrine of the Little Flower loaned $2,000 to the NUSJ.

By 1935, Father Coughlin saw the National Union as the beginning of a great political and social movement which could be decisive as a third force, counteracting and holding the balance of power between the Democratic and Republican parties and as a lobbying agent within the legislative and executive branches of government. To implement that goal the NUSJ received constant publicity in the radio broadcasts of the second most dynamic public figure in the United States. But after the 1936 political campaign Coughlin would come to realize that direct participation in politics was costly and success difficult to achieve. He would also become convinced that the two-party system was too solidly entrenched to be dislodged by his third-party movement. Thus, after the elections he would devote most of his attention and energy to the publishing of his weekly journal, *Social Justice*, and to delivering his radio broadcasts. But prior to that election Father Coughlin saw himself and his organization as being omnipotent. He feared no one — not even the President.

But Father Coughlin's public attitude toward President Roosevelt was positive. He was enthusiastic about Roosevelt's State of the Union Message calling for a public works program and pledging a renewed effort to end the depression. Recalling his earlier support of Roosevelt, Coughlin stated:

I coined the phrase "Roosevelt or Ruin" because I believed in him when he openly avowed that he would drive the money changers from the temple and hand America back to the Americans. Today I believe in him as much as ever. Today it is "Roosevelt and Recovery" provided he veers neither to the right nor to the left.[17]

This pro-Roosevelt attitude changed when the President proposed to the Senate that the United States seek admission to the World Court. Father Coughlin reacted swiftly, warning listeners that United States membership in the World Court would result in a "stupid betrayal" of the country's independence.[18]

Father Coughlin saw in the World Court issue the first real test of the NUSJ's ability to influence legislation. He was certain that United States entry into the World Court was only the first step in creating a European-American community which would eventually reduce the American economic standard of living to the level of workers in European countries. If this came to pass it would only prove beneficial to such international bankers as "the Rothschilds and Lazard Freres, the Warburgs and Morgans and Kuhn-Loebs."[19] Although Father Coughlin did not mention the Jewish ancestry of these banking families, nevertheless, by innuendo, he was spotlighting their prominence and singling them out as the profit makers at a time when the country was in the throes of a bitter depression. Hurling his mightiest shafts at the World Court proposal, Father Coughlin urged his listeners "in the name of peace and justice to wire your senator in Washington this simple vital message: 'vote no on the world court, with or without reservations.' "[20] This appeal resulted in an estimated 40,000 to 200,000 telegrams bearing more than one million signatures reaching Washington. Congress was stunned by this outpouring of support for Father Coughlin's position. His efforts were aided within the Senate by the skillful parliamentary maneuvering of Senators William Borah and Huey Long.

The national debate over the question culminated on January 28, 1935, when Father Coughlin appeared with Monsignor John Ryan and Senators Joseph Robinson and Joseph Bailey on a special nationwide broadcast, arguing the pros and cons of United States admission to the World Court. The program was noteworthy for several reasons. First, Father Coughlin showed once again how persuasive a speaker he could be when utilizing the microphone, even when sharing it with others. It was his voice and his manner of presentation that set him apart from the other speakers and that made him most convincing to the listening audience. Second, this broadcast marked the first open clash of opinion between Father Coughlin and Monsignor Ryan, the scholarly, social-minded cleric who had earlier supported Coughlin in the Al Smith controversy.

Ryan participated in the program at the direct request of the President, who wished to have a priest speak for the World Court, thus countering any notion that Father Coughlin was speaking for the Catholic Church.

In the end, however, the deluge of mail sent to wavering senators at Father Coughlin's urging turned the tide and caused the legislation's final defeat. He was elated at his victory. Now he could increase his attacks on the international bankers. He was confident of his power to mold national policy. He began to see himself not merely in the vanguard of a powerful lobbying organization that could influence legislation, but rather in the process of leading an organization that could achieve political power itself.

During the World Court battle, Father Coughlin had been impressed with the political savvy of Huey Long. Long's "Share the Wealth Plan," which guaranteed every American a $5,000 annual income, and his success in dominating Louisiana politics attracted Father Coughlin's interest. Realizing that his influence on the Roosevelt administration was greatly diminished, Coughlin saw in Long an instrument for attaining the political power he now so desperately desired. As a priest, Father Coughlin could not be the presidential candidate to lead America out of the depression. He needed a front man, one who could attract sufficient strength to supplement his own considerable following. Father Coughlin thought that the senator from Louisiana might be that candidate.

James Farley considered Long to be the most dangerous man in America. The former Postmaster General remembers that a straw poll conducted by the National Committee of the Democratic party had indicated that Long, as a third-party candidate, would gather approximately three million votes. Farley believed that victory was practically guaranteed for Roosevelt in the 1936 presidential election, but as an astute politician and campaign manager for the President any doubts at all made Farley uneasy. Although Farley characterized Long as a "demagogic bastard," he had great respect for the political skills of the Louisiana senator.[21]

For his part, Long knew that he needed support that would make him more attractive to Catholics in the Northeast and Midwest. He observed the falling out of Coughlin with FDR and was sure that Coughlin would be susceptible to the idea of forming a political alliance.

Whenever Long was in Washington he resided in a suite in the Broadmoor Hotel, where, according to T. Harry Williams, his biographer, he frequently entertained Father Coughlin. Their alleged discussions lasted for hours and centered on how to create a political alliance which would culminate in Long's defeating Roosevelt for the presidency in 1936. Each man saw himself as the dominant figure in any possible relationship. Coughlin realized that Long was a clever, persuasive individual who would be difficult to restrain.[22] There was a mutual feeling of distrust under the surface of public cordiality, for both were men of immense egotistical dimension. Both were vain and accustomed to giving orders rather than carrying them out. And so the alliance was never achieved. Long's dislike for Coughlin was typified by a statement he is said to have made after a particularly difficult meeting with the priest. As Coughlin left Long's suite, the frustrated Louisiana senator supposedly shouted, "Coughlin is just a political Kate Smith on the air. They'll get tired of him."[23] None of Long's bodyguards or aides, present in the room, said a word. When the Kingfish was this upset it was best to keep quiet.

Father Coughlin, however, claims he met Long in the Broadmoor Hotel only once, when Robert Harriss, a mutual friend, arranged the meeting. Harriss had told Coughlin that Long, sick in his Washington hotel room, wished to see him. Coughlin then asked Harriss if Long were a Catholic and Harriss replied, "Only when he is talking to Catholics who can do him some good." Coughlin had been hesitant but Harriss was insistent. "You can do me a good turn. Long is very sick. Go up and say hello to him and say a prayer for him." Coughlin went, but he is adamant that it "was the only time I met him face to face, in Washington." Coughlin maintains that Long was in bed, quite ill, and that their meeting was brief, although it did center on politics.[24]

In evaluating these conflicting stories it is difficult to believe that Long used Harriss to approach Coughlin. It is more probable that Coughlin used Harriss to approach Long, because the priest frequently used him to arrange meetings and to serve as part of his brain trust. For example, Gerald L. K. Smith, then a Long adviser, and later an associate of Coughlin, stated that his first meeting with the priest was arranged by a Coughlin emissary — Robert Harriss.[25] Also, a number of Long's aides have said that a series of meetings occurred between Coughlin and Long.

Although it is fanciful to speculate that the combined forces of Coughlin and Long could have defeated Roosevelt in 1936, it is quite possible that they could have been successful in radicalizing the American political scene, something which even the extreme Left in the 1960s, despite its vociferousness, marches, sit-ins, riots and bombings failed to do. Coughlin and Long were hell-raisers who, for a time, succeeded in channeling the discontent and frustration of America's people for their own political and personal advantage. It is not important to know how many times Long and Coughlin met. What is important is that no real political alliance was made.

When Coughlin publicly branded Long's Share the Wealth plan "unthinkable radicalism," their nonalliance became a *fait accompli.* Coughlin made it clear that his own economic theories did not envisage an equal distribution of the national wealth as a means of ending the depression.[26] But Long did his best to promote the belief that he and Coughlin were working together:

I think Father Coughlin has a good platform and I'm 100 percent for him and everything he says. What he says is right down my alley. He is advocating the same things I have been for a long time. I think our programs jibe perfectly.[27]

Later, Long announced that Coughlin would support Share the Wealth meetings in Des Moines, Iowa, and Reno, Nevada. Coughlin promptly repudiated Long's claim.

In spite of his failure to reach an agreement with Long, Coughlin was still very critical of Roosevelt, asserting that the President was in collusion with the very money changers he had promised to drive from the temple in his 1933 Inaugural Address. Father Coughlin cited as proof the failure of the administration's policies to end the depression and halt the domination of the plutocrats in government and industry.

Father Coughlin still asserts that Roosevelt's failure to end the depression was a major factor in his decision to split with the President. He lists two other factors which entered into that decision. First, says he, Bishop Gallagher had received a visit from the bishop of Guadalajara, Mexico, who told him that "your man Coughlin must stop supporting the United States government the way he is . . . because the government is supporting communists in Mexico." The bishop then gave Gallagher a photostatic copy of a check purportedly sent by a high-level Treasury Department official to the head of the Mexican Communist party. Coughlin recalls that this check was for "several millions of dollars." Gallagher was very upset by this incident and he told Coughlin: "You listen! Until we scrutinize this whole thing, you stay away from Washington." Thus it was done, for "all Michael had to do was say a word to me and I obeyed him."[28]

Second was a disagreement over the wording of the Wagner Act. In 1933, Roosevelt had told Coughlin that he would welcome a comprehensive piece of labor legislation. Coughlin told his friend Louis Ward of Roosevelt's desire for a bill. Ward recruited several other attorneys, who met with Coughlin in the evenings in the kitchen of the priest's church. After several weeks a draft of the bill was completed and forwarded to the President, who passed it along to his own attorneys for revision. Coughlin said that "the Wagner bill was very similar to the one I had submitted — with one rather important exception. It ended up that the responsibilities of labor, which I had included in the bill, were stricken out and just the rights of labor were included."[29]

In spite of Coughlin's claims of millions of members, the NUSJ announced in early 1935 that it was over $40,000 in debt and urged supporters to contribute as much money as possible. Furthermore, on February 3, 1935, Coughlin told his radio listeners that he had borrowed $40,000, which had to be repaid within a month. The response of his followers must have been positive, for on his February 10 broadcast, Coughlin announced that the needed financial support was forthcoming and he thanked contributors for their generosity in preserving the NUSJ. He also accused the Roosevelt administration of having communist tendencies, and at the same time he labeled Roosevelt a capitalist tool. Even Coughlin's staunchest followers were at a loss to explain this seeming contradiction.

In a March broadcast Coughlin continued his attacks on Roosevelt and the New Deal, by characterizing their existence as "two years of compromise, two years of endeavoring to mix bad with good, two years of surrender, two years of matching the puerile, puny brains of idealists against the virile viciousness of business and finance."[30] He attacked the National Recovery Administration for its failure to keep wages on a par with price increases. General Hugh Johnson, the fiery head of the National Recovery Administration, replied by declaring that Coughlin and Huey Long were representatives of a lunatic fringe which was a real threat to the democratic process. Johnson also questioned Coughlin's status as an American citizen and his right as a priest either to participate in or to lead a revolutionary party. Johnson also intimated that Coughlin had profited personally from the fiscal policies he advocated and warned Americans to beware of a Coughlin-Long alliance.

These two men are raging up and down this land preaching not construction, but destruction — not reform but revolution, not peace but — a sword. I think we are dealing with a couple of Catalines, and that it is high time for someone to say so.[31]

Reaction to the Johnson speech was quick and generally favorable. On March 6, 1935, the *New York Times*, for instance, although upholding the right of dissenters to criticize the Roosevelt administration, nevertheless lauded Johnson for standing up to Coughlin and Long and thereby stiffening the spines of many whose fear of this new axis had caused them to endure with silence their outbursts.

Commonweal, a liberal Catholic publication which was usually quite critical of Father Coughlin, disagreed with Johnson. The journal pointed out that Coughlin, "although a priest, was indeed an American citizen and, as such, was entitled to participate in politics."[32]

In response to Johnson's attack, Senator Gerald P. Nye of North Dakota took the Senate floor on March 7, 1935, to defend the priest as "an unceasing and uncompromising champion of social justice."[33] Nye acknowledged that, while not always agreeing with Father Coughlin, he still recognized the priest as a "giant." Nye went on to urge that support be given to a bill he was sponsoring which if passed would create a central bank to control money and credit. Nye admitted that Coughlin had assisted him in drafting the bill, but denied that this was his reason for defending the priest.[34]

Two nights later, addressing the Rhode Island Bar Association, General Johnson reiterated his charges without mentioning Coughlin by name. The priest no longer left his defense to others. Accepting an NBC offer to reply to Johnson on March 11, Father Coughlin described himself as an American citizen who had the same privileges as other Americans to speak out on important issues of the day in collaboration with "Catholic, Protestant, Jew and irreligionist to solve a common problem. . . . It is still my prerogative to vote. It is still my privilege to be interested in good government."[35] He made it clear to his listeners that when he spoke out on an issue he did so as an American citizen and not as a representative of the Catholic Church. He then went on to include himself with George Washington and Thomas Jefferson, as individuals who had been termed "revolutionary" when they were actually patriots. The priest also claimed that in this period of history it was Johnson and Wall Streeters like Bernard Baruch who had "become distorters of history and perverters of logic as they, the unjust aggressors, garb themselves in the raiment of patriotism and cast upon those who have suffered from their misdeeds the scarlet cloak of the rebel."

In replying to Johnson's accusations that he had profited personally from silver speculations, Coughlin first stated that he had never taken a vow of poverty. He did admit that the Radio League of the Little Flower had gained more than a $12,000 profit as a result of silver speculations, but he claimed that the original investment had been made at the public urging of FDR, who had pleaded with Americans to show their confidence in the nation's future by ceasing the hoarding of money which was deepening the fiscal problems created by the depression.

His personal affairs disposed of, Father Coughlin proceeded to attack General Johnson:

But the doctrines which I preach are important. While you were content to vomit your venom upon my person and against my character, the American public is fully cognizant that not once did you dare attack the truths which I teach. I need not condemn you before the court of public opinion. You have condemned yourself. More than that, you have appeared before a jury of 80 million people — your own figures, General — who, through your lack of Christian charity and justice, are today prejudiced against you.[36]

Coughlin labeled Johnson a "chiseler . . . a cracked Gramophone record . . . a chocolate soldier . . . a creampuff who had never faced an enemy or successfully faced an issue . . . a red herring, but a dead one . . . a political corpse whose ghost had returned to haunt," and a front for Bernard Baruch, "his Lord and Master," and the other Wall Street manipulators who created and profited from the depression. Baruch was subjected to almost as much criticism in this talk as Johnson himself. In a final disclaimer, Coughlin denied Johnson's accusation that he had split with Roosevelt in 1934. The priest stated emphatically that "I still proclaim to you that it is either 'Roosevelt or Ruin': I support him today and will support him tomorrow."[37]

Coughlin went on to applaud Roosevelt for his policies in 1933 and 1934 which tried to "drive the money changers from the temple," but which had failed because of the opposition of Johnson and Baruch. As a final salvo, Coughlin, referring to Johnson, reminded his audience of the ethical axiom "De Mortuis nil nisi bonum" — "Of the dead speak kindly."

The next day the *New York Times* carried a statement by Baruch in which he denied that he was a banker. NBC said that over three hundred telegrams and phone calls were received in praise of the Coughlin talk along with only a handful of critical comments.

Johnson replied to the Coughlin blast by issuing a statement calling Coughlin and Huey Long public enemies. He claimed that there was "less national harm in the 100 worst gunmen than there is in these two political racketeers."[38] On March 30, speaking from Chicago to a national radio audience, Johnson accused Coughlin of trying to establish himself as the American Hitler. He said:

Someone sent me a parallel of what both you and Adolf Hitler proposed and preached and they are as alike as peas in a pod. As a foreign-born you could not be a president but you could be a Reichsführer — just as the Austrian Adolf became a dictator of Germany. . . . Are you a Jack-in-the-Pulpit who jumps up one moment in the collar of Rome, ducks and reappears the next moment in a necktie?"[39]

Johnson continued the comparison by saying to the priest, "You have not chosen the swastika. You have a more sacred device. . . . No swastikas for your Nazis — but a cross."[40] He went on to state that the priest was promoting the false belief that the Catholic Church was building a fascist order in the United States.

Father Coughlin, although furious over these continued attacks, did not respond to the March 30 talk. He was hurt, however, by the fact that Roosevelt had not silenced Johnson. When in April, 1935, Harold Ickes, Secretary of the Interior, referred to Coughlin as a man "whose rich but undisciplined imagination has reduced politics, sociology and banking to charming poetry which he distills mellifluously into the ether for the entrancement of mankind,"[41] Father Coughlin was certain that Roosevelt had no desire to halt the attacks upon him, and Louis Ward even suggested that Roosevelt himself might have instigated Johnson's offensive against the priest.[42] But Coughlin refused to believe this. And James Farley states that Roosevelt had told him that Ickes' attack on Coughlin was "unwise."[43] The President was sufficiently sensitive to Coughlin's feelings to send Frank Murphy to Royal Oak to see if some kind of accommodation could be worked out.

Murphy was soon to split with Father Coughlin and to later become Governor of Michigan, Attorney General of the United States and a Supreme Court Justice. The mission was unsuccessful because Coughlin had already come to regard Murphy as a once-good man who had become too politically ambitious and who was being used by a devious President to prevent him from speaking out on the critical issues of the day.

Looking back, Father Coughlin laughs as he recalls the things he said about General Johnson. He maintains, however, that General Johnson indeed was "more expert in facing a powder puff than in facing the powder of a gun." He is still certain that Roosevelt did not precipitate the attacks against him. "I know enough about big government to know that the President can't be responsible for everything that is done by his subordinates."[44]

In 1935, however, Father Coughlin was not as forgiving of Roosevelt as he is today. Angered by the attacks against him, he began to discuss, more and more frequently, with his close advisers, Robert Harriss, Francis Keelon and Louis Ward, the possible impact of a third party on the 1936 presidential election. The more he discussed it the more certain he became that a third party, fighting for the principles of social justice under his leadership, could exert a definite influence, and might even emerge victorious, in a three-way presidential election. Coughlin believed that political victory might be achieved by combining the personal appearances of a candidate on the hustings with his own effective exploitation of the radio to reach a voting public which traditionally had voted for one of two major parties. He knew the task ahead of him was not an easy one. Yet he was confident that the American voters would support him, because they would come to understand the truth of the principles of social justice, while becoming disenchanted with the broken promises of the New Deal.[45]

In April, 1935, Father Coughlin announced that his series of broadcasts would be extended for an additional thirteen weeks and that he would embark on a series of personal appearances around the country to familiarize voters with the NUSJ. The purpose of the tour was to prove conclusively that the priest was a political powerhouse. Large, enthusiastic crowds could make the political leaders of both parties take notice and illustrate to millions of American voters that should Coughlin support a third-party candidate for the presidency, a vote for that man would not be a futile gesture. But before starting on this intensive political campaign — one that he considered to be the most crucial mission of his life — Father Coughlin again sought and received the public support of Bishop Gallagher. On April 21, Coughlin turned over part of his radio broadcast to Gallagher, who proceeded to voice his trust in and support of the priest in the strongest of terms:

> I pronounce Father Coughlin sound in doctrine, able in its application and interpretation. Freely I give him my imprimatur on his written word and freely I give him my approval on his spoken word. May both be circulated without objection throughout the land.
> Under my jurisdiction he preaches the just codes of the old law and its commandments. Father Coughlin preaches the doctrine of social justice to all. Until a lawful superior rules otherwise, I stand steadfastly behind this priest, Father Coughlin, encouraging him to do the will of God as he sees it and as I see it, each according to his lights.[46]

In placing an imprimatur on the writings and speeches of Father Coughlin, Gallagher gave his unqualified stamp of approval to the priest's enunciations. It is obvious that Gallagher did not see any breach of faith, morals or canon law in Coughlin's talks. There were some Church members who disputed Gallagher. Father Edward V. Dargin, canonist for the New York archdiocese, stated in the July issue of the *Ecclesiastical Review*, that Father Coughlin's political activities had violated canon law of the Catholic Church and that he should be punished for his transgressions. But it was Gallagher's and not Dargin's support that Father Coughlin required.

And so it began. On Wednesday night, April 24, 1935, 15,382 persons each paid twenty-five cents to enter Olympia Auditorium in Detroit to see Coughlin kick off his cross-country campaign. With all the seats occupied, over one thousand standees crowded

into the hall. The three-hour meeting afforded the audience ample
time to hear a number of prominent speakers, including Congressman William Lemke of North Dakota; Edward Kennedy, secretary of the National Farmers Union; Congressman William Con-
nery of Massachusetts, the co-sponsor of the Wagner-Connery
labor bill; Senator Gerald Nye of North Dakota; Congressman
Thomas O'Malley of Wisconsin; Congressman Martin Sweeney of
Ohio; and Senator Elmer Thomas of Oklahoma. The rows closest
to the platform were occupied by the speakers and some of the
most prominent individuals in the Detroit area. Among them were
Elmer O'Hara, Michigan chairman of the Democratic party; William Dorn, state chairman of the Young Democrats; Rabbi Leon
Fram of Temple Beth El; Aaron Kurland, the former head of the
Michigan Bank Depositors League; and many former Michigan
state office holders.

Each time a speaker mentioned Coughlin by name, the crowd
applauded and screamed. Each time a speaker mentioned a cause
Coughlin denounced or an individual Coughlin opposed, the crowd
booed and hissed. Prime objects of this type of vocal manifestation
were General Hugh Johnson, the international bankers, the World
Court and the League of Nations.

When Father Coughlin moved to the podium to deliver the final
address the crowd stood as one and let loose an ovation which
lasted over five minutes. They simply would not let the priest
begin his talk. The din created by the ovation vibrated the very
walls of the auditorium. When finally he was able to speak,
Coughlin told the audience that the first objective of the National
Union for Social Justice was the unification of the workers of the
Michigan auto industry into a cohesive force capable of bargaining collectively for its rights.

The lights and the smoke made Coughlin hot and uncomforta-
ble as he spoke. The sweat poured down his face. He mopped his
forehead — but he did not stop talking. This was his ecstasy! The
listeners were his flock, his parishioners. He was their father, their
leader, their idol. While some men dreamed of becoming million-
aires, or of making love to beautiful women, Coughlin made his
dreams a reality by addressing large crowds such as these.

Michigan, the most disorganized laboring state in the union, shall become our spearhead; the success of the National Union is to be gauged by the automotive industry which confronts us. . . . I call upon the broken lines of Michigan society to come and unite under the one banner of the National Union for Social Justice.[47]

The large, enthusiastic audience which flocked to hear Coughlin, and the presence of so many influential figures, caused some observers to voice their fear of the potential political power possessed by the priest's National Union for Social Justice. Raymond Gram Swing left little doubt about how he viewed Coughlin. In his book *Forerunners of American Fascism*, Swing expressed fear that the influence of Coughlin, Long and others holding beliefs similar to theirs was rapidly growing. Swing's views were supported by Norman Thomas and Walter Lippmann, although the latter cautioned that Coughlin had failed, as yet, to translate his seeming popularity into votes at the polling booth.[48]

On May 7, 1935, Colonel Frank Knox, publisher of the *Chicago Daily News*, who was to be the Republican vice-presidential candidate in 1936 and Secretary of the Navy under Roosevelt in 1940, criticized Coughlin in a speech at Dearborn, Michigan:

Only a few miles from where we gather tonight the voice of a visionary impractical priest has summoned literally millions of our people to the support of a fantastic theory that the whole remedy for the evils from which we suffer is to be found in currency inflation and political control of credit.[49]

Undeterred, Father Coughlin addressed an enthusiastic crowd of over twenty-five thousand people in Cleveland, Ohio, on May 8. The crowd roared with approval when Coughlin castigated Roosevelt for his support of the Eccles bill, which was an attempt to directly control the money market through the federal government rather than through private bankers. Coughlin believed that this measure, sponsored by the new chairman of the Federal Reserve System, did not go far enough.

The stage was now set for the main event. On May 22, Father Coughlin arrived at Madison Square Garden to address a jam-

packed audience of over eighteen thousand listeners who paid
from fifty cents to two dollars each to hear him. The audience was
enthusiastic, but not quite up to the vociferous standards set by
the Detroit audience five weeks earlier. Coughlin devoted his
speech to attacking Bernard Baruch and others associated with the
New Deal. His most vituperative remarks were reserved for President Roosevelt, whom Coughlin criticized for pursuing fiscal
policies which were causing unendurable hardships for America's
plain people, and for vetoing a bill providing veterans of World
War I with a bonus. Each mention of Roosevelt's name drew
hisses and boos.

Father Coughlin's appearance at Madison Square Garden netted
him an estimated $10,000 profit. He had paid $4,000 to rent the
building and approximately $1,000 to cover the expenses of the
speakers and advertisements. The total receipts were estimated at
$15,000 to $17,000. Father Coughlin maintains that he did not
profit personally from his speaking tour. He says that whatever
money was netted was poured back into the campaign.[50]

Following his Madison Square Garden appearance, Coughlin
spent several days at the sprawling Larchmont estate of his friend
Francis P. Keelon, a foreign exchange broker. Keelon, Harriss and
George LeBlanc, a banker, formed the backbone of Coughlin's
eastern financial base. Father Coughlin saw no inconsistency in
condemning international bankers and such Wall Streeters as Bernard Baruch in his broadcasts, personal appearances and writings,
and at the same time hobnobbing with financiers like Joseph Kennedy, Keelon, Harriss and LeBlanc. Many of these financiers stood
to profit immensely from the enactment of Coughlin's inflationary
monetary policies.[51]

Father Coughlin's efforts to stir up his supporters were temporarily halted when the Chicago Park Commission refused him
permission to rent Soldiers' Field for a speaking appearance, on the
grounds that the park's facilities were not supposed to be utilized
for the dissemination of propaganda. Coughlin commented that
"the refusal is hardly worth commenting on."[52] He did seek to
reverse the decision, but his efforts were fruitless, although the

reasons cited by the Chicago Park Commission for its ban were hardly convincing, particularly the claim that Coughlin's appearance might prove objectionable to a large number of people. Although it appeared to violate Coughlin's constitutional rights, the decision stood. It should be pointed out that the Communist party supported his efforts to get the park permit.

The Coughlin tour moved on to St. Louis, where the priest again addressed an estimated crowd of over eighteen thousand people which applauded his attacks on the Federal Reserve System and his call for unity among the nation's workers. Coughlin cited government statistics to prove that over 85 percent of the nation's wealth was divided among 4 percent of its people. He also continued to urge the passage of the Wheeler-Rayburn Public Utilities Act, which made illegal the existence of economically superfluous holding companies. He emphasized that it was the ruinous fiscal policies of the Roosevelt administration which allowed the continued exploitation of the poor and the downtrodden.

While in St. Louis, Father Coughlin stated that "the Jews have enemies — Bernard Baruch, the motion picture industry, and Eddie Cantor." Cantor, who was very active in helping European Jewish refugees come to America, quickly responded by describing Coughlin as a man without "an atom of sincerity in his entire system." Coughlin remained silent but Cantor was to become his lifelong enemy.

The oppressive summer heat caused Coughlin to curtail his activities until the fall. Although a vigorous forty-four, Coughlin dreaded the hot weather, which seemed to drain his strength. He usually vacationed in Canada or Europe or sharply decreased his priestly duties during the summer months.

He did take time out from his summer hiatus to address the Massachusetts House of Representatives. He was accompanied to the House chamber by the colorful rogue of Massachusetts state politics, Governor James M. Curley, who was certainly not his friend or supporter. In his address to the legislators the priest said that it was up to them to see to it that democratic government was not overthrown by "Nazism, Communism and that other form of dictatorship which is now insinuating itself into state and federal government."[53] Coughlin was loudly applauded by the legislators when he concluded his address.

In early September, Coughlin, while having dinner at his parents' home, received a phone call from Joe Kennedy, who asked, "Where are you keeping yourself?" Coughlin replied, "Home, I'm busy." There was silence for a few seconds before Kennedy said, "The Boss wants to talk to you." Coughlin knew at that point that Kennedy was calling either from the White House or from Hyde Park. "Where are you, Joe?" Kennedy replied laughingly, "Up the river." An instant later Coughlin heard the distinctive voice of the President of the United States at the other end of the wire say, "Hiya, Padre." The President, who always addressed Coughlin as "Padre," told him that he was lonesome and would like him to visit with him at his home in Hyde Park. Coughlin responded by telling the President that he had to attend a very important funeral. But Roosevelt was insistent, so Coughlin told him that he would call Kennedy the next day with a reply to his invitation. Coughlin was eager to visit with the President but he had been admonished by Bishop Gallagher to stay away from Roosevelt. He therefore went immediately to see Gallagher, who gave his consent to the visit. In addition, he gave Coughlin the photostatic copy of the check for the Communist party that the Mexican bishop had brought to him and told Coughlin to ask Roosevelt for an explanation.

Coughlin remembers, "I called Joe Kennedy to tell him to meet my train in Albany. When I got off the train there were boys on the platform selling newspapers and shouting 'Extra! Extra! Huey Long is dead.' " A reporter at the station asked Coughlin for his reaction to Long's death, and he responded by calling it "the most regrettable thing in modern history."[54] Coughlin today regards this as something of an overstatement, but he meant it to be such when he made it. "Why not? After the poor man was gone, or any other man, for that matter, one should say nice things about him. Remember, there is family left behind."[55]

Joe Kennedy was waiting in his Rolls Royce for Coughlin at the station and together they drove through the early morning mist, arriving at Hyde Park at about 5:00 A.M. The front door of the big house was open and totally unguarded. They let themselves in and went to the kitchen to prepare breakfast for themselves. It was daylight when they finished eating, but still too early to awaken the President. Instead, they went into the library, where they chatted about Coughlin's political plans and Kennedy's desire to resign as head of the Securities and Exchange Commission. After an hour or so, they heard a noise from the top of the stairs and Coughlin went to see if it was the President.

Coughlin recalls:

The Boss was at the head of the stairs. He had the most powerful arms — he had to. He walked on his arms, the poor fellow. His legs weren't of much use to him: I ran up the stairs with the newspaper under my arm for some reason or another. I was going to give him my shoulder. That was the custom in the house. . . . I said, "By the way your boyfriend is dead." That was the first he heard that the wounded Long had died. . . . He blanched white. It was a shock to him.[56]

The three men went to the kitchen, where Coughlin prepared breakfast for the President, and then he and Kennedy joined him for a second breakfast. The President came to the point very quickly. "Cards on the table, Padre. Cards on the table. Why are you cooling off to me? Why are you criticizing the things I'm doing?"

I told him that I wasn't criticizing anything that he was doing, but only some of his administrators. He said, "Come on, Padre, the truth." I said, "We have had bad news from Mexico. This is it." I took the photostat of the check from my pocket and showed it to him. As he was looking at it I told him that "Michael Gallagher's afraid we are going soft on communism." After a pause the President asked, "How in the name of God did this thing ever get into your hands?" So I told him.[57]

Roosevelt promised Coughlin that he would investigate the origins of the check. Coughlin claims that he later found out that "somebody in the Treasury Department had slipped the check down there unbeknownst to Mr. Roosevelt. Now that's how far the communists had infiltrated our government."[58]

The conversation with Roosevelt lasted from 7:00 A.M. to 2:00 P.M. Coughlin urged the President to abolish the Federal Reserve System and follow more inflationary fiscal policies. Roosevelt, while cordial, refused to commit himself, and instead tried to woo Coughlin back into the fold by stressing the nation's dire problems and the catastrophe that would confront them should a Republican President be elected in 1936. He told Coughlin that a third party led by the priest might result in a Republican victory. But Coughlin, too, was noncommittal.

When the meeting was terminated, Kennedy drove Coughlin to Great Barrington, where the priest had a dinner date, and on the way informed him that he was going to resign as chairman of the SEC. Kennedy told Coughlin that he still retained his liking and respect for Roosevelt but that the SEC job presented no further challenges to him. A short time later Kennedy's resignation was made public.

As he thought back on the day's events Coughlin was certain that a reconciliation with Roosevelt was an impossibility and that only direct political action could improve the economic life of the nation. The only remaining question in Coughlin's mind about his relations with Roosevelt was how and when to make the irrevocable move into the political arena against a "charming, likeable, popular and very astute President."[59]

6

The Election of 1936

AFTER the Hyde Park meeting, Coughlin waited for the appropriate moment to make official his break with Roosevelt and announce his support of a third-party presidential candidate. Meanwhile he worked to cement his image as a social reformer and an important political figure by inviting two prominent foreigners to visit his Royal Oak home. One of them was William Aberhart, the newly installed premier of the province of Alberta, Canada, who had been elected on a party platform which advocated that each adult man and woman in Canada be paid twenty-five dollars a month. Coughlin pointed out to the press that Aberhart's program was similar to his own and that "both he and Alberta are to be congratulated on having made this forward step, which the forefathers of the United States attempted to make, but in which they were frustrated by the Alexander Hamiltons and their successors."[1]

A week later, on September 22, 1935, the Very Reverend Hewlett Johnson, Archbishop of Canterbury, an advocate of social credit, visited Coughlin. After their meeting the archbishop matched wits with the press. In response to a request that he pose with a cup of coffee in his hand, the archbishop said, "Gladly, and if you will drop in this evening, perhaps you would like to snap me in my bath." When asked to stand closer to Father Coughlin for picture-taking purposes, he protested, "But my dear sir, the

Father and I couldn't be much closer spiritually."[2] Father Coughlin was satisfied that the well-publicized visits of these two digni-
taries had propagated the impression that they had come to pay
homage to him.

Now it was time to get down to the real task at hand — electing
a President. He shifted the complete responsibility for running the
Shrine of the Little Flower to an assistant, the Reverend Albert
Hutting. This led to speculation that Coughlin was going to resign
his pastorate and seek the presidential nomination for himself. The
resignation rumors became so widespread that Coughlin had to
publicly deny them; Father Hutting, he announced, would assume
the pastor's duties until he had concluded his twenty-seven-week
broadcasting season.

In November 1935, Coughlin resumed his broadcasting series on
a coast-to-coast network numbering thirty-two stations. He led
off with a stinging attack on congressmen who supported Roosevelt's domestic policies and those foreign policies which, he
claimed, were leading to United States involvement in a second
world war. His break with Roosevelt could not have been more
"official" than when he announced that the country was now
faced with a situation where continued support of the administration would lead to "Roosevelt and Ruin."[3]

But what could he do to provide a viable alternative? With
Long dead, Coughlin lacked the potential attractive candidate who
could win an election. He concluded that his only chance at victory lay in forging a political alliance with Dr. Francis Townsend
and the Reverend Gerald L. K. Smith. To do so was not to be a
simple accomplishment.

Townsend was an aged California physician — a tall, gaunt, almost emaciated-looking individual — who had attracted a huge
following among the frustrated and frightened elderly people of
the country. While many of the nation's senior citizens had come
to regard Roosevelt with affection, they were still susceptible to
the promises of men who claimed to have fast, simple solutions to
complex problems. Townsend seemed to have such a solution —
the Townsend Plan — which promised to give each citizen sixty
years of age and over a monthly stipend of two hundred dollars,

which he would be required to spend within thirty days. The money to finance this plan was to be raised by a 2 percent business transaction tax which, according to Townsend's estimates, would give the government $1,600,000,000 each month.

Reverend Gerald L. K. Smith had initially been a bodyguard of Huey Long and later one of his advisers. He was a thickset, broad-shouldered man, with a prominent nose and thick curly hair. After Long's assassination, Smith had become a national figure because of the stirring emotional eulogy he had delivered from the steps of the State Capitol in Baton Rouge to more than one hundred thousand mourners. Smith fancied himself to be Long's successor in Louisiana; with his tremendous oratorical power he was able to convince many people of this — Father Coughlin among them.

In November, Townsend visited Father Coughlin at his home and they agreed to form a loose alliance. Townsend promised Coughlin that he would support the NUSJ in local, state and national electoral contests; Coughlin agreed to throw the weight of the NUSJ behind those candidates who favored old age pension legislation, but persuaded Townsend that it would be politically astute to emphasize such legislation only after the 1936 election had resulted in victories for NUSJ candidates at the polls.[4] A month later, despite the agreements, Coughlin criticized the Townsend Plan as being "impractical."[5] He knew that political victories were not won by appealing only to the elderly. He called for social improvements for all classes and not just for citizens over sixty and did not support even the basic features of the Townsend Plan.

In early 1936, Father Coughlin sent Robert Harriss to meet with Reverend Smith in the New Yorker Hotel to explore the possibility of Smith's joining with Coughlin and Townsend to defeat Roosevelt. Smith agreed to an alliance. His goal was to use both Coughlin and Townsend to promulgate his candidacy for the presidency in 1940. Shortly after this meeting Smith went to see Coughlin in Royal Oak, where he agreed to be a featured speaker at the National Union Party Convention in July.[6] This was important to Coughlin. As a stump speaker, Smith had no peer. H. L. Mencken, after hearing Smith, was moved to comment that he

Father Coughlin at the White House to see President Roosevelt (Wide World Photo)

Coughlin with (left to right) Congressman Thomas O'Malley of Wisconsin, William Lempke of North Dakota, William P. Connelly of Massachusetts, and William Collins, representing the American Federation of Labor, forming the Union party in 1935. (United Press International Photo)

was "the gustiest and goriest, the loudest and the lustiest, the deadliest and damndest orator ever heard on this or any other earth."[7]

Coughlin vehemently denies that he was allied with either Smith or Townsend. Whenever Smith's name is even mentioned, Coughlin reacts: "Smith was a viper . . . a leech . . . who was anti-Christian, anti-Semitic and anti-God. I had no more of a relationship to him than I had with Spartacus and the gladiators."[8] The facts, however, tend to contradict him. Coughlin's own newspaper, *Social Justice*, featured a picture of Townsend, Smith and Coughlin on page one of its July 27, 1936, issue, under the headline "Forces United!" The caption under the picture read:

> The National Union in no sense surrenders its identity. However, the above trinity determines to focus attention upon the unholy trinity of Roosevelt, Landon and Browder. Dr. Townsend, Reverend Gerald Smith and Father Coughlin as they form their holy alliance against the unholy money changer's system.

With the alliances accomplished and with functional units of the NUSJ in 302 of the 435 congressional districts in the United States, Coughlin was satisfied with his political progress. He felt powerful enough to warn unfriendly congressmen that the NUSJ was going to destroy their political careers.[9]

Coughlin was determined not to be sidetracked in his efforts to build a political machine. To this end he decided to increase the tempo of his political activities by publishing a weekly journal that would give additional exposure and credence to the candidates that the NUSJ would support. Although his Sunday afternoon radio broadcast was heard by millions, Coughlin believed that a newspaper would keep his name and message before the people as they rode the subways, ate dinner or relaxed after a hard day's work. It would serve to combat the increasing criticisms directed at him by many of America's larger newspapers. And perhaps his readers would heed more readily requests for financial aid to defray his broadcasting and electioneering costs.

In December, he announced his intentions to his radio audience and asked that one million of his listeners write to him in support of the venture. Although the replies fell short of the one million responses called for, the tens of thousands of letters he received in a three-week period gave Coughlin cause to be optimistic about the potential success of his newspaper.

Coughlin's activities were being carefully watched from Washington. First startled, and then moved to concern by the boldness of Coughlin's political activities, Jim Farley thought it wise to try to reconcile the differences between FDR and Coughlin, if only to avoid any possibility of the priest upsetting what appeared to him to be a certain Roosevelt victory in the coming election. But FDR was not convinced that he should meet with Coughlin. By now, he had cultivated a strong dislike for the priest. Farley finally convinced the President and sought out Coughlin. Although he had attacked Farley periodically, Coughlin believed that the Postmaster General was basically a good man. Besides, a visit to the President still did wonders for his ego, particularly when he was convinced that he had the upper hand.

But the atmosphere in Roosevelt's office that January 8 was strained — so strained that at one point Roosevelt, in an effort to be polite, could only ask how Coughlin's Great Dane, Pal, was feeling. Coughlin replied, "Fine. How is Fala?" After a while Roosevelt tried to pin Coughlin down on his future political plans, and Coughlin tried to find out FDR's plans for legislation, in the event he was returned to office in 1936. Both were unsuccessful. After three-quarters of an hour, the meeting ended.[10]

Coughlin shrugged off an attack by James Rowland Angell, president of Yale, who in a February, 1936, alumni address had assailed the "teachers' oath bills," which compelled the president of Harvard, James Conant, to take a loyalty oath while allowing "a recently naturalized foreign priest to escape such an oath and pour out weekly, over the radio, under the blessed name of social justice, the most poisonous and inflammatory economic and social nonsense."[11] Says Coughlin as to his lack of reaction: "After all, the presidents of Yale always were and still are a little soft-headed."[12]

On March 13, 1936, Father Coughlin published the first issue of his weekly journal, *Social Justice*. From then until April, 1942, this journal was his most important vehicle in propagating his views. Before publication began, Father Coughlin appeared before Josephine Arnold, notary public for Wayne County, Michigan, to sign the Articles of Incorporation. The stated purposes of the Social Justice Publishing Company were

to carry on business as a proprietor and publisher of newspapers, journals, magazines, books and other literary works and undertakings; and also to carry on business as a printer, bookseller, bookbinder, papermaker, stationer, engraver, photographer, photographic printer, stereotyper, electrotyper, lithographer, or any other business as manufacturers in connection with and incidental to the above.

The company's Board of Directors consisted of Charles E. Coughlin, Eugenia Burke and Amy Collins. All three listed their address as Twelve Mile Road and Woodward Avenue, Royal Oak, Michigan, the address of Father Coughlin's church. The Board of Directors assumed the power to mortgage and convey the assets of the corporation. The officers of the company were: Father Coughlin, president; Eugenia Burke, vice-president and secretary; Amy Collins, treasurer. Father Coughlin's stated aims in publishing *Social Justice* were to enlist additional support for the Union party candidates in the elections of 1936, and to be of "assistance to the millions of Americans who are attempting to rid this nation of want in the midst of plenty."[13] There is no evidence available to indicate whom Father Coughlin consulted prior to the publication of the journal. But as a priest he did need at least the tacit approval of Bishop Gallagher. In a conversation with J. Pierrepont Moffat of the State Department, Michael Francis Doyle of Philadelphia, a good friend of the bishop, said: "Father Coughlin could not do what he is now doing without the support and backing of his Bishop and thus far his Bishop has been staunchly supporting him."[14]

The first issue was devoted, in good part, to the Frazier-Lemke bill, which called for the federal government to buy up all outstanding mortgages on farms and then allow farmers who lived on those properties to gradually liquidate the mortgages while paying only 1½ percent interest on the money owed. The mortgage money was to be raised by the government through a three-billion-dollar issuance of paper money. The goal of the bill was to make the federal government the country's largest owner of farm mortgages at a time when hundreds of farmers were losing their farms daily because of their failure to meet the high interest rates of creditors.

The measure had evoked considerable support, particularly in state legislatures, thirty-three of which passed resolutions supporting its passage in Congress. Its support in Congress, however, was nominal. It ran into a good deal of opposition, especially from congressmen who represented areas in the North and Northeast with large numbers of private homeowners. These homeowners were also in difficulty with creditors and the foreclosure rates on their homes were high. Yet they were excluded from the provisions of the Frazier-Lemke bill. In spite of this weakness Coughlin had fully supported the measure, maintaining that it was noninflationary because the three billion dollars issued would have the real wealth of the United States behind it. In addition, the real value of the farms being saved from foreclosure was valued in excess of twenty billion dollars, and Coughlin believed that this value could be utilized as excellent collateral for the money loaned under the bill's provisions.

The bill was pigeonholed in the House Rules Committee, which was under the chairmanship of Congressman John O'Connor of New York, whom Coughlin considered to be a Roosevelt lackey. To get the bill reported out of O'Connor's committee, Coughlin had sent Louis Ward to meet with Marvin McIntyre. There is serious disagreement over what transpired at this meeting. McIntyre said he was told that if Roosevelt did not get O'Connor to get the measure to the House floor, then Father Coughlin would devote his full energies to attacking the Roosevelt administration.[15] Coughlin, however, denies vehemently that Ward ever bullied or threatened McIntyre. He maintains that Ward was given vague answers by McIntyre, who insisted that Roosevelt lacked the necessary influence to get the bill out of committee.[16] Despite his denial of the use of threats, Coughlin continued to assault the Roosevelt administration and O'Connor for their failure to support the Frazier-Lemke bill.

Roosevelt remained silent, since he believed that a policy of nonresponse was the wisest course to follow in the face of these attacks. O'Connor, however, did reply, and set off one of the most raucous verbal battles ever to involve a member of Congress. In a telegram to Coughlin, the contents of which were released to the press, O'Connor said:

Just read your libelous radio rambling. The truth is not in you. You are a disgrace to my church and any other church and especially to the citizenship of America which you recently embraced. You do not dare to print what you said about me. If you will please come to Washington I shall guarantee to kick you all the way from the Capitol to the White House with clerical garb and all the silver in your pockets which you got from speculating on Wall Street while I was voting for all the farm bills. Come on![17]

The telegram had given Coughlin convulsions of anger. He was anxious to go to Washington to accept O'Connor's challenge. He still fancied himself an athlete, and although a little out of shape he thought he could still kick the hell out of O'Connor. He made plans to work out in a gym. Then he contacted Congressman Martin Sweeney of Ohio, and asked him to announce on the House floor that he would accept O'Connor's challenge. His friends could not persuade him that he was degrading himself. Finally, Bishop Gallagher thought it wise to intervene and tell Coughlin not to be intemperate in his actions. While Gallagher was so instructing Coughlin, Sweeney, following Coughlin's instructions, was shouting to O'Connor in the House, "He accepts your challenge and he will be here at ten o'clock tomorrow morning [February 18]." O'Connor responded by once again denouncing Coughlin for his intrusion into politics:

Every decent Catholic in America has been ashamed of him since he came to this country. . . . Just because Father Coughlin is an egomaniac he thinks he can run the government. He stepped into the bonus and world court issues, but had as much to do with Congressional action on them as any elevator operator in the Capitol.[18]

Bishop Gallagher was able to convince Coughlin of the foolish-ness of engaging in a common brawl with O'Connor. But Cough-lin could not forget O'Connor's assault. On his radio show and in the very first issue of *Social Justice*, Coughlin was at his sarcastic best when he asked:

My dear John, is it politics to plead for the poor? Is it politics to emulate the gentle Master who castigated the Scribes and Pharisees? In fear and trembling, I ask you, John, is it politics to attempt, even at an infinite distance, to follow in the footsteps of Him, Who, when reason and prayer had failed drove the money changers from the temple by physical force? John, if these be politics, I humbly submit that I am a politician.[19]

Support for the Frazier-Lemke bill was, however, a losing bat-tle. The bill finally got out of the House committee on April 30 and was decisively voted down 235 to 142 in May. Prior to this vote a letter written by William Green, president of the American Federation of Labor, was read in the House chamber. It urged House members to vote against the measure because it was infla-tionary. Coughlin regarded Green's intervention as an attempt of the powerful eastern labor leaders of the AFL to work against him, personally.

Green's actions notwithstanding, Coughlin left no doubt where he placed major responsibility for the defeat of the Frazier-Lemke bill. "The Frazier-Lemke bill is a corpse on the steps of the White House." Coughlin went on to accuse Roosevelt of killing the bill through "use of the gag, the political stiletto." Then Coughlin bid farewell to the Frazier-Lemke bill with a flourish.

Alas poor Frazier-Lemke bill, cold and stiff in your stark death, you might have known that, because there was contained within the ar-teries of your body the red blood which dared challenge the money changers in your effort to restore to Congress its right to coin and regulate money of this nation — you might have known that you could expect no kinder fate![20]

By the spring of 1936 Father Coughlin decided that his would be the last word on which candidates the NUSJ would support for Congress. He hoped that NUSJ support of selected candidates would be the key factor in the outcome of congressional races throughout the country. On April 28 the NUSJ received its first political test at the polls. The Pennsylvania congressional primaries saw the NUSJ support twenty-four candidates, twelve of whom emerged victorious. Father Coughlin believed NUSJ support was the decisive factor in the victories. But the NUSJ had given its support to the candidates only one week prior to the primary and at a time when economic conditions in the state had improved over what they had been in 1935, thus facilitating the renomination of incumbents, who had the political machinery of office behind them. Ten of the twelve victorious candidates were incumbents.

The NUSJ looked forward to its next test in the Ohio primaries. In his public appearances and in the pages of *Social Justice*, Coughlin vigorously supported the NUSJ-backed candidates. On May 10, Coughlin addressed a Cleveland rally of more than twenty thousand. In a fiery talk he urged Ohioans to vote for NUSJ-supported candidates and emphasized the importance of Martin Sweeney's renomination. Sweeney, a loyal Coughlin supporter, was being opposed for renomination by the Democratic machine. He and twelve other NUSJ-supported candidates emerged victorious in the primaries. Coughlin, overlooking the fact that seventeen of thirty-two NUSJ-backed candidates were defeated, believed that his support was again the decisive factor in these victories.[21] The outcome of the Ohio primary, however, moved the *New York Times* to comment on May 14 on the power that Father Coughlin's third-party effort seemed to possess.

Coughlin sat back, confidently waiting for Republicans and Democrats to woo him for his support. He would have his price; one which he did not consider exorbitant. He wished to become a close adviser to the President, whomever he happened to be. Such a position would bring power, and power was what he was seeking. He hoped that the Democrats would approach him first. He had no respect for Alf Landon, the Republican presidential candidate, whom he considered a "mental lightweight."[22] But the phone never rang. Apparently, the two major political parties needed further convincing of his political power.

On May 29, Coughlin sent out a political feeler, through the pages of *Social Justice*, in which he intimated that he would support a third party in the November presidential elections. He hoped that both the Republicans and Democrats would respond by making concessions to him; they remained silent. Coughlin then decided to renew his attacks on the President. He denounced him, in particular, for his failure to multiply job opportunities for youths. "Youth asked for bread and he gave them a stone, a gravestone."[23] Roosevelt was "the Democratic promise breaker," said *Social Justice*, and "your erstwhile saviour whose golden promises ring upon the counter of performance with the cheapness of tin."[24]

Although the President was furious at the attacks, he made no attempt to reply to them. When James Farley sounded out the President on the idea of meeting Coughlin again to get him to cease, or at least tone down, his attacks, the President remained adamant.[25] Coughlin claims that his criticisms of the President were based on his belief that the administration was intent on precipitating a communist revolution that would culminate in a dictatorship with Roosevelt the dictator. He was certain that if Roosevelt were to be stopped it would have to be done in 1936 because the President's reelection would threaten the very existence of the Constitution, personal liberties and states' rights.[26]

Since the Republicans continued to ignore him, Coughlin's remaining alternative was to make certain that his own political movement did well in the 1936 elections so that it could provide the foundation for victory in the 1940 presidential election — if indeed such an election were to be held. He had no choice now but to unveil the Union party as a third force on the American political scene.

First, he went to the communications center of the nation, New York City, where he issued a formal statement saying that although the NUSJ was not a political party it would endorse candidates in the November national elections. He emphasized that, at that moment, the NUSJ was primarily interested in congressional elections and predicted that at least 275 congressmen would be elected because of its support. The NUSJ, he repeated, would support neither Roosevelt nor Landon, and he broadly hinted that he would announce the formation of a third political party in the very near future.[27] In the meantime, he urged his readers and his radio listeners not to commit themselves politically.

Finally, on a special nationwide broadcast on CBS on June 19, 1936, Coughlin announced his support of Congressman William Lemke of North Dakota for President of the United States on the slate of his newly organized Union party, the formation of which had been announced six hours earlier. Coughlin closed his broadcast by stating:

This is a new day for America with its new "Union party." Lemke has raised a banner of liberty for you to follow as you carry it unsullied into the ranks of the money changers' servants now occupying the White House and the halls of Congress.

Behind it will rally agriculture, labor, the disappointed Republicans and the outraged Democrats, the independent merchant and industrialist and every lover of liberty who desires to eradicate the cancerous growths from decadent capitalism and avoid the treacherous pitfalls of red communism.[28]

In spite of the importance Coughlin placed on the broadcast announcing his support of Lemke, it was anticlimactic. Gerald L. K. Smith, never one to stand in the background and watch Coughlin or anyone else become the focal point for the news, had already announced the formation of the Union party. He had also disclosed that the party, which would support Congressman Lemke for President, consisted of supporters of himself, Townsend and Coughlin. By beating Coughlin to the punch, Smith succeeded in irritating the priest no end. For the remainder of the campaign, his aides and employees would strive mightily not to mention Smith's name in Coughlin's presence. For to do so was to invite an icy glare.

William Lemke was the best candidate for the presidency of the United States that Coughlin could muster. He seemed to be the personification of middle-class America. He was born in Minnesota, grew up in North Dakota, and overcame the loss of an eye to become sufficiently proficient in his studies to be graduated from the University of North Dakota and then from Yale University Law School in 1905. It was at the University of North Dakota that he became friendly with Lynn Frazier, his collaborator on the bill bearing their names. After becoming involved in an unsuccessful land speculation deal in Mexico, Lemke established a law practice in Fargo, North Dakota, and in 1920 was elected state attorney general, the same year Frazier was elected governor. In 1921 both were recalled because of a dispute over the operation of the Bank of North Dakota. Cleared of any wrongdoing, Lemke ran for governor in 1922 as an independent, but lost by 20,000 votes. In 1932 he was elected to the House of Representatives and was reelected in 1934. Lemke's home life seemed to exemplify the American ideal. He was married in 1910. He liked to spend time with his wife, Isabelle, and their children, William Jr., Robert and Mary, go fishing, raise flowers, and romp with his dogs. Thirty-four years after the 1936 election Gerald L. K. Smith described Lemke as "a complete composite of unattractiveness. He looked like a hayseed. He wore a cap. He was not eloquent and all he could talk about was money and agriculture."[29] Father Coughlin could never tolerate sharing the stage with anyone. He could not abide formidable intellects. He became irritated when he had competition from within his ranks. William Lemke was the perfect foil for Father Coughlin.

When asked why he didn't choose either of his two friends Senator Elmer Thomas of Oklahoma or Senator Burton Wheeler of Montana for the presidential nomination, Coughlin chuckled and said, "They were good friends of mine."[30]

Thomas O'Brien, the Union party vice-presidential candidate, had overcome poverty to graduate from Harvard and eventually become the District Attorney of Boston. His political achievements were nil, but it must be pointed out that candidates just as inadequately prepared have been elected vice-president. Circumstances have even catapulted several of them to the presidency itself. Coughlin liked O'Brien for his guts and determination.

In supporting Lemke and O'Brien, Coughlin had ample evidence of the problems he faced without the help of Huey Long. Smith had wanted the Union party presidential nomination, but Coughlin would have none of that. Lemke may have lacked color, but he was definitely preferable to the irksome Smith. For although Coughlin had no respect for Lemke's intellectual prowess, he believed that the congressman would follow his orders and that "he could not tell a lie."[31]

Throughout the battle over the Frazier-Lemke bill, Lemke had said very little. He had been virtually ignored by the news media. It was to become a common occurrence in the 1936 presidential election. Just as Lemke was the forgotten espouser of the bill bearing his name, so would he be the forgotten presidential candidate of the 1936 election. Not only forgotten by the theoretically neutral mass media, but even largely neglected by his chief supporter, Charles Coughlin, who kept the North Dakota congressman in the background throughout the presidential campaign. Lemke was not even present to answer questions from the press when his candidacy was announced. This lack of attention was exactly what one should have expected, given Lemke's personality and Coughlin's desire to be in the limelight.

To provide some legitimacy for Coughlin's lackluster candidates it was crucial that they be approved by the Townsend Convention, which would meet in Cleveland in July, and by his own Union party delegates. Coughlin, however, was not idly waiting for those two conventions. He embarked on a series of public appearances in Brockton, Trenton, Philadelphia and Chicago, all in the effort to rally behind him the millions of voters he needed for a good showing at the polls. Just as important as his public appearances in these cities were his behind-the-scenes meetings with regional leaders of the NUSJ, meetings which swiftly convinced him that they would prove virtually worthless in the upcoming election. He knew now that he would have to depend on his personal charisma and the followers of Smith and Townsend for electoral success.

Coughlin attacks the Roosevelt administration before the Townsend National Convention in July, 1936 (Wide World Photo)

Gerald L. K. Smith, Coughlin, and Dr. Francis E. Townsend at the Townsend Convention in Cleveland, July, 1936 (United Press International Photo)

To solidify support for Lemke, Coughlin was scheduled to be the main speaker at the Townsend Convention. He realized that his talk to the aged Townsend followers would have to be a good one because of his earlier criticism of the Townsend program. That he and Townsend did not warm to each other aggravated his task. Their relationship was polite, but not friendly. The priest was further upset by the fact that Townsend seemed to have taken a liking to Smith. In Coughlin's eyes, Smith was using the old doctor for his own political ends, although it is hardly necessary to add that so was Coughlin.

Smith had advised Townsend to refuse to appear before a congressional committee investigating the doctor's activities. Taking the proffered advice, he walked out in the middle of the hearing, proclaiming his dislike for the manner in which the committee was prying into his affairs. Smith led Townsend out of the hearing room and to a taxi which took them to Baltimore. In order to avoid receiving a contempt citation, Smith took Townsend to the home of his good friend H. L. Mencken.[32] While he was in hiding, the sympathy of the American people and the mass media swung sharply in Townsend's favor and Congress temporarily dropped any attempt to serve the contempt citation on him. The end result of this incident was that Townsend leaned heavily on Smith's advice.

The scheduling of the speakers for the Townsend Convention resulted in Smith's preceding Coughlin by one day. Smith had put on quite a show, raking the Roosevelt administration with grapeshot and broadsides. He accused the New Dealers, wheat speculators and Wall Street bankers of being one and the same. He went on to urge all God-fearing, patriotic Americans to seize control of the country. The speech was a rousing success. The Townsendites roared and cheered every time Smith denounced Roosevelt. A day earlier, when Gomer Smith, the Townsendite candidate for senator from Oklahoma, had applauded the President for saving America from communism, the crowd had roared its approval. But Gerald Smith was a spellbinder and he was at his best that day. With each line, the perspiring young Bible-spouting reverend set off sparks of emotion in his listeners. Everyone had been impressed. H. L. Mencken wrote that Smith was

the master of masters, the champion boob bumper. . . . Twice at
Cleveland, I saw the rev. gentleman torpedo even the press stand. In
that stand were journalists who had not shown any human emotion
above the level of cupidity and lubricity for twenty years, yet he had
them all howling in ten minutes.[33]

When he had concluded, the audience let loose a thunderous
ovation. Smith was ecstatic.

Father Coughlin, however, was not. How the hell could he top
this sly, aggressive rabble-rouser? Coughlin knew that Smith's performance would be hard to match and almost impossible to surpass.

The next morning, Coughlin mounted the speaker's platform,
accompanied by Smith and Townsend. The crowd roared its approval. Coughlin, standing between the other two, put his arms
over their shoulders, looked up at the audience, smiled, and said:
"We stand united together against the unholy trinity of Landon,
Roosevelt, and Browder. We're all working toward the same
end." The crowd gave them another thunderous ovation.

Smith and Townsend then withdrew from the platform, and
Coughlin was ready to begin in earnest. He startled the audience
by roaring out, "Martin Sweeny, stand up and tell them where
you stand on the Democratic party." Sweeny jumped to the microphone and played Charlie McCarthy to Coughlin's Edgar
Bergen. "Because Roosevelt is a double-crosser, Father, I stand
with the National Union for Social Justice."[34] This interlude
over, Coughlin continued, his booming voice catching the fancy
of the Townsendite listeners. They cheered and applauded his
criticisms of Roosevelt and the New Deal. Each round of applause
sparked Coughlin to greater criticism of the President. By the
time he reached the conclusion of the talk, he was almost shrieking
at the crowd. He was completely immersed in its reaction to him.
He had the crowd eating out of his hand. He hoped Gerald Smith
and his idiotic admirer, H. L. Mencken, were still in the audience.

His notes were forgotten. He reminded the audience that FDR stood for "Franklin Double-crossing Roosevelt." Most of the crowd cheered this remark, but a number of people started to boo. Dr. Townsend quickly strode to the podium and said in a soft voice, "Will the sergeant-at-arms put those booers out." Frank Arbuckle, the convention chairman, then shouted at the audience, "There is no place here for that." The booing subsided. When Father Coughlin resumed his talk he asked why it was that the communists were supporting Roosevelt. He then ripped off his Roman collar and in an almost hysterical voice labeled the President of the United States a "liar" and "betrayer." The crowd was frenetic. It was going wild. Coughlin was on the verge of physical exhaustion, but it had been worth it. Gerald L. K. Smith, the world's greatest rabble-rouser, indeed!

Later that same day Gomer Smith, vice-president of the Townsend movement, once again took to the platform. Addressing the same crowd that had earlier hissed, booed, and stomped at the mention of Roosevelt's name, he delivered an earnest and vigorous defense of Roosevelt and his policies. Within five minutes from the time he began, Gomer Smith had the crowd of thirteen thousand cheering at every mention of Roosevelt's name. He attacked Townsend's attempt to stampede the convention into support of a third party against Roosevelt. He urged the good people in the audience not to

become involved with men who reach into their pockets for the Holy Book of God to make a demagogic speech and then so far forget their self respect as to heap personal abuse on the Chief Magistrate of the nation.[35]

It did not seem to matter much what the elderly delegates heard. They were cheering everybody and everything.

Townsend, however, was not cheering. Instead, he promptly moved to expel Gomer Smith from his organization for being discourteous and for attempting to disrupt the movement. But the national board of directors of the organization, all hand-picked by Townsend, balked at punishing Smith and adjourned without taking any action in the matter. Under the provisions of the organization's charter, Townsend had the power to remove and replace the board of directors at his discretion. But he chose to do nothing. The refusal of the board to get rid of Smith indicated that there was a lively opposition within the Townsend movement to supporting Lemke and tying in with Coughlin.

The Townsend Convention's endorsement of Lemke's candidacy went almost unnoticed because of reaction to Coughlin's speech criticizing Roosevelt. Jim Farley, speaking for the Roosevelt administration, publicly downgraded the effects of Coughlin's speech; the accusations, he said, would hurt Coughlin and the Union party more than they would Roosevelt.[36] Coughlin's speech also set off a furious chain reaction of queries on the position of the Vatican in tolerating such attacks on the President of the United States. Although it had stated publicly, in June of the same year, that Coughlin's activities had not violated canon law, the Vatican viewed them with consternation. Direct Vatican intervention in disciplining Coughlin was ruled out for the moment because that was considered to be the responsibility of his bishop. The Vatican also pointed out that before any action was taken regarding the disciplining of an American priest, the matter would first be referred to the Apostolic Delegate in Washington, D.C.[37]

July of that year found Bishop Gallagher in New York City preparing to sail for Rome and a visit to the Vatican. Gallagher reiterated his support for Father Coughlin, but he did concede that he had told Coughlin that his language criticizing Roosevelt was a "little too strong." He refused to censure Coughlin for his actions and denied that he would discuss Father Coughlin's activities with the Vatican "unless they speak of it."[38] He did admit that the Vatican was aware of Father Coughlin's political activities and kept a record of all of the priest's speeches. While waiting for Bishop Gallagher to arrive in Rome, the Vatican simply announced that Coughlin's portrayal of Franklin Roosevelt as a liar had created a "painful impression."[39] In fact, Pope Pius XI was angry. He became even angrier when he heard that Bishop Gallagher, just before leaving for Rome, had insisted, "I absolutely cannot speak contrary to Father Coughlin."[40]

Coughlin at the opening of the convention of the National Union for
Social Justice (United Press International Photo)

The Vatican was faced with a situation where one of its priests was attacking the President of the United States in language so strong that it was not utilized even by candidates for political office. Since the issuance of *Rerum Novarum*, the Catholic Church had tried to ameliorate the social upheavals created by the Industrial Revolution and the rise of nationalism. It was difficult for this ponderous, medieval institution to change direction and its efforts were often perfunctory. The Vatican failed to see how Coughlin's intemperate remarks and his direct involvement in politics could improve the image of the Church. It instructed its Apostolic Delegate to the United States, Ameleto Cicognani, to inform Father Coughlin that an apology was to be made immediately to President Roosevelt and that his political activities were to be "toned down."

Even prior to being so informed, the radio priest was having misgivings about his remarks. He realized that he "had no business saying those things about President Roosevelt."[41] Bishop Gallagher had phoned him and communicated his displeasure with the matter. When Gallagher asked Coughlin to back down on his statements Coughlin was only too happy to do so,[42] and on July 23, he publicly apologized to President Roosevelt. He explained that he had been carried away in the passion of his speech and this had caused him to use such intemperate words as "liar" and "betrayer." Coughlin also pointed out that he had been an early supporter of Roosevelt and had helped him become President.

Bishop Gallagher denied that the Vatican had forced Coughlin to apologize and that he was being called to Rome, as the *New York Times* claimed, to discuss Father Coughlin's activities.[43] Actually, both the Vatican and Gallagher were upset by Coughlin's remarks and both had requested Coughlin to apologize. Coughlin made his apology and then promptly continued to lambaste the President, although not in such language as he had used in Cleveland.

After his apology, Coughlin embarked on another series of public appearances. First, he went into upstate New York, where he attacked Governor Herbert Lehman, a Democrat and staunch Roosevelt supporter, who was seeking reelection. In Buffalo,

Coughlin labeled as false and malicious continuing reports that the Vatican had told him to restrain his activities. Then, as if to underline the point of being unrestricted in his activities, Coughlin appeared before ten thousand followers in Hamburg, a suburb of Buffalo, to renew his attacks on Roosevelt in more civil terms. He made it abundantly clear that his apology to the President was behind him and that "I have no apologies to offer the gentleman in the White House who lies on the rotten meat of broken promises." But Coughlin did not content himself with criticizing Roosevelt. He attacked Alf Landon as well as the Republican party, which he claimed was totally dominated by William Randolph Hearst, the newspaper baron. He pointed out that in Landon's state, Kansas, farmers raised sunflowers for parrot food and the "Republican papers are being fed the parrot food by the lord of San Simeon."[44]

From New York Coughlin moved on to Hankinson, North Dakota, for a rally to celebrate Lemke's homecoming. Several thousand farmers heard Coughlin tell them that if Roosevelt were reelected they "should repudiate their debts, and if anybody tries to enforce them, repudiate them also."[45] Later, Coughlin denied that he had urged the repudiation of farm debts, and blamed the poor public address system for distorting what he had said. He asserted that he had actually told the farmers that if something were not done to alleviate their problems, then they would not be able to repay their debts.

In early August, Coughlin campaigned in Massachusetts and Rhode Island, where he was greeted by large crowds that cheered him when he launched his tirades against Roosevelt and Landon. These warm receptions buoyed his spirits, but left him exhausted. He returned to Cleveland for the opening of the national convention of his own National Union for Social Justice.

The day before the opening of the convention Walter D. Davis, convention marshal, said that Dr. Francis Townsend and Gerald L. K. Smith would not be allowed to address the NUSJ convention. This directly contradicted an earlier announcement by Sylvester McMahon, national secretary of the NUSJ, that both men would address the convention. McMahon had said that Coughlin had personally invited Townsend and Smith to address the NUSJ.

Davis called Coughlin and was told to add the two names to the speaker's list. Davis, in explaining his actions, said that he merely wanted "to keep the NUSJ out of politics. . . . This is not an open forum. . . . This is not going to be another Townsend Convention if I can help it."[46]

Father Coughlin chuckled when recalling the incident. "Just a little trial balloon. Just a little trial balloon."[47] He had actually wanted to prevent Smith from speaking but, in the interest of party harmony, he did not do so. He also wanted to impress Townsend by letting it be known that it was through his direct intervention that the old doctor would address the convention. But by scheduling Smith and Townsend to speak to the delegates on the Saturday prior to the big Sunday finale, Coughlin ensured that they would do so in relative obscurity.

On August 13, the NUSJ delegates were welcomed to the convention by the keynote speaker, Senator Rush Holt of West Virginia. From the start the audience was Coughlin's. They idolized him; they elected him president of the National Union by unanimous vote and, with only one dissenting vote, acceded to his request that the National Union endorse Lemke and O'Brien.

The convention moved toward its Sunday conclusion with only a minimum of dissent. Father Coughlin anticipated that a packed house of over seventy thousand followers would jam into Cleveland Stadium for the convention finale. The actual turnout, estimated between twenty-five thousand and forty-two thousand, was a disappointment.[48]

Nevertheless, the crowd was an enthusiastic one. It stomped, applauded and cheered as Lemke attacked Roosevelt, Alf Landon and the New Deal. He labeled Roosevelt "a bewildered Kerensky who doesn't know where he is going." And displaying the delusion that has afflicted political candidates from time immemorial he shouted to the crowd: "We are going to win!"[49]

Vice-presidential nominee O'Brien found the Democratic and Republican parties guilty of "treason to the masses."[50] Some of his words made sense, but his presentation was boring. The crowd grew restless. After what seemed an interminable wait, Coughlin moved to the microphone.

The hot sun beat down on his bare head as he began to speak. Sweat poured down his face. Aides kept giving him fresh hand towels with which he wiped away the perspiration running into his eyes. He promised the crowd to cancel his radio broadcasts "if I don't deliver nine million votes for Lemke."[51] After speaking thirty-five minutes in the sweltering sun, he admonished his people, "Go to your homes. Ring door bells and organize until your members are at least as numerous as the unemployed." Suddenly, he began to sway and he whispered into the microphone, "I'm sorry but I cannot address you further. I've been up all night. I must leave you now. God bless you."[52] Supported by his aides, Coughlin was taken by car to his hotel room, where he was treated for heat fatigue and nervous indigestion by Dr. George O'Malley, a good friend.

When Father Coughlin left the podium, many in the audience did not realize that he was ill. They thought that he had simply concluded his speech. They moved toward the podium, which stood where second base would have been for a baseball game, milled about, took pictures, stood on the podium and, in general, seemed in a festive mood. On this note, the NUSJ convention ended.

Coughlin's physician prescribed ten days of complete rest. While recuperating at his parents' home, he disclosed that for ten minutes before he finally stopped speaking, the audience had been a blur. He had felt a choking sensation and visualized thousands of fantastically shaped figures dancing before his eyes. "Then everything went black. . . . I couldn't see anything although I knew there was bright sunshine."[53]

Coughlin soon recovered from his illness, but all was not well within the Union party. In addition to the feelings of antipathy between Coughlin and Smith, Townsend was disturbed by some of the individuals whom Coughlin had brought into the campaign. The most prominent example was Newton Jenkins, who was entrusted with a great deal of responsibility in the day-to-day operation of the Union party. Townsend considered him to be pro-Hitler, and Jenkins' activities seem to have borne out the doctor's view. In 1935, he had participated in a meeting with a number of pro-Nazis, pro-Fascists and "superpatriots" in Chicago. The purpose of the meeting was to unify these varied fascist elements to provide support for a powerful political third force as an alternative to the Democratic and Republican parties. Among the prominent American fascists present were William Dudley Pelley, Harry Jung, Walter Kappe, Fritz Gisibl and George Christians.[54] The meeting had accomplished little more than a tenuous agreement to cooperate in the struggle against Republicans and Democrats. But this was not the end of Jenkins' pro-Nazi flirtations. On October 30, 1935, he appeared in Lincoln Turner Hall, which was guarded by uniformed would-be storm troopers wearing swastika armbands. In his talk, Jenkins blamed the country's troubles on Jewish politicians who, he claimed, controlled the government. Townsend did not like Jenkins, but made up his mind to tolerate him because he believed that the Union party was the vehicle to make his own program a reality.

Given associates like Jenkins, coupled with some of his own unflattering references to persons of Jewish descent, it was no wonder that Coughlin would soon be called an anti-Semite. Philip Slomovitz's *Detroit Jewish Chronicle* assailed him for mentioning only Jewish names when he spoke of the money changers and the international bankers.[55] The priest did not respond, but an article in *Social Justice* denied these charges, while at the same time it spoke of "good Jews" and "atheistic Jews," and concluded that there was a "Jewish question" in the United States.

The Jewish Advocate stated that the priest's remarks had resulted in his emergence as a "challenger of the Jews . . . his anti-Semitic utterances are definite causes for alarm."[56] *The Detroit Jewish Chronicle* stated that Coughlin had utilized an old trick of Jew-baiters in referring to different classes of Jews — the good Jew and the atheistic Jew. But rather than feeling anger toward Coughlin, "we are rather inclined to believe that he ought to be pitied."[57] It should be pointed out that in the late 1930s, when his followers physically assaulted Jews in the streets, Coughlin never explained how the "good" Jew could be identified.

Monsignor John Ryan said that Father Coughlin's remarks were "unjust to Jews and unfortunate in the political campaign."[58] Another Catholic, Congressman Joseph A. Conroy of Massachusetts, accused Coughlin of trying to "arouse class discontent and fan the flames of religious bigotry."[59]

Osservatore Romana, which usually presented the Vatican's views, not only strongly criticized those priests who attacked the supreme social authorities of the countries in which they resided but, in addition, strongly rebuked Bishop Gallagher for having said that the Vatican approved of Father Coughlin's activities. Indeed, its editorial stated that Gallagher's statement did not "correspond with the truth," and that the bishop knew what the truth actually was.[60]

Upon his return from Rome, Bishop Gallagher was greeted by Coughlin and the press. With Coughlin standing beside him, Gallagher denied the accuracy of the *Osservatore* editorial and claimed that Father Coughlin's difficulties were the result of a campaign by greedy capitalists trying to put him out of business. Gallagher went on to say, "It's the voice of God that comes to you from the great orator from Royal Oak. Rally round it!"[61] Coughlin was beside himself with joy. He had received the complete support of the only man, with the exception of the Pope, who could muzzle him. Given this strong statement of support, he could hardly believe it when the bishop went on to state that Franklin Roosevelt was the best-qualified candidate for the presidency.

Having been spiritually fortified by his superior, Coughlin was ready to resume campaigning. He went on to Chicago where he met with his aides Philip Johnson and Alan Blackburn, a pair of brilliant graduates of Harvard University. They had originally been part of Huey Long's brain trust, and had joined up with Coughlin after Long's assassination in 1935. Their main function was to see that *Social Justice* was published on time by Cuneo Press of Chicago. They worked without salary and, in fact, had sufficient personal funds to contribute $5,000 to Lemke's campaign.[62] Johnson would eventually become a foreign correspondent for *Social Justice* and, years later, one of America's foremost architects. Johnson and Blackburn were the organizers of the rally in Riverview Park, Chicago. They did their job well, for eighty

The opening of Father Coughlin's National Union for Social Justice, showing the delegates from Pennsylvania and Massachusetts, August, 1936 (Wide World Photo)

A crowd of 80,000 greets Father Coughlin in Riverview Park, Chicago, September, 1936 (United Press International Photo)

Coughlin, taken ill, leaves the Cleveland mass meeting (United Press International Photo)

thousand Chicagoans paid fifty cents each to hear Father Coughlin denounce the New Deal and reiterate that his political activities had not been curtailed.

The organizers of an Ebbets Field rally did not fare as well, for only twenty thousand followers in his eastern stronghold of Brooklyn turned out to greet Coughlin. His close friend Patrick Scanlan, editor of the *Brooklyn Tablet*, the official newspaper of the Brooklyn archdiocese, had been pushing hard for a large show- ing for the priest. A large number of priests in the archdiocese had used their pulpits to press their parishioners to turn out for Coughlin. Given these efforts on his behalf, it was no wonder that Coughlin was unhappy about the size of the gathering. His disap- pointment did not prevent him from savaging the New Dealers, particularly those who were supporting the Loyalists in the Span- ish Civil War. He said noticeably little about Lemke and the polit- ical alternatives offered by the Union party. But he did take time to mock Landon's speech-making abilities and advise him to hire "a good tutor and practice his speeches."[63]

From Brooklyn it was on to New Haven, Des Moines, St. Louis and Cincinnati. As always, he was greeted at the train platform by crowds of well-wishers who surged forward in an effort to touch his coat, while shouting words of devotion and encouragement to him. And as always there was a considerable number of special police on hand to protect Coughlin because of the usual number of crank calls threatening his life. As the campaign tempo in- creased, he became exhausted, sick and irritable. He refused to talk to reporters. "I am a very sick man. I need to see a doctor rather than reporters."[64]

The political impact of these public appearances was muted although in the Michigan senatorial primary, Coughlin-supported Louis Ward lost to the regular Democratic party candidate, Pren- tiss Brown, by only 3,799 votes, and in the Boston mayoralty primary, Coughlin-backed Thomas O'Brien did gather 37,000 write-in votes against the irrepressible Jim Curley. In addition, on November 7, 1936, O'Brien, running on the Union party ticket, would draw enough Irish Catholic votes away from James Curley to enable the Republican Henry Cabot Lodge, Jr., to squeeze out a victory.

Coughlin was appalled by the September primary results and the days up to the November 7 election were painful ones. The months of campaigning, the heartaches, the frustrations were "all for nothing. Down the drain . . . I knew then that victory on election day was out of the question."[65] Nevertheless, he continued his campaigning on behalf of candidates who were supported by the NUSJ.

The instructions to Gallagher to have him "tone down" Coughlin's activities were apparently not being interpreted strictly enough to satisfy the Vatican. Furious with Gallagher for his strong statements on Coughlin's behalf, which gave many Americans the impression that Coughlin spoke with Church approval, the Vatican now felt compelled to restrict Coughlin's activities. It sent Eugenio Cardinal Pacelli, Vatican Secretary of State (Later he was elected Pope Pius XII) to confer with Archbishop McNicholas, the powerful and highly respected head of the Cincinnati archdiocese, about the political and social ramifications within the United States of any decision made concerning Coughlin.

Gallagher, upset by Pacelli's visit, determined to go to Cincinnati to meet with him. He wanted the cardinal to hear his side of the story. He convinced Archbishop Schrembs of Cleveland to accompany him. Gallagher and Schrembs reached Archbishop Mc-Nicholas' residence early in the morning, at a time when the Cincinnati prelate and Pacelli were already in conference. After they had waited in an outer office for the better part of the day, a priest was sent to inform them that they would not be given an audience by Pacelli. Angry and frustrated, the two churchmen, who were referred to by their fellow priests as the "Gold Dust Twins" because of their close friendship, returned to Detroit. The next day, Gallagher was instructed by Pacelli to exercise closer control over Father Coughlin and to inform him that he was not to participate in political campaigning once the 1936 election was over.[66]

His work done, Pacelli returned to Rome to report to Pope Pius

XI, and Coughlin continued his political campaigning. Although reluctant to discuss all of the outcomes of Pacelli's visit, Coughlin did confirm that after the 1936 elections the Vatican forbade him to directly lead a political movement. He stressed, however, that as an American citizen he had the right to voice his opinions and that he did continue to do so, even after the 1936 elections.

In recalling the incident, Father Coughlin is still angry at the rude treatment accorded Gallagher and Schrembs. "Can you imagine! Keeping two wonderful bishops waiting all day, and then sending a secretary out to dismiss them. Why, you don't treat a dog like that!"[67]

According to Gerald L. K. Smith, who says he was planning strategy for the final days of the Lemke campaign with Coughlin at the latter's home, Bishop Gallagher came to the house on his return from Cincinnati, quite visibly depressed, and asked to see Coughlin alone. They retired to another room and when Coughlin returned he, too, seemed shaken. In a low voice he told Smith, "The arm of Jim Farley is long. Mr. Roosevelt has served notice on the Pope that he will not send the Church a fraternal delegate to Rome unless Father Coughlin is silenced."[68] Coughlin, however, denies that Smith was with him when Gallagher told him of Pacelli's instructions. The priest states that he "would not believe Smith on a stack of Bibles. I never remember him being at my house."[69]

Pacelli's visit was not the only jolt Father Coughlin received in October. Harold Ickes, Secretary of the Interior, delivered a stinging attack on the Union party, labeling Lemke a "Father Coughlin–Landon stooge" and insinuating that Coughlin was in cahoots with the Republicans to defeat Roosevelt.[70]

But Coughlin continued his offensive in a Boston press conference when he labeled as communists both David Dubinsky and Felix Frankfurter. John Barry, a reporter for the *Boston Globe*, who knew Frankfurter well, took exception to this description of the Harvard law professor. There was some additional verbal give and take between the two men before the press conference concluded. Soon after, Coughlin met Barry by chance at the Hotel Biltmore in Providence, where he had delivered a speech. Tired and overworked, he berated the Boston newspaperman and then suddenly lunged at him. He ripped off the reporter's glasses and punched him in the face before Thomas O'Brien finally succeeded in restraining him. Barry said that since Coughlin "was a priest of the Catholic Church there was nothing for me to do but stand and take it."

The next morning, upon his return to Boston, Coughlin was still fuming as he told reporters, "If I had him here I'd choke him . . . If I see that fellow I'll tear him to pieces."[71] The Boston police department assigned six policemen equipped with tear gas bombs and guns to Coughlin. Whether they were to guard him or to restrain him was not made clear.

Another blow against Coughlin was struck by John H. O'Donnell of Pittsburgh, an NUSJ member, who filed suit against Coughlin and the other members of the board of trustees of the NUSJ on the grounds of "mismanagement, unlawful conduct, bad faith, negligence and breach of trust."[72] O'Donnell, who had cast the only vote against NUSJ endorsement of Lemke at the Cleveland convention, claimed that Father Coughlin had become dictator of the organization and that funds had been mismanaged. Coughlin labeled the charges a "big laugh," and stated firmly that he "did not think the suit [would] ever come to trial."[73] He was right; the suit was dropped without ever going to court. But he remained angry with Frank Murphy, his erstwhile friend, whom he believed had put O'Donnell up to making the charges against him. He resolved to strike back at Murphy by endorsing the incumbent Republican governor, Frank Fitzgerald, who was running against Murphy. Speaking in Detroit's State Fair Coliseum before 6,000 people on October 17, Coughlin announced his support of Fitzgerald, claiming that in so doing he was "putting principles above friendship." The crowd roared its approval. In the confusion that prevailed, one Woody Hockaday of Wichita, Kansas, dressed in a red shirt, white trousers and an Indian headdress, made his way to the platform. In spite of his garish clothes, his yelling and chanting made him seem like part of the pro-Coughlin audience. He wasn't. He leaped onto the stage, scattered a large bag of chicken feathers over Coughlin and others standing near him, grabbed the micro-

Coughlin at a New York rally in Brooklyn, September, 1936 (United Press International Photo)

phone from the startled Coughlin, and shouted, "You can't talk politics here!"

It took a few seconds for bystanders to understand what had happened. Soon, however, Hockaday was in the midst of a brawl with five Coughlin aides and three policemen. The crowd was in an uproar and surged toward the platform. After putting up a tremendous battle, Hockaday was overcome. People in the crowd were screaming, "Kill him! Hit him!" Luckily for Hockaday, Coughlin intervened. Regaining control of the microphone, he shouted, "Don't lay a hand on him! . . . Get back! Back, back . . . Let him alone; I love to talk to communists." The crowd was surly but it responded. Hockaday was arrested and hustled out to a police car.

Coughlin resumed his speech, calling Hockaday a communist who had been purposely sent to disrupt the meeting. Hockaday, for his part, said, "People think I'm a nut. That's why I can get away with this stuff. A nut can do things other people can't."[74] Was Hockaday trying to tell America something?

(As a result of this incident, Father Coughlin applied for and received a permit for a thirty-eight caliber chrome Smith and Wesson revolver with a white pearl handle which he carried under his clerical garb.)[75]

Shortly after being attacked by Hockaday, Coughlin was confronted with more troubles. Herman Koenig, president of NUSJ Unit 66 in St. Louis, resigned from the organization: "I think," he said, "that Father Coughlin has gone mad." A weary Coughlin returned to Cleveland, the scene of his most severe denunciations of Roosevelt, and startled his audience by calling Roosevelt a "scab President."[76]

If October was not a good month, November was to be worse. All pretense of a working alliance with Townsend and Smith had ended, and with it the hopes for the millions of votes he had expected from their supporters. Their dislike and distrust of one another had resulted in their going their separate ways. Now, practically on his own, Coughlin wound up his campaign with a swing through the East: Scranton, Newark and finally New York City. Again and again he hit out at Roosevelt and the New Deal. He warned voters that communists had infiltrated the government, and that Roosevelt's reelection would be a national catastrophe. In a final Saturday night broadcast, he told his listeners that the Social Security Act only guaranteed the "continuance of the money changer in power and the retention of an immoral wage system." He used this opportunity to apologize for calling Roosevelt a "scab President" and also "for any hurt which such words might have done this person."[77] But he followed up these conciliatory remarks by accusing Roosevelt of pushing legislation which would result in a form of government similar to the governments of "Mussolini, Stalin, and Hitler."[78]

On November 2, Farley told Roosevelt, "You will carry every state but two — Maine and Vermont."[79] On election day, Roosevelt carried forty-six states; Landon two — Maine and Vermont; Lemke none. Lemke's national vote was 882,479 out of 45,646,817. The Lemke vote was highest in his native state of North Dakota. Even here, it was a mere 13 percent of the votes cast. Only in North Dakota, Massachusetts, Minnesota, Rhode Island and Oregon did Lemke receive more than 5 percent of the vote. In the heavily Protestant South, an area in which Coughlin's broadcasts were not carried extensively, Lemke received a vote of 4,386. Not a single congressional candidate who ran solely with Union party support was elected. It was a slaughter, and Coughlin was the chief victim.

The enormity of Lemke's defeat can be partially attributed to the fact that the Union party was on the ballot in only thirty-six of the forty-eight states and in only thirty of these thirty-six states was its label on the ballot. In Pennsylvania, Lemke appeared as the candidate of the Royal Oak party; in Michigan, as that of the Third party; in Illinois, the Union Progressive party; in New Jersey, the National Union for Social Justice. The Union party was not on the ballot in any form in the states of New York, California, and Louisiana. New York City had a large number of Coughlin supporters. California was Townsend's home state, and Louisiana was Smith's base at that time. All of these states cast significant electoral votes.

There were other, more basic reasons for the magnitude of

Coughlin's defeat. The National Union for Social Justice and the Townsend movement were social movements rather than political instruments. They were the creatures of two men. Having no viable political organizations, they had no professional machines for getting out votes. Without Coughlin and Townsend they would have ceased to exist. Both organizations were autocratic in structure and suffered from an absence of young supporters who would have brought energy and zest to the election campaign. In addition, Father Coughlin's egocentricity prevented the Union party from hiring a professional staff capable of running a successful political campaign. Coughlin, Smith and Townsend had no practical political experience, nor were they willing to delegate authority to people with such experience.

As a candidate, Lemke was the personification of the nonentity. He probably caused many voters to turn away from the Union party. His selection by Coughlin was only one of the numerous serious errors the priest made during the campaign. Coughlin's dictatorial control of the NUSJ may have led many of his non-Catholic followers to reject Lemke on the grounds that it would be a Catholic priest who would be making policy in the United States. His use of such terms as "liar," "betrayer," and "scab" to describe Roosevelt was still another error which alienated many who had thought highly of both Coughlin and Roosevelt.

Traditionally, third parties in presidential and congressional elections have fared poorly. In addition, the Democrats had an immensely popular, politically astute President leading their ticket, a man who had restored the faith of many citizens in America's future and who was at the zenith of his popularity in the fall of 1936. He was unbeatable.

Another factor in the poor showing of the Union party was the distrust and dislike that Smith and Townsend had for Coughlin and he for them. There was neither cooperation nor communication between them during the campaign. At one point, discussing the role of Townsend and Smith in the campaign, Coughlin said, "I don't know *what* they did!"[80] He should have added "nor did I care." The election proved that Smith's boasts were empty ones; he had never inherited Huey Long's following and he was able to deliver few votes to Lemke. And Americans over sixty, who ordinarily might have been influenced by Townsend, in the sanctity of the voting booth cast their votes for Roosevelt. In the final evaluation the American people thought that Roosevelt, not Lemke and not Landon, was the man.

The real surprise of the election results was Coughlin's failure to translate into Lemke votes his vast and loyal radio audience. There were millions of voters who listened to Coughlin, but few who voted his line. Even many Catholics in the urban areas of the Northeast, who were staunch Coughlinites, probably voted for Roosevelt in the belief that a vote for Lemke would be wasted. After all, the important thing was to prevent a Republican from gaining the presidency. They remembered only too well the depression and the previous Republican administration of Herbert Hoover. Coughlin claims that he did not expect Lemke to win in 1936, and that the Union party was formed to protest against the policies of the Democrats and Republicans. But he never believed that his candidate would do as badly as he did.[81]

Saddened and disheartened by the election results, Coughlin announced in November that he would fulfill his campaign pledge to cease his broadcasts if Lemke did not receive nine million votes. He also informed his Sunday afternoon radio audience that the National Union for Social Justice would cease to exist as an active organization.[82] "What else could I do? I had told millions of people what I would do. So I left the airwaves — for a short time."[83]

7

The Return to Action

THOSE Americans who had hoped that the disaster suffered at the polls by the Union party in November, 1936, and the subsequent cessation of Father Coughlin's radio broadcasts would terminate his career as a public figure were to be sadly disappointed, for the priest was soon presented with the opportunity to renew his broadcasts. On January 20, 1937, Bishop Gallagher, whom Coughlin proclaimed "the champion of the people in the battle for rights,"[1] died, and four days later Coughlin's promise to stay off the air was thrown to the wind when he resumed his broadcasts stating that such was Gallagher's dying request.

Father Coughlin's new Church superior was Archbishop Edward Mooney, a brilliant scholar, who was appointed head of what was now the Archdiocese of Detroit. Ordained in 1909 Mooney served under Archbishop Schrembs from 1916 to 1922, first as headmaster of the renowned Cathedral Latin School in Cleveland and then as pastor of St. Patrick's Church in Youngstown, Ohio. Although Father Coughlin describes Mooney as "one of the finest gentlemen that it was my privilege to meet — not necessarily a friend of mine, but a gentleman,"[2] it is with considerable anger that he gives this account of Mooney's disobedience as a priest in the 1920s:

Archbishop Schrembs asked Mooney to substitute for him at a public function and read a text that he had prepared. Mooney agreed, but after scanning the speech, he told Schrembs that he did not agree with the speech's contents and could not present it. Schrembs told Mooney that whether or not he agreed with the content of the talk was immaterial, and ordered Mooney to deliver the speech. He refused. Schrembs was furious and he removed Mooney from his post as principal of the Cathedral Latin School and made him pastor of a church in Youngstown, Ohio, a post which he knew Mooney would find distasteful. It was Mooney's first parish and he found it a difficult assignment. As a result of his unhappiness, Mooney got his brother, a member of the United States diplomatic service, to wrangle a position at the Vatican. In 1923, he was appointed spiritual director of the North American College in the Vatican.[3]

Mooney performed quite well in his new position and in 1926 Pope Pius XI appointed him Apostolic Delegate to India, where he remained until 1931, at which time he was appointed bishop of Rochester. It was from Rochester that Mooney was appointed Bishop Gallagher's successor.

The period immediately following Mooney's installation as head of the Detroit archdiocese was a relatively quiet one. Although Coughlin still delivered his radio broadcasts and spent considerable time getting out *Social Justice*, much of his effort was devoted to his new church and its attendant pastoral duties. He took time, however, to lash out at President Roosevelt's effort to remake the Supreme Court in order to circumvent its rash of decisions holding much of his New Deal legislation unconstitutional, and then returned to his business. When on October 4, 1937, in a press interview, Father Coughlin referred to the "personal stupidity of President Roosevelt," and on the pages of *Social Justice* the same day declared that no Catholic could belong to the CIO, because "Catholicism was as incompatible with the CIO as Catholicism was incompatible with Mohammedanism," his "quiet" period came to an end.

There can be little question that Father Coughlin had a personal stake in opposing the CIO. In 1935, the priest had been the prime mover in the creation of the Automotive Industrial Workers Association (AIWA), an independent labor organization, initially established in Chrysler Corporation plants and then in other plants where it soon came into conflict with the emerging United Auto Workers, which was tied to the CIO. Father Coughlin had hoped that the AIWA would be able to organize the nation's auto workers and to this end had promised it the full support of his National Union for Social Justice.

Coughlin's control of the AIWA had been exercised through that organization's secretary, Richard Frankensteen, a devoted Coughlin admirer. By 1936 the UAW and the AIWA were trying to arrange for a merger of interests. But these efforts were slowed by the intransigence of John L. Lewis, then leader of the CIO. In a speech before the annual convention of the AFL, Coughlin first supported labor's right to unite and then criticized the CIO and Lewis, whom he described as a labor dictator, and a communist tool being used to prepare the way for the eventual victory of Marxism in the United States.

Coughlin believed that communists held key posts in the CIO and that the principles of that organization ran counter to Christian teaching, and when he said so in a press interview on October 4, 1937, Archbishop Mooney responded quickly and sharply. In a personal statement carried in the *Michigan Catholic* on October 7, he disassociated the archdiocese of Detroit from Coughlin's views, and voiced sorrow that Father Coughlin had not utilized "the prudent counsel of a friendly critic" before making his statement.

Father Coughlin drew up a response to the archbishop's statement and was startled when he was denied permission to issue it. But the archbishop wanted to clear up any lingering misunderstandings about Father Coughlin's remarks, so he requested Monsignor John Doyle, chancellor of the archdiocese, to ask E. Perrin Schwartz, editor of *Social Justice*, to print verbatim Father Coughlin's press interview and the archbishop's statement related to CIO membership, which had been only partially printed in *Social Justice*. Doyle wrote to Schwartz:

Archbishop Mooney urges me to direct you to publish in your next issue the exact text of the published statements of Father Coughlin and Archbishop Mooney touching matters referred to in your article. . . . This action of the Archbishop is taken with a view to supplying the

correcting influence of full information and thus safeguarding your
Catholic readers against misleading and disturbing inferences which
the Archbishop fears they might, without such full information, draw
from your article.[4]

In a stinging rebuke, E. Prewitt Semmes, Father Coughlin's attorney, rejected this request.

Social Justice is now and always has been published by the Social
Justice Publishing Company. It is not and never has been a Catholic
publication. . . . I am directed to inform you, and through you, his
Excellency, the Archbishop of Detroit, that while the columns of *Social Justice* are open at all times for any contributions which the
officers of the corporation feel will be of interest to its readers, the
corporation will continue to edit and publish *Social Justice* without
supervision of anyone except its own officers.[5]

The fact that his ecclesiastical superior had rebuked him must
have come as a shock to Father Coughlin. He had been accustomed
to the support of Bishop Gallagher. According to Semmes, it now
seemed clear to Coughlin that Archbishop Mooney wished to exercise censorship over his statements.[6] Rather than submit, Father
Coughlin canceled his radio series for the 1937–1938 season and
announced that Walter Baertschi, a Toledo businessman, had assumed control of *Social Justice*. In a press release, Semmes stated:
"It was quite apparent that Father Coughlin would be permitted
only to talk platitudes that mean nothing, that he could not say
what he thinks, but only what the Archbishop thinks."[7]

A campaign to return Father Coughlin to the air was immediately inaugurated. Baertschi appealed over Mooney's head to Pope
Pius XI to grant Father Coughlin permission to speak without
ecclesiastical censorship. Public rallies calling for the end of censorship of Father Coughlin's activities were held in Detroit, Cleveland, Cincinnati and Toledo. But these efforts had little effect.
Pope Pius XI, replying to Baertschi's appeal, instructed Archbishop Ameleto Cicognani, the Apostolic Delegate to the United
States, to say that Archbishop Mooney's corrections of Father

Coughlin's remarks were fair. Cicognani's statement went on to say:

Every bishop has not only the right but the duty to supervise Catholic teaching in his diocese. Any priest who feels aggrieved by the action of the bishop has the right of orderly recourse to the Holy See, but in loyalty to the Church, he also has the duty of using his influence to keep the matter from becoming the occasion of public agitation and thus possibly creating confusion in the minds of many Catholics.[8]

Father Coughlin then publicly urged his followers to cease the fight on his behalf. He also confirmed his loyalty to his Church.

On November 22, 1937, the *Free Press* congratulated the Vatican for silencing Coughlin, who was, it said, best known for "his venomous attacks . . . his slanderous utterances . . . his wickedness." The *Detroit News*, on November 23, 1937, editorialized:

It had long been evident that the public activities of Fr. Coughlin constituted a problem in which the Church would finally exert internal discipline. . . . The episode therefore is closed, and becomes an entry in church history and democratic experience, bearing in the former on the question of how far the priest as an individual may go in expressing himself in matters outside the direct purview of the Church, if these expressions eschew the personal and concern themselves with social ideas and programs. In this, the priest continues to enjoy a wide latitude. As a political incident, the case is one of a multitude which have proved that recklessness and intemperance of utterance in a prophet not only limit his appeal and usefulness, but eventually are the seeds of his destruction.

But, as after the 1936 elections, those who concluded that Father Coughlin's public career was over were mistaken. Walter Baertschi disregarded the Apostolic Delegate's statement and on November 29, *Social Justice* carried a page-one appeal from Baertschi to all readers:

I know that Father Coughlin is an obedient priest. He cannot give his consent to our rallies, but in two years of association with him I

know how his great heart loves social justice. As chairman of the
Committee of Five Million I cannot let the people down. No fewer
than 40,000 persons this week have begged me to carry on this fight
for social justice and the restoration of our great leader to the radio.
We cannot stop. We must Carry On! In these pages there will be no
change of policy, there will be no change in the staff employed by
Father Coughlin, there will be no change from Royal Oak to Toledo or
to any other place.

Every hour of every day will find me together with the members of
the corporation and the staff of SOCIAL JUSTICE, being guided in
every word we write by the spirit of the radio priest of Royal Oak
whom circumstances have forced for the time being to withdraw from
us in body.

According to E. Prewitt Semmes, Baertschi was never a policy
maker for *Social Justice*.[9] Thus it is very likely that Father
Coughlin was responsible for Baertschi's actions.

The Vatican continued to be deluged with mail from loyal
Coughlin supporters. Thousands of copies of a form letter sent by
his followers must have had an impact on the Pope:

His Holiness, Pope Pius XI
Vatican City
Rome, Italy

Most Holy Father:
    With sorrowing heart I write Your Holiness begging aid most ear-
nestly to restore to us Father Charles E. Coughlin in his Radio Broadcasts as heretofore, under the late, highly esteemed Bishop Michael J.
Gallagher of Detroit, a true, courageous Bishop, who publicly stated
— "I made no mistake in putting him [Father Coughlin] before the
microphone. . . . He has accomplished much for the future of mankind
and . . . the Church. I do not term him a national leader, but . . . a
world leader. His arguments cannot be refuted, nor withstood."
    Holy Father, encyclicals of Your Holiness were but classics, some-
thing heard of and laid aside quickly — until Father Coughlin thun-
dered forth the teachings of Your Holiness to the world and brought
back to us, the fact, that the Church and Your Holiness in particular is
solicitous for the poor.
    Father Coughlin has courageously and self-sacrificingly given him-

self to promulgate Your teachings on the living annual wage; the evils of concentration of wealth in the hands of a few; the irresistible power in the hands of those who control the wealth and credit, the bloodstream of the nation, of our beloved country.

Before Father Coughlin came to the radio, we were as lost sheep straying in the wilderness, bewildered and unconsoled. Then came Father Coughlin, the fearless shepherd who gathered us together, even as a hen would gather her young under her wings, and we found solace and courage . . . but, there were and are those who . . . have finally prevailed to keep the voice of our beloved shepherd from us. . . .

Holy Father, we plead for our Father Coughlin — Have him continue his Radio Broadcasts in the same heartfelt way, not in censored platitudes which defeat the dignity God bestowed on man, but as an "Alter Christus," fearless and outspoken, going about doing his Father's business, spreading the doctrine of the Mystical Body — a brotherhood of man with a fatherhood in God — to confute the Atheistic Communism and other Godless isms — to continue to espouse the cause of the poor, for the rich have ample means . . .

The only argument the enemies can find is that Father Coughlin followed the explicit command of Your Holiness and has "thrown into the conflict all the energy of his mind and all the strength of his endurance." Holy Father, many of us were tricked by artful propaganda, but now humbly ask Your Holiness to give us back our Father Coughlin, as he should be — free and unrestrained in preaching the doctrine of Christ to the poor and to all who will listen.

Most respectfully yours,

In a similar vein, a handbill to supporters of Father Coughlin said that the cancellation of the priest's radio broadcasts that fall was due to censorship by his immediate superior, who not only restricted the priest-teacher but contradicted him in so many ways that his broadcasts would be only a waste of time and money. In December a meeting between Father Coughlin and the Apostolic Delegate concluded with an announcement that the priest would resume his broadcasts on January 9, 1938. The announcement was followed by a statement from Archbishop Mooney that Father Coughlin's return to the air "represents an exercise of liberty of action which he has always enjoyed in the matter."[10]

If Coughlin were to be allowed to voice his opinions unfettered

by Mooney's control, then obviously this policy reflected a change
in the thinking of the Vatican. The records of the Vatican and the
Detroit chancery are still unavailable. Only Father Coughlin has
broken the silence to tell of the circumstances leading to his return
to the air.

It's simple. The archbishop had overstepped himself. I was more than
he could take on. I had lots of friends at the Vatican, people who
could not agree with me publicly. But they knew that I spoke the truth.
They knew that I recognized the communist threat to the Church.
Well, they finally reached the Pope and when they did, he came to his
senses and he saw the righteousness of my ways. So, of course, instructions were sent here to halt any restrictions on my activities. Also, I
had many priests in the archdiocese who were upset by the manner in
which I was being treated. They knew I was telling the truth and they
told Mooney so.[11]

Several years later, Archbishop Mooney was to say:

It is not too much to say that the fate of our country in a critical
day depends upon our finding moderate men on the side of capital and
labor who are willing to sit down together in patient and considerate
good will to talk out their difficulties in an effort to further interests
which are essentially in harmony and not in conflict. The extremists on
both sides will lead us to ruin.[12]

Extremists had indeed wrought much damage in the United
States in the 1930s. Particularly effective was the propagation of
anti-Semitism by individuals and extremist organizations on the
Right. From January 31, 1933, the day of Hitler's appointment as
chancellor of Germany, to the outbreak of World War II on
September 1, 1939, 121 right-wing anti-Semitic organizations appeared in the United States.[13] All of them shared at least one common belief: that an international communist conspiracy led by
Jews menaced the very existence of the United States. The leaders
of these organizations represented nearly everything that was
medieval, bigoted and hateful in American society.

William Dudley Pelley, in his book *The Door to Revelation*, tells how, inspired by Hitler's success, he founded his Silver Shirts on January 31, 1933. The Silver Shirts were patterned after the Nazi SS, and Pelley was fond of referring to himself as the "American Hitler."[14] The organization attracted many former members of the Ku Klux Klan. Catholics were not formally barred from membership, but many local chapters did discourage them from joining.[15]

The Silver Shirts distributed much right-wing literature in the United States. Through his control of Pelley Publishers, located in Asheville, North Carolina, Pelley issued a great deal of literature emphasizing mysticism and anti-Semitism, copies of which were sent to Germany.[16] Among them were *Liberation*, later called *Pelley's Weekly*, and *Silver Legion Ranger*, a weekly newspaper which propagated his anti-Semitic, pro-Hitler viewpoint. Pelley distributed Hitler's *Mein Kampf* throughout the United States and collaborated with Ulrich Fleischauer, head of *World Service*, the official English-language propaganda organ of Goebbels' Ministry of Information, and with Julius Streicher, the editor of *Der Stürmer*, a vicious anti-Semitic journal. Streicher was to be one of the twelve major German war criminals condemned to death at Nuremberg.

A sampling of Pelley's views can be ascertained from the following quotes from his writings:

America must join the trend toward Fascism as a matter of world momentum. . . .[17]

America may undergo a brief bath of violence . . . but it will be the same cleansing bath that awakened Italy, that awakened Hungary, that awakened Spain, that awakened Germany. It will awaken thousands of Americans to a realization of menace.[18]

Let us understand thoroughly that if a second civil war comes to this country, it will not be a war to overthrow the American government, but to overthrow Jew-Communist usurpers who have seized the American government and bethought themselves to make it a branch of Moscow.[19]

Now, if ever, the Sons of Jacob must take a last desperate gamble and find out if they can actually seize the government of the country before the vigilante storm breaks and a major part of the 7,000,000 Yiddishers who have managed to get into this country over the past ten years are slated for deportation — or worse.[20]

Sooner or later, when the country is quivering and absolutely supine, a strong leader must arise who shovels out the burglars by strongarm expedients. If such a leader does not arise, if he does not succeed in putting the Jewish Reds in their places, the nation . . . is to be known as the United States of Soviet America. To oppose such a colossal sabotage, to make such shoveling effective, to reestablish orderly government and industrial prosperity, civic aphorisms are but silly. Someone must do the job and talk the ethics of it afterward. The Jewish Red beclouds the issue purposely by screaming that this is Fascism.[21]

In Wichita, Kansas, the Reverend Gerald Winrod issued a monthly journal called the *Defender*, which enjoyed great popularity in the corn and wheat belts of the Middle West. His appeal to lower-class members of evangelical Protestant sects was widespread. Winrod's attacks on Jews, communists, Catholics and Negroes were well received by his readers. The *Defender* was founded in 1925 as a Fundamentalist response to the growth of Modernism. By 1935, after Winrod met with Streicher and became friendly with Fleischauer in Germany, the *Defender* preached a virulent form of religious and racial hatred. It referred to Jews as "Christ killers" and to Catholicism as the "harlot of the Bible."[22] In its pages, Winrod stated that "Jews and Jesuits are charting the course for the Roosevelt Administration."[23] By 1937, the *Defender* achieved a monthly circulation of 100,000.

Elizabeth Dilling, who, in 1934, wrote *The Red Network*, a scathing attack on liberal, socialist, and communist organizations, visited Germany in 1938 and on her return wrote the violently anti-Semitic work *The Octopus*. While in Germany, Miss Dilling attended the annual Nazi Party Congress at Nuremberg. In 1942 she was tried for sedition; the case ended in a mistrial because of the death of the trial judge and she continued to campaign on behalf of former German-American Bund leaders.[24]

After taking power in Germany, the Nazis allocated funds to pro-Hitler movements around the world. One of the prime recipients of this assistance was the German-American Bund.[25] Originally called "The Friends of New Germany," it was led by Fritz Kuhn.

Kuhn had been an officer in the German army in World War I but later migrated to the United States. He was employed as a chemist by the Ford Motor Company in Detroit. It should be remembered that, in the early 1920s, Henry Ford was responsible for the English-language publication and dissemination of the "Protocols of the Elders of Zion," first in his *Dearborn Independent* and then in a book entitled *The International Jew*. The "Protocols" was a forged document purporting to detail a Jewish plot to take over the world.[26] *Social Justice* reprinted the "Protocols" in serial form in 1938. While on the Ford payroll, Kuhn was able to travel around the country to fulfill his obligations as Bundesführer of the German-American Bund.

In 1936, Kuhn met Hitler in Berlin. Bolstered by this meeting, Bund membership grew rapidly in major American cities. The Bund not only stressed the growth of its own membership rolls, but "also served to give impetus to many other organizations which though nominally anti-communist, are actually anti-Semitic and to a lesser degree anti-Catholic."[27] The zenith of Bund activities in the United States was reached on the night of February 20, 1939, when over nineteen thousand people packed Madison Square Garden, ostensibly to celebrate George Washington's Birthday.

The flags however, were not all American flags. Just as prominent, but more in evidence, were flags so well known to the American public and the whole world as the emblem of Nazi Germany, the hated swastika. Inside the hall there seemed to be two kinds of officials — one of the familiar policeman, the other much like the Storm Troopers of Germany, the "O. D.'s or Ordnungs Dienst." The brown shirt was replaced by a gray with Sam Browne belts, arm bands and American Legion trousers. It seemed as though a private army had taken over a small portion of New York City. So-called ushers, the O. D.'s paraded up and down the hall with long searchlights in their hands which could easily maim or kill. Huge banners were placed about the Garden with the following propaganda: "Wake up America," "Smash Jewish Communism," "Stop Jewish Domination of Christian America," and perhaps the most startling banner of them all contained the following: "1,000,000 Bund Members by 1940."[28]

Kuhn was soon convicted for embezzling Bund funds, some of which were used to transport the furniture of a female friend across the country. When such revelations were made public, Bund membership stagnated.

Lawrence Dennis, in his books *Coming American Fascism* and *The Dynamics of War and Revolution*, dealt with the advantages of fascism over democracy. His skill as a writer and lecturer gained him a widespread audience on the extreme Right. As early as 1933, Dennis was a loyal supporter of Hitler's and during his frequent visits to Germany met with two of the Führer's close advisers, Alfred Rosenberg and Ernst Hanfstaengl. During a visit to Italy, he met with Mussolini. He also worked closely with George Sylvester Viereck, an officially registered German agent. Dennis regarded himself as the American Alfred Rosenberg, in that he believed that he was the intellectual leader of American fascism.[29]

Edward J. Smythe, president of the Protestant War Veterans Association, had close connections with the German-American Bund. Smythe also established lines of communication with the Ku Klux Klan and tried to organize its merger with the Bund. Although he failed to resolve personal differences between leaders of these organizations, he continued to praise the Bund and spout pro-Nazi propaganda.[30]

James True of Arlington, Virginia, was the publisher of the anti-Semitic *Industrial Control Reports*, which were sent to the German embassy in Washington and to various German consulates throughout the country. He consistently praised the activities of the German-American Bund and was a close associate of the Reverend Gerald Winrod. True, George Deatherage and Robert Edmondson publicly declared themselves the leaders of the American fascist movement. By 1941 these three were in the process of cementing their relationship through the formation of an American fascist political party. Personal jealousies and the absence of sufficient financial aid, however, ended this venture.

True was near psychotic in his anti-Semitism; for example, he attempted to patent a large club which he called a "Kike Killer." True saw, everywhere, a Jewish plot aimed at destroying the sanctity of the southern white woman:

... rich Jews have hired "big buck niggers" to attack white women. These Jews give the "niggers" plenty of money and tell them to go after the white women. Yes, these fellows down there are going to kill every Jew in their section of the South. Doesn't sound very nice does it? Call it a pogrom if you want to, but it is the language the Jews understand. The Jews, you see, are guilty of sex crimes just like the "niggers." ... I don't see anyway out except a pogrom. We have got to kill the Jews.[31]

In 1935, George Deatherage gave impetus to the rebirth of the Knights of the White Camellia, the 1930s version of the Ku Klux Klan, when he obtained a West Virginia charter for this organization to operate out of his home in St. Albans, West Virginia. Deatherage claimed that the aim of his organization was to join in the worldwide drive against communism, which he saw as a movement financed by the "international Jewish bankers." In the summer of 1938, Deatherage called for the convening of a meeting of all Christian organizations to campaign against communism. He urged that this assemblage adopt as its emblem the same fiery swastika he used on his publications.[32]

Robert Edmondson was director of the Economic Research Service, a publishing house which disseminated material from *World Service*. He was also a contributor of Winrod's *Defender*. His publications were widely circulated in Nazi Germany and the United States. In 1937 the *World Service*'s anti-Semitic Congress meeting in Erfurt, Germany, commended Edmondson for his tenacity and moral courage in fighting against the attempts of Jews to dominate the world. Edmondson's closest colleagues in the United States were George Deatherage, James True and leaders of the German-American Bund.[33] Edmondson, like True and Pelley, began his anti-Semitic, anti-communist activities after Hitler's ascension to power on January 30, 1933. He devoted considerable time and energy to trying to prove the Jewish ancestry of Franklin D. Roosevelt. His feelings toward the Jews were typified by these words he composed to be recited at most meetings which he conducted:[34]

Morning, Noon and Night the Jew-Controlled Press, Radio and Movie News-Reels are flooding this country with Propaganda deliberately aimed at involving us in WAR. International Jew Baruch, "Fellow-Traveller" Ickes, Dorothy Thompson, Levy Kosher LaGuardia and the whole "Jew Deal" crowd, are Baiting Friendly Nations. The American People have no quarrel with Germany or Japan. They do not want to fight either Nation, and neither do the Germans nor the Japanese want to fight us.

The Only People Who Want War Are . . . THE JEWS. Will the Jews do the Fighting? No, They will make the profits.

But hundreds of thousands of Christian American Boys are to be killed and crippled for life, or blinded on the Altar of Jewish Communism because Germany in Europe and Japan in Asia ARE THE ENEMIES OF JEWISH BOLSHEVISM. If Germany chooses to get rid of Jews that is HER business . . . not ours. We exclude OTHER ASIATICS. . . . The Chinese and the Japs.

The German purge of Jews has been BLOODLESS. What a contrast to the Jew-Communist Mass-Murder of Millions of Christians in Soviet Russia. . . . Which still goes on, while the Bolshevik Ambassador is entertained by our "Jew Deal" Officials in Washington, and OUR PRESIDENT CONGRATULATES THE SOVIETS ON THE ANNIVERSARY OF THEIR REVOLUTIONARY SLAUGHTER.

Did our Jew-CONTROLLED ADMINISTRATION PROTEST THE TORTURE AND BLOOD MASSACRE OF HALF A MILLION CHRISTIANS BY MOSCOW'S JEW-COMMUNIST LOYALISTS IN SPAIN?

NO——NOT ONE WORD.

Did it protest the Soviet-Backed Communist-conquest of One Quarter of China by a campaign of Wholesale Murder and Burning? No, but it

lends $25,000,000 of American Tax payers Money to the Kuomintang-
Communist Government of China.

Did the Jew-Controlled Press rave in FLAMING HEADLINES
against these "Gentile Liquidations" by the Jew-Financed-and-Organ-
ized "TERROR"? No. The News was CENSORED AND SUP-
PRESSED.

But when Germany takes a few shekels from these INTERNA-
TIONAL SHYLOCKS AND Japan defends itself against COMMU-
NISM, the BARUCH-FRANKFURTER-ROSEMAN-MORGAN-
THAU-B'NAI-BRITISH ADMINISTRATION BECOMES BEL-
LIGERENTLY INSULTING AND the Jewish Hired Propagandists
fill our eyes and ears with lies, shriek "PERSECUTION" and flatly
demand *WAR*.

WARS ARE JEWS' HARVESTS——Jew-Lover Sombart, Author of
"Jews and Modern Capitalism."

Eugene Sanctuary was very active in the Ku Klux Klan in the
1930s. He was the author and publisher of its official history,
Knights of the Ku Klux Klan. Sanctuary was also a frequent contributor to Winrod's *Defender*, and distributed the "Protocols of
the Elders of Zion." Sanctuary was listed by the American Section
of *World Service* as a man who could be counted on to collab-
orate with the Nazis. He also served as director of several small
Protestant mission societies of extremist tendencies, and consequently was fond of referring to himself as a "church speaker."[35]

Joe McWilliams was a young tough who organized the Christian Mobilizers in New York City, a group dedicated to bringing
Nazism to the United States by the use of street fighting along the
lines of Hitler's storm troopers. McWilliams thought very highly
of Father Coughlin and Hitler, and he consistently praised them
for their leadership qualities and for the policies they advocated.

All of these men had followings of hundreds of thousands of
bitter, bewildered, frustrated Americans who were especially vulnerable to the propaganda preached by the hate-mongers on the
Right. But what made the right-wing movement relatively ineffec-

tive was the inability of its leaders to form a cohesive major organization. The attempts to achieve a unified front ended in failure because the leaders could not agree on who would be in charge. Each sought notoriety, power or simply money. Each had latched onto the most salable commodity created by the depression — bleak, mindless hatred.

Charles Coughlin's move to the extreme Right of the American political scene did not immediately follow the disastrous 1936 election. The competition for leadership of the Right was too intense and Coughlin was a late entry into the struggle. Eventually, he would be grouped with these men. For he too sought fame, power and money, and he too sold hatred to the American people. By the late 1930s most of these groups would pay homage to him as their leading spokesman, although none of them was willing to subvert its own identity to become part of a more broadly based movement led by him. Father Coughlin might have been the man to galvanize the movement — he had the largest following, the drive and the charisma. But he was also a Catholic priest, and as such, he represented a Church which many on the extreme Right viewed with hostility and suspicion. He eventually gained the respect and admiration of the leaders and followers of the extreme Right because of the policies he voiced support for on his radio broadcasts and in the pages of *Social Justice*.

On January 9, 1938, Coughlin again resumed his broadcasting activities. *Social Justice* hailed his return to the air and suggested that Archbishop Mooney would come "to love the pastor of the Shrine of the Little Flower."[36] His broadcast was carried over sixty-three stations. He did, however, lose WOR, his New York City outlet, an occurrence that convinced Coughlin that Jews controlled the nation's communication system and that they were responsible for his difficulties in securing broadcasting outlets. By using *Social Justice* as his major instrument of communication he felt certain of not being susceptible to the pressures and opinions of broadcasting executives.

In an effort to rejuvenate his political fortunes and to inspire renewed loyalty to Father Coughlin, *Social Justice*, in the spring of 1938, announced the creation of the Million League. This organization was to be subdivided into smaller units called Social Justice platoons that could "be merged into a great thinking army that can swing our teetering nation back to sanity and right thinking."[37] Eyebrows were raised over the use of the military term "platoons," but it seemed to be in keeping with Father Coughlin's new image as the militant leader of a devoted following striving to defend the nation from the threat posed by Roosevelt, the Jews and the communists, all three of whom were soon to become synonymous to him. But except for that vague call to membership nothing more was said about the Million League. Shortly after, Father Coughlin launched a second organization which he said would exemplify the ideals of America.

The first chapter of the Christian Front originated in Brooklyn and subsequent chapters were organized throughout the country. Father Coughlin lauded the bravery and zeal of the Christian Front in combating communism. He urged Christians to understand that although the United States was a Christian country, its politics, education, industry and finance were controlled by communists, non-Christians and pagans. It was over these facets of American life, therefore, that the priest urged Christian Fronters to seek control. On June 27, 1938, *Social Justice* proclaimed:

Forces of destruction in the United States today are seriously grinding away the keystone of American liberty. Human minds, clever and scheming, are engineering the mechanism of a juggernaut of hatred, slavery and death . . . the saving of America must be a Christian Front.

On July 11, 1938, the journal stated:

When Communism, Fascism or any other "ism" strikes at the heart of America, it is plunging its dagger into YOU. Beware of smugness. Don't console yourself with the now hackneyed phrase "it can't happen here."

IT IS HAPPENING HERE RIGHT NOW! Communism is all about us — in our factories — our theatres — our schools — our government — EVEN OUR CHURCHES! It is eating slowly — slowly — into our national vitals. America sits supinely as a person rooted to a spot by the glint in the eye of a serpent about to strike. America MUST MOVE or the poison will be shot into her arteries and then — DEATH!

A UNITED CHRISTIAN FRONT IS OUR LAST-DITCH DE-FENSE AGAINST COMMUNISM! If the Christians of the United States — men and women of all Christian creeds — stand shoulder to shoulder against the intruder, the battle can be won.

You belong on the Christian Front. You are badly needed there. Regardless of age or creed, your country needs you today more than during the blazing days of war. The enemy now is much more insidious than one which fights on the battlefields. TODAY'S ENEMY IS SLINKING, DODGING, LYING, CRAWLING. It calls such tactics "boring from within."

The Christian Front excluded Jews from membership in its ranks, and was to be "made up of Catholics and Protestants." Christian Fronters were not concerned about being called anti-Semitic because Coughlin told them that "anti-Semitic" is only another phrase of castigation in communism's glossary of attack.[38]

Although the Christian Front attracted many members and much support, even from bishops within the Church, the organization was comprised predominantly of the most malcontented and frustrated of America's "Christian" population. Chapter meetings presented them with opportunities to drink beer through the night, praise Father Coughlin, berate the English, and curse the Jews and their leader, Franklin Delano "Rosenfeld."

Many Christian Fronters espoused Nazi ideals and utilized Nazi methods. They organized "buy Christian only" movements and in 1938, 1939, and 1940 made the streets, subways and movie theaters of many cities in the United States unsafe for Jews. Elliott Shapiro, then associated with the Anti-Defamation League, recalls: "The ADL received many complaints from Jewish people in Brooklyn who were being beaten by gangs of individuals who screamed that they were 'Father Coughlin's brownshirts.' . . . We arranged for meetings with Church officials of the Brooklyn archdiocese, but they were, on the whole, quite unsatisfactory in their outcome. They merely shrugged and said that they could not control the everyday acts of Brooklyn parishioners. Of course, they also denied any knowledge that it was Catholics who were beating up the Jews."[39]

This was not a surprising position; the official archdiocesan newspaper, the *Brooklyn Tablet*, under the editorship of Patrick Scanlan, Father Coughlin's friend and a frequent contributor to *Social Justice*, consistently lauded both Father Coughlin and the Christian Front.

Father Coughlin was well aware of the activities of many of his Christian Fronters. Harold Tietz, a German Jew seeking information about Coughlin's relationship to the Christian Front, wrote to him to relate what transpired at one Christian Front meeting held on a New York City street corner:

a tall chap of some twenty-two years deigned to ask permission to pose a question. Immediately the mob turned on him following the boy for about a block while the police were forced to protect him. The lad was loudly professing to be a United States army man (there was a soldier in uniform with him) and also a staunch Irish-American. The crowd would have torn and beaten him and he had not as yet asked his question. Cries of "Communist!" were raised everywhere.[40]

Father Coughlin wrote in reply:

Your letter of July 10th relative to the Christian Front came to my desk this morning.

Please pardon me for refraining from criticizing either positively or negatively this organization. I have nothing to do with it. Moreover I do not, nor will I belong to it. Moreover I do not propose to enter into more discussion concerning it other than what I said publicly over the radio last Sunday.[41]

Perhaps James Wechsler best described the almost total silence and inaction which the violent, Nazi-like activities of the Christian Front in New York City evoked from the police department and public officials.

New York's experience with Coughlinism has visible national significance. The City has become a laboratory for carefully developed fascist experimentation, nourished by the heterogeneous character of its population and by the timidity of press and public officials. Ultimately, however, the problem is national. What the rest of the country can learn from New York is the failure of the silent treatment. For silence has merely encouraged rumors, halftruths, and bizarre reports which create panic among Coughlin's foes almost as deadly as the hysteria which obsesses his followers. What is needed is swift official attention.[42]

But not everyone was silent. The Christian Front had attracted only a modest percentage of American Catholics and its creation had led to the organization of some Catholics who opposed Father Coughlin, his principles and his Christian Front. One such organization was the Committee of Catholics for Human Rights. Its executive board was composed of such prominent clerics and laymen as Monsignor John Ryan of Catholic University; John Brophy, national director of the CIO; Dr. Harry McNeil of Fordham University; and the Reverend Charles Miltner of Notre Dame University. Included in the membership of the Committee were such Catholic notables as Bing Crosby, former governor Alfred E. Smith and John Ford, the movie director. The Committee also published a newspaper, the *Voice for Human Rights*, which was blunt in its criticism of the Christian Front, describing it as the greatest "mass manifestation of intolerance, bigotry, violence and uncharity ever to be promoted by Catholics in this land where the record of the Church is thus far unblemished," and "a perversion of the spirit of Christian social principles."[43]

By late 1939, Christian Fronters became closely allied, in the public eye, with the German-American Bund and the policies of Adolf Hitler, and Father Coughlin's all-out support of the Christian Front faltered. For in many of America's large cities Christian Fronters were being arrested for attacking Jews who were frequently old men, children and women. In New York City, for instance, two men convicted of disturbing the peace shouted that they "wished to see Jewish blood flow all over America," and that they would like to see "every Jew in the United States hanged."[44] The resultant publicity of this and other incidents caused some Coughlin followers, those who were poor, forlorn, frustrated but nevertheless decent individuals, to voice their complaints about these activities.

When seventeen members of the Christian Front were arrested in Brooklyn and charged with plotting the overthrow of the United States government, Father Coughlin stated that he had only approved the anti-communist principles of the Christian Front, "not its leadership or actions."[45]

Commonweal's reaction to the arrests was to the point:

These men were members of the Christian Front, a hazy organization claiming to be devoted to Christianity and the Christian Way and inimical to Communism and atheism. But the Christian Front idea of Christian society and the American way is very strange. So are its ideas of proper political, economic and social action. Destruction of the Jews was one of these. "Direct Action" street demonstrations, control of the gutters — bombs and rifles and setting up a dictatorship by force are some more."[46]

Commonweal went on to accuse Father Coughlin and the *Brooklyn Tablet* for the difficulties in which these seventeen misguided individuals found themselves.

In the January 22, 1940, issue of *Social Justice* Coughlin wrote:

I am neither the organizer nor the sponsor of the Christian Front and moreover, it is not becoming for me to identify myself with this organization. . . . However, if Christians as individuals or as groups desire to establish a Christian Front with the objective in mind of incorporating the spirit and the doctrines of Christianity into our social life, that is commendable. Nevertheless, as a clergyman, I do not find it compatible to identify in any way whatsoever. I prefer to remain entirely outside all organizations.

The priest commented the following week that although he did not condone sedition against the United States government he was not "running out on the fine body of New York Christians who make up the membership of the Christian Front."

Although the guilt of the seventeen Christian Fronters was not proven, opposition to the organization increased, as evidenced by a January 18, 1940 telegram to Attorney General Robert Jackson, signed by a number of well-known individuals including A. Philip

Randolph, Franz Boas, Robert Lynd, Harold Urey and young Adam Clayton Powell, which demanded that Father Coughlin's connection with the Christian Front be thoroughly investigated. The telegram was superfluous, as J. Edgar Hoover had already taken personal charge of the investigation of the Christian Front.[47]

Coughlin's involvement with the Christian Front and his continued public controversies made it increasingly difficult for him to utilize the radio. His 1938–1939 broadcasts were carried on only forty-six stations, including WMCA in New York.

On November 20, 1938, Father Coughlin justified Nazi treatment of the Jews as a necessary defense mechanism against the spread of communism:

German citizen Jews were not molested officially in the conduct of their business. The property of German citizen Jews was not confiscated by the government, although a few synagogues and stores were destroyed by mob violence. The children of German citizen Jews were permitted to attend public schools with other children. The German citizen Jewish bankers pursued their business as usual. The German citizen rabbis were permitted the practice of their rites. Until this hour no German citizen Jew had been martyred for his religion by government order although restrictions were placed upon Jewish professional men.

While it is true that foreign citizen Jews resident in Germany were disparaged and expelled, it is likewise true that many social impediments were placed in the pathway of Catholics and Protestants by the Nazi government — impediments which are revolting to our American concepts of liberty. But despite all this, official Germany has not yet resorted to the guillotine, to the machine gun, to the kerosene-drenched pit as instruments of reprisal against Jew or gentile. . . . Since 1923 when Communism was beginning to make substantial advances throughout Germany, a group of rebel Germans — under the leadership of an Austrian-born war veteran Adolf Hitler by name — organized for two purposes.

First, to overthrow the existing German government under whose jurisdiction Communism was waxing strong and, second, to rid the Fatherland of Communists whose leaders, unfortunately, they identified with the Jewish race.

Thus Naziism was conceived as a political defense mechanism against Communism and was ushered into existence as a result of Communism. And, Communism itself was regarded by the rising generation of Germans as a product not of Russia, but of a group of Jews who dominated the destinies of Russia.

Were there facts to substantiate this belief in the minds of the Nazi Party, I ask?[48]

The furor created by this broadcast was not overlooked in Berlin. Otto Tolischus, *New York Times* correspondent in Berlin, stated that "the German hero in America for the moment is the Rev. Charles E. Coughlin because of his radio speech representing National-Socialism as a defensive front against Bolshevism."[49]

In New York City, WMCA revealed that the station had received an advance text of Coughlin's speech, which it had turned over to Professor Johan Smertenko, director of the Anti-Nazi League. Smertenko had made a number of corrections of fact in the Coughlin text and returned it to WMCA. The station then returned the text to Coughlin, suggesting that the factual corrections be incorporated into the talk. WMCA also informed Archbishop Mooney of the controversial nature of Father Coughlin's talk as well as of the factual errors in the text. But Mooney, already humiliated by Vatican interference on Coughlin's behalf, did nothing.

Angered by the Coughlin broadcast, which it described as an effort to "incite religious and racial strife in America," WMCA promptly alloted time for Professor Smertenko to challenge Coughlin's alleged facts. WMCA also asked Father Coughlin to submit his radio texts to the station forty-eight hours prior to each of his weekly broadcasts. Father Coughlin refused to do this, whereupon WMCA refused to carry his broadcasts.

On November 27, it was WHBI, Newark, that carried his message to New Yorkers. Coughlin first denied that he was anti-Semitic, and then proceeded to state that American bankers of Jewish descent had financed the Russian Revolution. The reiteration of his earlier charges against the Jews created a storm of controversy. Dr. John Stanton, a University of Michigan history professor, replied:

To say that the Russian Revolution owes its origins to the activities of any group of foreign interests is to show only a superficial understanding of the facts underlying the events that led to the downfall of the Romanovs and the advent of the Bolsheviks to power.[50]

The *Michigan Christian Advocate* commented on December 8, 1938, that Coughlin's November 27 broadcast defending his previously stated position that the Jews were responsible for the bolshevik take-over of Russia was

an unsatisfactory defense, especially since his "documents" have been branded as fakes . . . the total effect of the broadcast was to stir latent hatreds against the Jews in an hour when a kindling of hatred might rush our own land into a devastating fire beyond all control. The Father seems to forget that the same class that can be stirred to hate the Jews is the very same class that can be stirred to hate the Catholics and the Negroes.

Frank Hogan, president of the American Bar Association, without mentioning Father Coughlin by name, took issue with his statements:

One hate breeds another. . . . Wherever Jews are persecuted, there too, other creeds and races will sooner or later be persecuted. . . . We Catholics cannot permit men of ill will to preach in America bigotry and anti-Semitism without raising our voices in protest. . . . Some Americans have swallowed hook, line and sinker the falsehood that the Jews are in league with the Bolshevik tyrants of Russia. I raise my voice against the spread of this lie. . . . democracy, Christianity and Judaism are all bound together by the silken strands of justice. . . . if there is an attack upon any of these then both the others will suffer.[51]

Officially, the Church was silent in this controversy. It was left to a handful of churchmen to speak out on their own. A statement by George Cardinal Mundelein of Chicago, one of the most powerful figures in the American Catholic hierarchy, merely shielded the Church from association with Coughlin's statements:

As an American citizen, Father Coughlin has the right to express his personal views on current events, but he is not authorized to speak for the Catholic Church, nor does he represent the doctrine or sentiments of the church.[52]

Monsignor John Ryan, however, accused the priest of being "eager or at least willing to promote anti-Semitism in the United States." The highly respected Catholic layman George Shuster stated that charges that a Jewish conspiracy was responsible for the Bolshevik revolution were "ridiculous fabrications."[53]

The *Detroit Jewish Chronicle* criticized Father Coughlin:

What a sensation Father Charles E. Coughlin would be if what he says were only fact. The one reason the world doesn't rock and shiver whenever he goes on the air is that he is so lamentably shy on accuracy.[54]

But Father Coughlin had supporters both in the United States and abroad who spoke out in his behalf. The German newspaper *Zwoelfuhrblatt*, which had reviewed Father Coughlin's broadcasts, concluded that

Jewish organizations campaigned so that the broadcasting company proceeded to muzzle the well beloved Father Coughlin subjecting his speeches to censorship. This attempt at veiling the truth shows not only enslavement and submission to Jewry but also is indicative of boundless cowardice. The dreary, slimy motivation of this step demands attention.[55]

The Jersey City Knights of Columbus Council announced that it had passed a resolution giving Father Coughlin a vote of confidence and approval, "for his broadcasts of November 20, and November 27."[56]

A crowd of more than six thousand persons in New York City attended a meeting sponsored by the Committee for the Defense of American Constitutional Rights to appeal for Father Coughlin's unhindered use of the airways. The crowd cheered at every mention of Coughlin's name and booed every mention of Roosevelt and the Federal Communications Commission. A resolution was adopted demanding that the license of Station WMCA be revoked for refusing to broadcast Coughlin's speeches. The crowd was addressed by Justice Herbert A. O'Brien of the New York Domestic Relations Court, State Senator John J. McNaboe and Queens Borough President George Harvey.

In early 1939, the Nazi newspaper *Der Stürmer* stated that "Father Coughlin in Royal Oak, in the state of Michigan, has the courage to speak his conviction. His conviction is that National Socialism is right."[57]

Father Coughlin responded to criticisms of his broadcasts by accusing the press, and by innuendo the Jews, of having "intentionally dodged the issue by endeavoring to confuse the public mind, particularly through the use of managed editorials and mismanaged interviews. For emphasis let me repeat that the controlled press has failed to face the issue which I presented."[58] Later he wrote: "Regardless of what my critics say they have not been able to disprove one of the statements which I uttered. Nor will they be able to do so."[59]

The priest's spirits were lifted by letters which promised loyal support for his efforts. Many of them evinced strong hatred of the Jews:

Did you read in the paper the other day that Mischa Elman plans to give twenty-five concerts in various cities, the proceeds to go to Jewish refugees? What do you think of it? He, Heifitz and Kreisler are a bunch of second raters and think they are tops. How long do they think they can get away with it and believe you me, I know something about it. They are the bunk. And I bet that Einstein fellow eats with a knife and is fooling everybody with his relativity — all the bunk. Some day the Jews will get what is coming to them. Just wait and see.

When I was in Germany in 1935, I read in the "Stuermer" a letter that told me a lot. You know how highly regarded Mr. Streicher is. In this issue there appeared a letter written by a little girl nine years old in which she said that there is so much fuss about the treatment of Jews in Germany and that in her opinion the Germans really didn't know how to treat the Jews. However, when she grew up she would really show them how to treat the Jews. I bet she will too.[60]

Coughlin was upset by reports from aides in New York City that many of his followers were not aware that he could be heard on a Newark station and consequently missed his broadcast of

November 27. In order to focus attention on what his followers considered to be an attempt to silence Father Coughlin and to keep public attention focused on him, plans were made to picket WMCA. Allen Zoll, a young right-wing extremist and the leader of the boycott, stated bluntly that the aim of the picketing was to punish the station for refusing to carry Father Coughlin's broadcast by putting it out of business. For the next several months, the station was picketed by pro-Coughlinites — sometimes by only a handful, sometimes by crowds estimated as high as two thousand. At times, pro-Coughlin and anti-Coughlin factions clashed in the streets.

In July, Donald Flam, president of WMCA, accused Zoll of trying to extort $7,500 from him in return for calling off picketing of the station. Flam claimed that he had already given Zoll a $200 down payment in marked bills. Zoll defended his taking of the money by maintaining that he was acting as an employee of the station in trying to halt the picketing. Zoll was arrested, but was later acquitted of the charges. This incident, coupled with press criticisms of police department handling of brawls involving pro and anti-Coughlin forces, resulted in Mayor Fiorello La Guardia's issuing a directive restricting to four the number of pickets at WMCA.

When Radio Station WJJD, Chicago, temporarily discontinued Coughlin's broadcasts, his followers launched a letter-writing campaign that bombarded that station with mail urging the return of the priest to the air. One letter stated:

If Father Coughlin is denied the air, who is the only living person today, who dares to tell the American people the truth, there is nothing left for us to do but quit listening to your station.
Unless there is a satisfactory explanation by your station in the next few days, of the injustice done to Father Coughlin, I shall write a letter to all of the sponsors of the broadcasts coming thru your station, that I and my family and intimate friends are not longer prospective customers for their advertised products.[61]

While still in the midst of the furor over his previous two broadcasts, Coughlin on his December 4 broadcast involved himself in another hot controversy involving Henry Ford and Rabbi Leo Franklin.

Ford, who, it will be remembered, had published the "Protocols of the Elders of Zion," had made a public apology in 1927 for any remarks that he had made which might have been construed as being anti-Semitic. In the summer of 1938, however, he received a decoration from Hitler — the Award of the Grand Cross of the German Eagle — the highest award that could be offered by Nazi Germany. Pictures of him accepting and wearing this decoration probably contributed to a decline in sales for the Ford Motor Company. And so Ford was advised to mollify the Jews by doing something for them through a prominent Jew.

Ford and his advisers selected Rabbi Leo M. Franklin, an outstanding Detroit civic leader, to be their man. Detroit University, a Jesuit school, had conferred an honorary doctor's degree upon him. Dr. Franklin was approached by two Ford employees of Jewish descent, Moritz Kahn and Harry Newman, a former Michigan All-American football player. Both Kahn and Newman told the rabbi that Ford was anxious to help German Jewish refugees. Before doing so, however, Ford wished to have a letter from Dr. Franklin requesting a meeting with him. The rabbi agreed. On November 26, 1938, he wrote to Ford, asking to see him. On November 29, Harry Bennett, Ford's closest adviser, telephoned Dr. Franklin to arrange the time and place.

The meeting was held in Bennett's office and Ford was most cordial, promising to give employment to many German Jewish refugees. Ford asked if the rabbi would join him in the issuance of a public statement expressing sympathy for the Jewish refugees. Dr. Franklin agreed and, assisted by William Cameron, former editor of the *Dearborn Independent*, immediately drafted a statement which Ford said he found satisfactory. Ford then requested that Rabbi Franklin issue the statement to the press. On December 1, the newspapers carried the statement, which, among other things, called for the United States to make itself "a haven for the oppressed." Surely this would placate the Jews and other boycotters of Ford.

On December 2, an anonymous caller telephoned Franklin and

warned him that he would be double-crossed by Ford, Bennett and Father Charles E. Coughlin. On Sunday, December 4, 1938, Father Coughlin denounced the release given the press by Rabbi Franklin as a lie. He assured his followers that Dr. Franklin's release was "a gigantic attempt to put into the mouth of America's foremost manufacturer words he did not say." Coughlin went on to say that Harry Bennett had given him a signed statement authorizing him to say the following:

1. The direct quotation carried in the paper is totally inaccurate and was not written by Mr. Ford but was composed by Rabbi Franklin.

2. Rabbi Franklin came to see Mr. Ford to ask him if his factory would assimilate Jewish refugees, the result of Nazi persecution. Mr. Ford said that he believed there was little or no persecution in Germany; if any, it was due not to the German Government, but to the war-mongers, the international bankers.

Moreover, while Mr. Ford expressed his humanitarianism for all people, yet he believed that Jews wouldn't be content to work in factories.

That was the essence of the talk between Mr. Ford and Rabbi Franklin. But the story handed to "The Detroit Free Press" was written by Rabbi Franklin and handed to it by Rabbi Franklin and not by Mr. Ford.[62]

The next day, the *Detroit Free Press* described Coughlin's broadcast as "his weekly attack on the Jews." It also accused Coughlin of having a "congenital inability to tell the truth." The *Free Press* declared that Bennett had told the paper that its story was "absolutely accurate. . . . The statement as it appeared in the *Free Press* was an exact copy of the statement prepared by Dr. Franklin and Dr. Franklin was authorized to make it on behalf of Mr. Ford." Father Coughlin immediately sued the *Free Press* for one million dollars for libel, but later dropped the charges.

The following week Coughlin broadcast a statement from Harry Bennett which contradicted the earlier statement Bennett had given the *Free Press*.[63]

A statement which resulted in casting reflections of an exceedingly serious nature upon the veracity of Father Coughlin appeared in the

Detroit Free Press, Monday, December 5th, 1938, based upon a statement which it was alleged I made. It labeled statements of Father
Coughlin regarding Rabbi Franklin's recent visit to the Ford offices for
the purpose of getting an expression of the Jewish situation in Germany as untrue. This is to definitely state that absolutely no interview
was given in response to Rabbi Franklin's request by Mr. Ford to be
printed as Mr. Ford's own statement in the press. . . .

Throughout the entire controversy, Henry Ford remained silent.
The old gentleman had much to gain from his silence. For as
Keith Sward, in his biography of Ford, pointed out:

Bennett's manipulation of the interview had been a masterpiece. It
cast Ford in a double image. To Jews and anti-Nazis and haters of
racial brutishness — and to potential boycotters of the Ford car — the
folk hero had been held up once more as the friend of the oppressed,
as the protector of the little man. But anti-Semites and pro-Nazis and
other assorted enemies of democracy had it on the authority of Father
Coughlin that the Ford-Franklin interview meant nothing of the sort; it
meant only that a wily Jew had put one over on Ford. The reaction-
aries also had it straight from Bennett that, in Ford's opinion, Germany's internal wrongs, if any, could not be laid to Hitler or the Nazi
system.[64]

Says Coughlin of his friendship with Ford: "We were great
friends. I had lunch with Henry Ford at least once a month . . . he
was a sincere man who knew the truth when he saw it. . . . Ford
was misled into the Jewish Protocols and anti-Semitism."[65] Misled? Perhaps. Yet this was the same Henry Ford who kept Fritz
Kuhn on his payroll and in the late 1930s financed some of the
activities of Gerald L. K. Smith.

Coughlin, now turning his attention toward foreign affairs, said
that the United States might be pulled into the war because Roosevelt was heeding the urging of Jewish leaders in other countries to
go to war for the sake of their brothers in Germany:

The three outstanding leaders in the world today are the three Jews,
Leon Blum, the radical of France; Maxim Litvinov, the reddest of red

Russians; and Leslie Hore-Belisha, minister of war in England. . . . Must the entire world go to war for 600,000 Jews in Germany who are neither American, nor French, nor English citizens, but citizens of Germany?[66]

The December 30, 1938, issue of the *New York Post* showed that excerpts from an article by Father Coughlin were, word for word, almost identical to that of a speech given by Joseph Goebbels, Hitler's propaganda minister. Coughlin even managed to exaggerate Goebbels' speeches, as illustrated by the priest stating that twenty thousand hostages had been murdered by the Bela Kun regime in Hungary while Goebbels said the total was twenty. Among the excerpts were the following:

GOEBBELS

On April 30, 1918, in the courtyard of the Luitpold Gymnasium in Munich, 10 hostages, among them one woman, were shot through the backs, their bodies rendered unrecognizable and taken away. This act was done at the order of the Communist terrorist, Eglhofer, and under the responsibility of the Jewish Soviet Commissars, Levien, Levine-Nissen and Axelrod.

On the 26th of December, 1918, one of the Socialist members of the Reichstag, the Jew, Dr. Ozkar Cohn declared that on the 5th of the previous month, he had received 4,000,000 rubles from Joffe for the purpose of the German revolution.

In 1919, during the Bolshevik regime of Bela Kun, a Jew whose

COUGHLIN

On April 30, 1918, in the courtyard of the Luitpold Gymnasium in Munich, 10 hostages, among them one woman, were murdered. This act was perpetrated by the direct order of the Communist terrorist Egelhofer and under the responsibility of the Jewish Soviet Commissars, Levien, Levine-Nissen and Axelrod.

On December 26, 1918, one of the Socialist members of the Reichstag, the eminent Jew, Dr. Oskar Cohn, declared that on the 5th of the previous month he had received 4,000,000 rubles from Joffe for the purpose of instigating a revolution in Germany.

In 1919, Hungary, a neighbor to Germany, was overrun with

real name was Aaron Cohn, in Budapest murdered 20 hostages. The truth of this report has been officially confirmed by the Geneva Red Cross.

Communists. The notorious atheist, Bela Kun, a Jew whose real name was Aaron Cohn murdered 20,000. The truth of this has been officially confirmed in the report made to the Geneva, Red Cross.

The Reverend William Kernan, rector of Trinity Episcopal Church, in Bayonne, New Jersey, in a February 23, 1939, broadcast over Radio Station WEVD said that

between Coughlinism and Americanism there is not now, nor can there ever be, any similarity. . . . Coughlinism, intent upon destroying American unity, uses every device within its power to divide our people. Its theme is: Gentile against Jew, Christian against non-Christian . . . note the similarity of Dr. Goebbels' language and Father Coughlin's words. . . . Coughlinism destroys Americanism. It begins by depriving one minority, the Jews, of their unalienable rights. It ends by destroying these rights for everyone. . . . It aims to cause so much strife, so much hatred, so much suspicion, so much fear as to paralyze those social, economic and political functions upon which a democratic society rests. It aims to prevent democracy from working. And then — the dictatorship.

Jan Masaryk, son of the founder of the Czechoslovak republic, in answer to Coughlin's frequent criticisms of the Czechs, labeled him "either a fool or a liar."[67] Coughlin did not respond directly, but his demeaning remarks about the Czechs continued.

Coughlin momentarily took time from his battles to comment on the elevation of Eugenio Pacelli to the papacy, the same Pacelli who had visited the United States during the 1936 election campaign to mute Coughlin's activities. Coughlin called the new Pope "another Hildebrand, who hates inequity and loves justice."[68] But his real view of Pius XII was and still is quite negative. Coughlin accuses him of having had "broken the neutrality and given all-out aid to Russia. The greatest faux pas in the history of the papacy. Nothing equaled it any time. He had no damn business going on either side. A Pope is supposed to be on God's side."[69]

His concern over Pacelli's becoming Pope was partially offset by his pleasure in having the Italian Fascist journal *Il Regime Fascista* describe him as a man who "appreciates our line of conduct. Italians cannot fail to express their sympathy to this apostle of Christianity."[70]

Not everyone in the United States, however, regarded Coughlin as an "apostle of Christianity." The Massachusetts Industrial Union Council adopted a resolution criticizing him for his "un-American and anti-labor attitude. . . . and making an attack on one racial and religious group and using as his sources, not facts, but Nazi pamphlets contrary to the denunciations for radicalism by His Holiness, the Pope."[71]

A statewide conference of the Michigan Civil Rights Federation demanded that the Federal Communications Commission investigate the veracity of remarks made by Father Coughlin on his radio broadcasts. If his remarks were found to be untrue, then, it was urged, the priest should be prevented from broadcasting.

The Reverend Leon M. Birkhead, national director of Friends of Democracy, lumped Coughlin with Hitler and Mussolini as "a world troublemaker":

> Under the guise of Americanism, Father Coughlin is doing a job alarmingly similar to that being performed by German spokesmen under the mask of Aryanism. No matter by what name it is called the philosophy of fascism still smells — and not so sweetly. Father Coughlin . . . is not going to become the American Fuehrer. But . . . he is important, he is typical of the anti-democratic radio propagandist.[72]

But Father Coughlin was not deterred from continuing to voice his opinions, as evidenced by the following form letter, dated April 11, 1939, that he sent to *Social Justice* subscribers:

> Anti-Christ is riding high, wide and handsome. Meanwhile, the Jews of America have not condemned Communism. Meanwhile, the government of America is fostering relations with Communistic states. And meanwhile, the people of America are suffering from the rule of those who are opposed to our Christ.
> It is very well to quote the Scripture and say "Father, forgive them,

for they know not what they do." But it is just as appropriate to remember that our battling is not against flesh and blood but against powers and principalities and rules dwelling in high places.

Let's be militant and fight these people to the bitter end, cost what it may. Our Christ Who was crucified was no weakling when He drove the money changers from the temple by physical force. The day has come when we must stand up and fight for all that we hold dear.

The Reverend Father James R. Cox of Old St. Patrick's Catholic Church commented:

Father Coughlin has produced forged documents, misquotations and delivered misrepresentations as evidence of his accusations against the Jews. Only a Communist or Nazi Court would permit such so-called evidence as he used to bolster his alibis for retailing alien propaganda . . . his attacks upon the Jews are abhorrent to everyone who believes in the Fatherhood of God and the Brotherhood of Man.[73]

The *Christian Century*, on May 24, 1939, castigated Coughlin as "Hitlerish in outlook, in method and the effect he produces." The General Jewish Council published a thin volume called *Father Coughlin: His "Facts" and Arguments*, which documented the priest's distortions, misquotations and lies. Father Coughlin reacted to this publication by publishing *An Answer to Father Coughlin's Critics*. Supposedly written by "Father Coughlin's Friends," it was compiled, in the main, by the priest and the editor of *Social Justice*, E. Perrin Schwartz.[74] It tried to repudiate many of the accusations made against the priest in *Father Coughlin: His "Facts" and Arguments*. In conclusion the book stated: "We assure you that anti-Semitism and anti-Christianity are listed among immoralities which we neither practice nor condone. Nevertheless, there is a Jewish problem in America as there is a Christian problem."[75]

In an open letter to the priest, published in the May 22, 1939, issue of *Social Justice*, John Cogley, the eminent Catholic writer who was to become well known as editor of *Commonweal*, tried, by appealing to his sense of fairness, to get Coughlin to restrain many of his followers from perpetrating un-Christian acts on Jews.

In a sense you are the most powerful Catholic voice in the United States today. . . . You are a unique priest. You are heartily disliked. You are genuinely beloved. You are a definite, undeniable force on what novelists like to call the American scene. Your opinions sway millions; you dismay millions more. . . .

You were a pioneer, and nobody who is devoted to the cause of social justice can forget that it was you who first made the word encyclical a part of America's working vocabulary. . . .

But there is an unmistakable group of your faithful friends, violent supporters of you and your program, that have come popularly to be called "Coughlinites." They get into people's hair. They get into mine. At times they probably get into yours. . . . They are probably good simple people who don't have much sense, and it should not reflect on you that they have rallied 'neath your banner. . . .

This "fringe" has become notorious for its burning anti-Semitism, and they have persisted in canonizing you as the patron of prejudice. They have become psychotic on the question of Jews. They are using your controversial Russian revolutionist figures to justify a senseless, un-Christian attitude toward Mrs. Cohen, the delicatessen lady around the corner, and Meyer, the insurance collector. They have confused your anti-Communism campaign with an anti-Semitism campaign. . . .

These Christians, many of them Catholics who are known as "Coughlinites," have the thing all balled up. Something should be done to set them right. Somebody should talk to them. They would listen if you did. . . . What you could say would help to make up for the pain and insult many innocent, godly Jews have received from your confused followers.

Coughlin denied that "a single paragraph can be found in any radio speech ever delivered by me in which I have launched a sweeping denouncement of the Jewish people."[76] But his troubles were not over; the attacks against him increased.

Archbishop Spellman of New York received numerous complaints from Catholics and varied organizations about the activities of Christian Fronters, approximately 90 percent of whom were also Catholic. A number of priests, it was pointed out, were vigorously supporting Christian Front activities from their pulpits, thus conveying the impression to parishioners that the organization had the official support of the New York archdiocese. Archbishop

Spellman, however, felt that since the Christian Front was not exclusively Catholic and was not affiliated with the Catholic Church, there was little he could do. In addition, he was probably wary of incurring the wrath of Father Coughlin and some of his more fanatic followers.[77] Thus the pro-Coughlin priests continued their preaching.

Elliott Roosevelt described Father Coughlin's pronouncements as nothing more than "anti-Semitic oratory." On July 23, 1939, Father Coughlin's friend Father Edward Lodge Curran of Brooklyn replied to the young Roosevelt's criticisms, stating that Father Coughlin

is a believer in racial and religious tolerance. . . . Father Coughlin is consumed with denouncing Jewish as well as non-Jewish Communists. . . . No Catholic priest that I know of is anti-Semitic. . . . The charge of anti-Semitism has been part and parcel of the communistic campaign to militate against the anti-communist campaign of Father Coughlin. . . .

No real American Jew resents criticism any more than criticism is resented by any real American Christian. Only certain leaders who have no other way of crowding their temples on the Sabbath try to twist bona-fide criticism of the actions of some Jewish leaders into a libel on the Jewish race or into an act of anti-Semitism.[78]

Coughlin himself responded to Elliott Roosevelt's charge by calling him a "defamer," and then proceeded to attack the entire Roosevelt family. "Does he know what he is talking about since he and his family have been on rather friendly terms with the Communists?"[79]

But Fritz Kuhn's appearing before the Dies Committee, which was investigating the activities of the German-American Bund, added to his discomfort: Kuhn testified that the Bund had "the same aims and purposes" as Father Coughlin.[80] Attacks from other sources continued as well. Frank Martel called Coughlin "the Number One Fascist of America."[81] Events, however, were moving faster than words. In late August the signing of the Soviet-German nonaggression pact made it difficult for Coughlin to sin-

gle out communism and not fascism, for his attacks. He resolved
the problem by saying that "neither communism or nazism would
have been born if capitalism had accepted Jesus Christ."[82]

On September 1, 1939, Coughlin's difficulties were compounded
by the outbreak of war in Europe. German successes created
much American sympathy for the Allies, but Father Coughlin's
views remained the same. He threw his support against efforts of
the Roosevelt administration to repeal the arms embargo: "Our
task is to retain American neutrality." He asked his listening audience to "organize Christian American pressure" on Congress and
President Roosevelt to fight the pressure being exerted on the
government by Congressman Sol Bloom, Chairman of the House
Foreign Affairs Committee, and his supporters in New York, to
enact legislation allowing arms to be sold to belligerents on a "cash
and carry" basis.[83] Such legislation would have favored England
with its large surface fleet. The priest was simply leaving little
doubt that Sol Bloom and his supporters were the Jews. But his
appeal was effective. Mail poured into the Senate urging its members not to lift the arms embargo.

Coughlin's use of the radio and *Social Justice* to fight against
any modification of the arms embargo caused many of his opponents, most of whom favored repeal of the arms embargo, to
lobby for his removal from the air. The Reverend Leon Birkhead,
in a fall 1939 memorandum to the National Association of Broadcasters, protested

Reverend Charles Edward Coughlin's use of the nation's airways for
the purpose of inciting to riot and civil war, and stirring up racial
prejudice and hatred among the American people. . . . In protesting
Father Coughlin's use of the airways, Friends of Democracy does not
believe it advocates a limitation of freedom of speech . . . true freedom
of speech on the airways can be attained best by granting free time to
reputable speakers for the purpose of expounding both sides of controversial matters. Perhaps Father Coughlin has the right to plead his
cause; if so, those who believe in democracy as a way of life have the
right to answer him. It should be the task of the FCC and the NAB to
strike the balance.

In any event, the members of Friends of Democracy urge that provision be made immediately to cancel Father Coughlin's contracts, or in the event that it is not possible, let it be understood that such contracts will not be renewed. Because of the fact that the temper and character of his radio addresses are such that they incite his vast audience to physical violence and racial hatreds, Father Coughlin has abused the radio as "an instrument of public service."

Protests such as these had their effect. In October, 1939, the Code Committee of the National Association of Broadcasters (NAB) adopted new rules which placed rigid limitations on the sale of radio time to "spokesmen of controversial public issues." The secretary of the NAB, E. M. Kirby, admitted that Father Coughlin's broadcasts were discussed by the committee, prior to the adoption of the new code. It was pointed out, in regard to Father Coughlin's opposition to the arms embargo repeal:

While all Americans desire to stay out of war and preserve neutrality, the methods of achieving and maintaining the same are matters automatically falling within the sphere of public controversial issues and as such should be presented on free time and not sold.[84]

The new code permitted controversial public issues to be discussed on the radio during free time made available for these broadcasts or for programs of the public forum type that were under radio station control. Manuscripts for all speeches of a controversial nature were to be submitted in advance to the appropriate radio station. The code, by denying individuals the right to buy radio time to advocate controversial positions, left virtually no doubt that Father Coughlin was its chief target.

WJR, Detroit, Coughlin's flagship station, immediately protested the NAB code, calling it a step "in the direction of censorship and abridgement of free speech.[85] The Reverend W. A. Burk, director of Station WEW, operated by St. Louis University, refused to abide by the new code. Burk mentioned Coughlin's enormous popularity with Catholics and Protestants in the St.

Louis area and went on to laud the priest for his "patriotic work" in opposing communism.

The new NAB code, providing that all existing radio contracts for controversial shows were to be honored, but not renewed, allowed Father Coughlin to retain most of his radio outlets for the 1939–1940 season, although there were prompt cancellations of his broadcasts in Indianapolis, Scranton and Milwaukee. These larger radio stations justified their actions by saying that they were abiding by the code.

In March, 1940, Coughlin wrote a concerned sympathizer, "I will be broadcasting without serious interruption until the end of November 1940. The radio stations, despite all publicity to the contrary, are standing by us and will not be influenced by any N.A.B. code."[86] But he was proved wrong, for although a few smaller stations did agree to renew the broadcasts, he decided that the small audience he would be able to reach would not justify the large expenditure of money, time and effort required. In the September 23, 1940, issue of *Social Justice*, he announced that he was temporarily retiring from the air. "I want it understood that I am not retiring from broadcasting permanently. I have been retired, temporarily, by those who control circumstances beyond my reach."

In a letter to subscribers of *Social Justice*, in October, 1940, it was pointed out that "the NAB code proved too great a hurdle for our champion to surmount. With a few exceptions the radio station owners bowed to the will of the administration to which they are obligated for their operators' licenses. It would have been bad business for them to have done otherwise — according to the present-day concepts. But regimentation is the vogue and it will not be stopped."[87]

The failure of Father Coughlin to gain access to the radio created a movement to return him to the air. On December 4, 1940, Congresswoman Anne E. Felix pointed out:

Father Charles E. Coughlin, with whose economics and politics one may or may not agree, has been virtually forced from the air. . . . The matter of whether Father Coughlin is always correct or always mistaken isn't in issue. The question is whether free speech in the United States is a universally applied principle or an ineffective, however, glorified abstraction.

Friends of Father Coughlin organized campaigns through Social Justice Distributors and the Christian Front to return him to the air. At meetings held in such Coughlin strongholds as New York City, Detroit and Cleveland, form letters were given to people in attendance to sign and mail. One such letter was to be sent to the Reverend Ameleto Cicognani, Apostolic Delegate to Washington.[88]

Reverend Ameleto Giovanni Cigognani [sic]
Apostolic Delegate
Washington, D.C.

Your Excellency:
In this time of world chaos, I respectfully and humbly ask your assistance. Knowing the ardent desire of the Holy Father for peace, I ask that you use your influence with the hierarchy of the United States to place Rev. Chas. E. Coughlin back in his rightful place at the microphone. He has militantly and fearlessly expounded the encyclicals of the Popes and is the only religious leader in the United States capable of coordinating the vast numbers of peace loving people in this nation in a Crusade for Peace.

In the spring of 1940, a group of 273 New York City Protestant clergymen urged all Christians to oppose the un-Christian Christian Front. The Social Service Commission of the New York Eastern Conference of the Methodist Church in its report commended all Christians who had repudiated Father Coughlin and his anti-Semitic activities. It further attacked the Catholic hierarchy for its general attitude of noninvolvement in controlling the activities of Father Coughlin. The report went on to accuse Father Coughlin of being the inspiration for this "storm troop organization," and because the Christian Front was predominantly Catholic and viciously anti-Semitic, it was described as the "Catholic Klan."[89]

So it was that Father Coughlin had come to symbolize an instrument comparable in aim to one of America's most violent anti-

Catholic as well as anti-Semitic and anti-Negro organizations, the Ku Klux Klan.

Father Coughlin claims that he had no control over those local units of the Christian Front that went wild in their anti-Semitism and that he was troubled by the criticisms directed at him.

> I suffered a lot for them. But I have accepted the suffering and I have grown up a bit. It does not bother me any more. But it's still not comfortable and not nice to go through life with people looking at you and saying this S.O.B. has done this and that. You cease arguing because the more you argue the more you stir up trouble.[90]

In the late summer of 1940, Coughlin suffered two important setbacks. Realizing that no third-party alternative was feasible in the 1940 presidential election, he had offered to support Wendell Willkie, the Republican presidential nominee. Willkie repudiated this offer in the strongest of terms. "I am not interested in the support of anybody who stands for any form of prejudice as to anybody's race or religion or who is in support of any foreign economic or political philosophy in this country."[91]

In September, Coughlin supported Louis Ward in the Michigan Democratic 1940 senatorial primary, but his showing was disastrous. Ward's defeat was an indication of the loss of Father Coughlin's following and influence. Politicians now considered his support a hindrance rather than a help.

The results of the 1936 election and the years of controversy following it had served to sour Coughlin on the spoken word as a means of communicating with the American public. With the microphone wrested from his grasp he turned his full energies to the pages of *Social Justice*, his only remaining avenue of expression.

> Faith cometh through communications. And there's no communication as potent as the written word. More potent than the televised word; more potent than the radio word. These are only wind and pass away. The book is there for years to come. I started *Social Justice* simply to put down in writing, probably in eighth grade style, faith the people could read and remember.[92]

8

"Social Justice"

To understand *Social Justice* and its editorial policies, it is important to also understand the origins of Social Catholicism, a movement which attracted many adherents in the last quarter of the nineteenth century in Europe. Its leaders were chiefly Catholic priests and aristocrats who hoped to halt the growing popularity of socialism — which was regarded as anti-Christian — by improving the life of the workingman. Social Catholicism opposed the policy of laissez-faire, holding that the state must be active in opposing the evils brought about by the Industrial Revolution. Its philosophy sanctioned the efforts of workers to form unions and to have collective bargaining rights. But unions were not to become involved in class conflicts; instead they would work with employers to establish contracts fair to both sides. Governments were to pass social legislation regulating working hours, prohibiting child labor, and restricting the labor of women.

In 1891 Pope Leo XIII had issued his papal encyclical *Rerum Novarum*, which stated Church views on social issues. *Rerum Novarum* officially committed the Church to policies directed at improving the life of the workingman, as advocated by Social Catholicism.

The Russian Revolution and the subsequent spread of communism seemed to threaten the very foundations of the Catholic

Church. By the 1920s communism had replaced socialism as the major enemy of the Church. In 1929, Italy and the Vatican signed the Lateran Accord. In Austria, Chancellor Engelbert Dollfuss, a semi-fascist, typified the Austrian Catholic animosity to the spread of communism. In Germany, Hitler destroyed the Communist party while Hitler, Mussolini and the Catholic Church supported Franco and his Falangists against the Stalin-supported Loyalists in the savage Spanish civil war.

In 1931 the policies of Social Catholicism were strengthened when Pope Pius XI issued *Quadragesimo Anno*, a papal encyclical which reinforced the principles enunciated in *Rerum Novarum*. Pius XI urged Catholics to put into practice the principles contained in the two papal encyclicals. When in 1936 *Social Justice* was first published, it reflected, in large part, the philosophy of Social Catholicism. Its editorial themes dealt with what it considered to be the real issues of the time and those which affected the mass of American citizens. And because of the events that had taken place in Europe and Russia, it was not surprising that the journal saw fascism as a bulwark against the spread of communism.

Social Justice expressed the view that many Jews had aligned themselves with communism and had contributed extensively to its successes. This view, however, did not prevent the journal from also condemning Jews for their widespread influence in international capitalism, which *Social Justice* held responsible for the Great Depression. It stated that it was the duty of the federal government to play a large role in alleviating the suffering resulting from the depression. It criticized President Roosevelt for not committing the full energies of the government to ending it. It consistently attacked him for pro-communist allegiance on the one hand and pro-capitalist sympathies on the other and for being pro-British and pro-Jewish. *Social Justice* expounded an anti-British point of view because, it said, Great Britain represented the stronghold of world capitalism and imperialism; in addition, England was a Protestant country which had treated Irish Catholics with great cruelty.

Social Justice was unique in that it was published privately by a Catholic priest.[1] Originally, the sixteen-page weekly which began publication on March 13, 1936, resembled a newspaper of standard measurement (such as the New York *Daily News*). By 1942, *Social Justice* was published with sixteen large-type three-column pages.[2] Although its format changed frequently and the number of its pages and columns varied, and although its articles ceased to carry bylines as it approached its demise, it remained consistently in favor of the activities of Father Coughlin. For Father Coughlin and *Social Justice*, in fact, were one and the same; there were few items which appeared on its pages that he did not personally approve. In 1939, for example, E. Perrin Schwartz, listed as president of the company and editor of *Social Justice*, stated: "I'm the President and editor but I'm just a technical man. I don't have a thing to say. I just carry out instructions. . . . I have nothing to do with the policy. Father Coughlin's the man to ask that. I'm just a newspaperman. I just carry out instructions. I'm just the technical help."[3]

Father Coughlin fervently believed that *Social Justice* would achieve a large circulation. In its August 3, 1936, issue, *Social Justice* claimed a circulation of one million. It is probable that this was an exaggeration, although the figure has been used by some social scientists. N. W. Ayer and Son, Inc., stated that the circulation of the journal was 228,678 in 1940 and 184,929 in 1941. These were the only two years for which circulation figures were made available.[4] Financial data indicating the amount of money paid to the Social Justice Publishing Company for subscriptions shows that the journal's circulation could not have approached one million, although Father Coughlin insists that it did.[5]

Frequently the pages of *Social Justice* were utilized to gain financial support from his followers. On May 16, 1938, it stated:

SOCIAL JUSTICE belongs to the people. It is a mirror of TRUTH for the Nation. Just as Father Coughlin is America's leader in the broad field of social justice, SOCIAL JUSTICE is the only magazine in the United States dedicated solely to economic and social reform along the lines of our 16 points.

THE NET PROCEEDS OF OUR SOCIAL JUSTICE MAGAZINE ARE USED IN DEFRAYING THE COSTS OF FATHER COUGHLIN'S NATIONAL RADIO BROADCASTS.

Those wondrous discourses are YOUR property, just as SOCIAL JUSTICE is, in effect, the property of every subscriber.

As an American, you need Father Coughlin's broadcasts. America needs them today more than ever before. The world in its sad plight needs application of his humane principles of conduct.

This year of 1938 will be momentous. Terrific events are in the offing. It is the year of Congressional elections. This FALL can bring to our country a sharp return to the Republic we know — or disaster. THINGS THAT CAN HAPPEN THIS FALL ARE VERY MUCH YOUR BUSINESS.

The voice of Father Coughlin, which is Your property as an American, MUST be made to ring week after week in the homes of millions of Americans. To see that it does is also YOUR business.

On December 4, 1939, Father Coughlin again told his reading audience that *Social Justice* and his broadcasts were in dire need of financial help and that unless this support was forthcoming, their very existence was threatened:

To be candid and honest with you, it is not possible to continue broadcasting because it will not be possible to pay our bills much longer, unless the sum of $200,000 will be forthcoming within the next few weeks. This money must come either from 200,000 new subscriptions from which there will be a profit to allocate for the broadcasting expenses or from direct donations from those who do not find it convenient to secure new subscriptions.

These facts I pass along to you, having learned them from the accountant's office and having inspected the books myself.

Almost the exact appeal was made again to *Social Justice* readers on December 18, 1939:

THERE MUST BE TWO HUNDRED THOUSAND DOLLARS IN THE BROADCASTING FUND WITHIN THE NEXT 30 DAYS. RADIO EXPENSE IS NOW CLOSE TO $10,000 PER WEEK.

This is not much money when spread over the 500,000 readers of SOCIAL JUSTICE magazine. Not much money if every reader, who can afford it, would help out with a donation of from $1 to $20.

But, in order to have weekly broadcasting assured, Father Coughlin MUST KNOW who is with him. He must know that at once!

Many letters aimed at increasing subscriptions were written by Father Coughlin. One, sent to a Miss Lecia Paas, said that "when I invite you to read *Social Justice*, I am inviting you to read the truth." After she had made a financial contribution, Father Coughlin thanked her and sent a picture of himself and Pal, his huge Great Dane, with an appeal to her to seek subscribers to *Social Justice*.[6] In the attempt to propagate his views and increase sales of *Social Justice*, Father Coughlin frequently mailed out souvenir crucifixes that, he said, had touched a relic of the True Cross.[7] He utilized a form letter to spur his readers to "be militant and fight these people [Jews and government leadership] to the bitter end, cost what it may."[8]

Another method of increasing sales was to have young children sell *Social Justice*. Each child was instructed by the journal's distributors to break into a loud wail when people walked by. When asked why he was wailing, the child was to reply, "A big Jew hit me."[9] It was then easier to peddle the journal and to stir up feelings against the Jews.

The most stable feature of *Social Justice* was the "Know Social Justice Contest," which was inaugurated with the September 14, 1936, issue. The contests, meant to increase the journal's circulation, were little more than a catechism of the views of *Social Justice*. A representative sampling of questions and winning responses follows:

Q: Why is Father Coughlin not a communist?
A: Because he believes individual rights are superior to State's rights.
Q: Why is Father Coughlin not a fascist?
A: Because he is opposed to political and labor dictatorship.
Q: Why should Father Coughlin be unmolested in his radio broadcasts?
A: Because he truly and accurately interprets the encyclicals of the Pope on labor.
Q: What is America's chief war menace?
A: British propaganda relative to her investments in the Far East.[10]
Q: To what does Father Coughlin chiefly attribute the rise of fascism and communism?
A: The evils of the Treaty of Versailles.

Q: How best can America at present keep out of foreign war?

A: By ignoring British propaganda.

Q: What is the chief weapon against world revolution?

A: Christianity.

Q: What is the ultimate source of American human rights?

A: God.

Q: What is the most serious political menace today threatening American liberty?

A: Too much centralization of power in the federal government.

Q: What sort of Jews and Gentiles does Father Coughlin principally oppose?

A: Atheistic Jews and Gentiles.

Q: Why is Father Coughlin not pro-Nazi?

A: Because he is opposed to state control of religion.[11]

Prizes included cars and bicycles and *Social Justice* devoted considerable space to publicizing the contest and its winners. Contest winners had their names, their addresses and, at times, their pictures in the journal. The space allotted to the contest, and its longevity as a feature, may indicate that the contest's sponsors were generally satisfied with its results.

A perusal of the names of people who contributed articles to *Social Justice* in its early years reveals that they represented diverse political, economic and social views. (For more detailed information on contributors see Appendix G.) The views that they expressed on the particular subject written about for *Social Justice*, however, generally reflected the views of Father Coughlin. Many of these contributors were not in agreement with all or most of Father Coughlin's other views. Their articles were usually concerned with the nation's fiscal problems and the distribution of wealth. Many of them tended to favor inflationary fiscal policies and were critical of the New Deal.

Many important politicians saw *Social Justice* as a significant vehicle for reaching the voting public. It must be credited to Father Coughlin's influence that so many of them chose to voice their opinions in the pages of *Social Justice*. Among them were Congressman Arthur Lamneck of Ohio, former Senator from Oklahoma and Chairman of the United States Committee on Banking and Currency Robert Owen, Senator Homer Bone of Washington, Senator William E. Borah of Idaho, Congressman Fred Crawford of Michigan, Congressman George Dondero of Michigan, Senator Lynn Frazier of North Dakota, Congressman Wright Patman of Texas, Senator Elmer Thomas of Oklahoma, Congressman William Lemke of North Dakota, Senator Henrik Shipstead of Minnesota, Senator Ernest Lundeen of Minnesota and Congressman John J. O'Connor of New York.

When *Social Justice* became overtly anti-Semitic, many of these people who had contributed articles while the weekly expressed pro-fascist sympathies ceased writing for it. By 1940 contributors to *Social Justice* were those willing to have their names associated with the anti-Semitic, fascist-oriented views of Father Coughlin.

Given the views of *Social Justice*, it is not surprising that in its pages one could find the words and opinions of many ardent advocates of what may be generally termed the Far Right. Some of the most notable of these were George Sylvester Viereck, Mrs. Jane Anderson DeCienfuegos, Francis Yockey, Philip Johnson and Hilaire Belloc.

Viereck, a famous poet, was a German-born, naturalized American citizen who was convicted of violating the Foreign Agents Registration Act. He expressed his high regard for Hitler and Mussolini and on May 9, 1938, reminded the readers of *Social Justice* "that the Swastika stands for order."

Jane Anderson DeCienfuegos, born in Atlanta, was the wife of a Spanish aristocrat. During World War II, she broadcast Nazi propaganda in English from Berlin. In 1943 she was indicted in absentia, along with Ezra Pound, as a traitor to the United States. In the pages of *Social Justice* (i.e., May 9, 1938, and August 15, 1938) Mrs. DeCienfuegos lauded Franco and his followers and told of Loyalist atrocities.

On August 2, 1939, an article by Francis Yockey in *Social Justice* related the difficulties he encountered in finding a job and criticized the New Deal. Prior to United States entry into World War II, Yockey was involved in pro-Nazi activity and visited Germany frequently. In later years Yockey was to write *Imperium*, regarded by some as the fascist counterpart of the *Com-*

munist Manifesto. The book is replete with vague generalizations and blatantly prejudicial remarks about Jews and blacks.[12] In 1960, Yockey committed suicide in a San Francisco jail where he was being held for passport fraud.

Philip Johnson, who designed the Seagram Building and the Museum of Modern Art in New York, and who is currently working for the Israeli government on plans to redesign Jerusalem, was a foreign correspondent for *Social Justice.* In this capacity he accompanied the German army into Poland. William Shirer, in *Berlin Diary*, labeled Johnson a German collaborator.[13] In a story appearing in the September 11, 1939, issue of *Social Justice*, but filed before the German invasion of Poland, Johnson wrote that in his visits to Polish towns "there were not even any Poles to be seen in the streets, only Jews." Nowhere does he note how he was able to differentiate the Jews from the Poles. In an article appearing in the November 6, 1939, issue of *Social Justice*, he described the United States as a "crown colony" of Great Britain.

Hilaire Belloc, world-renowned English essayist, novelist, poet and brilliant expounder of Catholic doctrine, was accused of having a fascist frame of mind because of the pro-Franco outlook and anti-Semitic beliefs he expressed in his book *The Jews.* In the 1937–1938 academic year, Belloc came to the United States as visiting professor of history at New York's Fordham University. During that stay he became a regular contributor to *Social Justice.*

By 1940 the editors of *Social Justice* found it difficult to obtain articles from individuals not directly employed by one of Father Coughlin's organizations. For by this time it was obvious that Father Coughlin represented an extreme point of view — a point of view that was becoming increasingly unpopular as the Nazis swept across Europe. As Father Coughlin says, "Some of my so-called friends wanted nothing to do with me then. They were afraid to have their names associated with mine. The heat was too much for them."[14]

Father Coughlin claims that he was never an anti-Semite, and until the summer of 1938 it would be difficult to classify him as one. Before then he had referred to the existence of a "Jewish question" and had also singled out the Jews as being overly sensitive to the criticisms of non-Jews and too slow to condemn fellow Jews for wrongdoing. But in July of 1938, *Social Justice* began to reprint the "Protocols of the Elders of Zion" in a weekly series. Father Coughlin published the "Protocols," he explains, not because he was convinced of their authenticity but because he was struck by their prophetic nature.

It is difficult to determine why Coughlin became actively anti-Semitic at that time. Perhaps he had become convinced of the validity of the anti-Semitic doctrines preached by Hitler, the Reverend Gerald Winrod and William Dudley Pelley, all of whom tied Jews to the birth and spread of communism. Perhaps he was looking for an issue to attract large numbers of supporters and hasten his recovery from the enormity of his defeat in the 1936 presidential election. Whatever his reasons, and despite his denial of ever being anti-Semitic, Coughlin openly espoused the anti-Semitic line.

He stated flatly that the Jews had caused the communist takeover of Russia as part of their grand design for world domination envisaged in the "Protocols." As a result, the only way for American Jews to avoid persecution, he said, was to join with Christians in combating communism just as vigorously as they were opposing Hitlerism. It thus seemed logical for *Social Justice* to repeat that its purpose in printing the "Protocols" was to mobilize Jews in the fight against communism, which it viewed as the greatest menace to the Christian heritage. In the August 22, 1938, issue of *Social Justice* Coughlin maintained that Jews "are identified with communism because communism protected them alone while it persecuted Christians."

Coughlin did not confine his anti-Semitic publishing to reprinting the "Protocols," but subsequently attempted to prove their veracity. He did so in a number of articles replete with misinformation.[15]

He often wrote of his belief that international Jewish bankers plotted the revolution that overthrew the Christian regime of Czar Nicholas II of Russia. The point that Jews had financed the Russian Revolution was hammered at time and time again. For instance, *Social Justice* said on August 29, 1938, that Jewish money was used to bring about "the mad slaughter of Christians which resulted from this revolution . . . and that Christians are exempted, persecuted, slaughtered and outlawed from every office of state and practice of religion." Coughlin's accusations and sources did not stand up to close scrutiny, but facts notwithstanding, he attacked Jews for maintaining dominant roles of power in the Soviet Union.[16]

Father Coughlin, holding that Jews were closely tied to a world communist conspiracy, believed that they should not expect Christians to protest Germany's persecution of Jews if American Jews did not protest the Soviet Union's persecution of Christians. *Social Justice* said that it was not anti-Semitic but rather, pro-Christian, and was upset "by milk-and-water Christians and Russian-loving Jews. *We regard every organization against War and Fascism as a menace until the officials of such organizations incorporate the war against Communism in their program.*"[17] Father Coughlin and *Social Justice* saw communism as a philosophy subverting every phase of civilized life. They saw the communist threat everywhere. Communism was the major menace to the Church, because each represented a universal ideology and each competed for the minds and allegiance of the masses; it was anti-Christian and a threat to the very existence of religion. "Communism or Social Justice: take your choice!"[18] demanded *Social Justice*.

The period from September 1, 1939, to December 8, 1941, was marked by a decrease in the amount of space the journal devoted to criticism of the Jews. This can be partially accounted for by the journal's preoccupation with attacking Great Britain. Furthermore, once Europe was at war there was less reason for accusing the Jews of trying to start a war, although the journal continued to claim that the Jews were responsible for its start. The criticisms that were made, however, were just as intense as in the years preceding World War II. Major emphasis continued to be placed on the supposition that the Jews had fostered communism.

Social Justice was generally consistent in its defense of fascism, which it described as a reaction to communism. For example, in the April 3, 1939, edition of *Social Justice*, a headline proclaimed that the "Rome-Berlin Axis Is a Firm Rampart Against Communism." The article stated:

> It should never be forgotten that the Rome-Berlin axis is the great political rampart against the spread of Communism. As such, the Rome-Berlin axis is serving Christendom in a peculiarly important manner.

An article in the April 11, 1938, issue of *Social Justice* said:

> It may be a novel thought to picture the German chancellor, and his so-called "fascist" allies, as the champions of Christian social order against the forces of anti-Christian chaos. However, in the interest of Christianity and civilization itself, the menace of Satanic disorder leaves the western nations no choice. It is Civilization or Communism; Christianity or Chaos.

For the record, however, the journal denied fascist sympathies. E. Perrin Schwartz, its editor, once took George Seldes to task for having insinuated that *Social Justice* was pro-fascist. Schwartz defied Seldes to cite even one edition of the paper that ever displayed such a view and further stated that "I'm afraid somebody is taking you in, and you and I both know who would try like the devil to do it."[19]

Social Justice expressed the belief that Hitler was able to take power primarily because of the inequities of the Treaty of Versailles, which had brought economic ruin to Germany, and because of the German desire to resist communism. The journal lauded Hitler as the foe of communism, the man who had driven the international bankers out of the country, the man who had rectified the injustices of the Treaty of Versailles. On occasion, the weekly did attack Hitler, as when he placed limitations on the rights of Catholics and the Catholic Church and when he attempted to extend secular control over monasteries. But it commented that German Catholics were working within the Nazi regime, and not against it, in trying to overcome temporary Nazi hostility toward the Catholic Church. The journal pointed out:

It should never be forgotten that if powerful anti-Christian forces are at work in Germany, the anti-Christian forces in France, in Great Britain and in America can hardly be regarded as less powerful or less dangerous.[20]

The journal contained many articles lauding Hitler. The following excerpts are representative of them.

Since 1933 Chancellor Hitler has broken with international finance. Through the industry of her people — freed from slavery to un-Christian financial internationalists — Germany has solved her domestic problems. There is today virtually no unemployment; the Reich is prospering. Despite malicious propaganda, Germany's internal prosperity has set an example that causes European leaders to ponder.[21]

and:

The European champion, the bitterest foe of communism, the savior of peace and civilization . . . Hitler today is one of the leading personalities of the world, is in his private life to be admired, a real puritan. He has made of Germany, the defeated a new, united, great nation. He has brought back to his father-land the pride of industrial achievements and scientific improvements.[22]

Hitler's move into Austria in 1938 was justified as being beneficial to the cause of anti-communism because of the exodus from Vienna of "anti-God radicals."[23] The Czech crisis provided *Social Justice* with another opportunity to display its pro-Hitler position. Konrad Henlein, the leader of the Sudetenland German minority, was described as having made minimal demands upon the Czech government in calling for national determination. Reports of Nazi terrorism were described as leftist propaganda. Another article which bore a marked similarity to a pamphlet issued by the Fichte Bund, an official German government propaganda organ (see Appendix I for a comparison), stated that Czechoslovakia was a "mongrel state" in which the Sudeten Germans had been persecuted and Hitler was merely determined to rectify this situation. The Munich Pact was described as the model by which countries could settle their differences without resorting to war; it was a victory for "peace, truth and justice," and a defeat for warmongers such as Joseph Stalin and Eduard Benes.[24] When Benes resigned as president of Czechoslovakia, *Social Justice* declared that the Czech people could now move forward to peace and prosperity without the man who had betrayed them.

Social Justice viewed Mussolini as a hero. In an early issue the journal had declared that fascist Italy was working itself into a state of nationalistic emotion which was a threat to the peace of the rest of the world, and that its growing tendency to look back to the glories of ancient Rome could result in a danger to the maintenance of European peace. But from late 1936 to its demise in April, 1942, *Social Justice* had only accolades for Mussolini — whom it described as a brilliant leader, eager for peace — who had put a disorganized and disheartened Italy on its feet for the first time since it had become a united nation. Il Duce's attack on Italian Jews was lauded because they were the group that had opposed fascism, had dominated the intellectual life of Italy, and had fought Italian racial discrimination in Ethiopia.[25]

It is clear that Father Coughlin was enamored of fascist philosophy. In fact, he suggested that the political system of the United States be restructured on the Italian model, openly advocating the establishment of a corporate state in which workers would be represented on the basis of occupation. The fascist system need "not necessarily be a dictatorial one"; in fact, it would be a means of perfecting democracy.[26] He characterized the democratic government of the United States as a mockery and considered the U.S. political party system outdated; partyism resulted in a "mobocracy."[27]

The July 11, 1938, issue of *Social Justice* described an alternative to the political party system in the United States:

Do not be deceived! Democracy has nothing to do with political partyism and political partyism is not even on speaking terms with democracy.

Political partyism is a democracy's greatest enemy — as great as Hitlerism, as insidious as Stalinism.

Political partyism, which always sought the aid and support of the international bankers and the concentrators of wealth, never once dared to offend the powers behind the throne . . .

When will the American people rise above partyism and overthrow the politicians who have perpetually protected the exploiters of the poor?

I do not insinuate that the people should set up a government of Fascism, of Communism, of totalitarianism.

I mean that the people should organize to set up a government of perfected democracy free from all political parties — a democracy where labor and capital are both represented; a government where the president is not a politician; a government which is not controlled by the international bankers, the insurance corporations, the Morgans, the Kuhn-Loebs, the Rothschilds, the Warburgs and their kept industrialists.

Once having established that there was a communist threat to the safety of the country, *Social Justice* proclaimed that only by following Father Coughlin could this menace be defeated.[28] The communist threat was so insidious that communism might even disguise itself as democracy.

Communism is holding a pistol to the head of your country today. Tighter and tighter the finger of Moscow is squeezing the trigger. The sinister mind back of the gun-barrel is pressing for the awful blast that will blow the United States into the oblivion of stark national death.

Communism is not as fair as the robber who holds you up. The bandit will not kill you if you surrender your property. Communism will not only take ALL property from Americans but, after having stripped them of worldly goods, will then proceed to murder them both physically and spiritually.

Russian Communism has committed the physical murders of 30 million Christians, and the spiritual murder of 180 million persons by denying to them and to their children knowledge of God.

Like the highwayman, Communism wears a mask — several masks — and the most deceiving of these is "democracy."[29]

The communist menace was said to have contaminated President Roosevelt. When Earl Browder and the Communist party supported Roosevelt's 1936 reelection campaign, *Social Justice* commented that: "the sleek-bodied honey-tongued New Dealers have made love to the filthy untouchables from Moscow."[30] Browder and his American followers were a "crimson gang" of murderers who were "lying Judas Iscariots" when they talked of defending the Constitution.[31] John L. Lewis was called an ally of the communists and a friend of "David Dubinsky, communist president of the New York Garment Workers' Union";[32] Harry Hopkins was a "red sympathizer";[33] Heywood Broun was "Haywire Broun."[34] Hearst columnist Arthur Brisbane "upheld the Communists on the front page while his supposed boss bastinadoed them on the back page."[35] The entire CIO was a Moscow tool teeming with communists who took their instructions from the American communist leadership and the communist Central Committee of the United States.[36]

The journal warned its readers against underestimating communism because the zeal of its followers made up for its lack of numbers. There was little difference between communism and socialism: "A bad principle cannot through application be developed into a good practice."[37] The French socialist Leon Blum was described as a man whose roots were embedded in the doctrines of Karl Marx and Lenin. When Blum became premier, *Social Justice* on August 3, 1936, commented that France was now a communist nation. "The red flag flies from the mast of the French navy. The hammer and sickle has supplanted the fleur-de-lis."

This same issue described the intellectual founder of socialism, Karl Marx, as a "philosophical panhandler, a scientific beggar and a literary plagiarist . . . the son of a Jewish lawyer." Another issue described Marx as having been born wealthy and as never having done an honest day's work in his entire life.[38] Distortions and half-truths of Marx's life continued to be published in subsequent issues of *Social Justice*.

Social Justice strongly supported Franco's forces against Loyalists in the Spanish civil war:

Communists are referred to in the daily press as "the loyalists." Those who oppose them are labeled as rebels. We have lived to see the day when one who upholds democracy, the rights of private property and the freedom of religion is classified with the Benedict Arnolds of civilization.[39]

In response to the argument that the Loyalists constituted the duly elected democratic government of Spain, *Social Justice* on April 4, 1938, replied that the Loyalists were not duly elected and anyway they had forfeited their right to govern when they had turned Spain into a totalitarian communist state. When Franco emerged victorious, *Social Justice* in its April 10, 1939, issue stated:

General Francisco Franco has put an end to "democracy" in Spain. He has put to flight the communist hypocrites. . . . No longer will Spanish "democrats" burn churches, tie nuns together in kerosene-soaked pits, massacre bishops, priests and ministers, mow down hundreds of thousands of innocent men, women and children just because they were Christians.

No longer need the American columnists, kept newspapers, paid Red agitators, Washington internationalists weep for "Spanish democracy" for it is now only a dark, red spot in history.

On the home front, *Social Justice* disagreed with Roosevelt on the means of relieving the depression. His failure to multiply job opportunities for jobless youths was deplored.[40] When Roosevelt sought to alleviate the problem by lengthening their period of education and by appealing to industry to hire youth wherever possible, *Social Justice* applauded, but agreement was rare; it usually regarded Roosevelt's attempts to alleviate unemployment and poverty as superficial and ineffective. For example, the May 22, 1936, issue of *Social Justice* contained a political cartoon labeled "child-labor slavery." It depicted a little girl with a weight chained to her ankle; she was praying over the grave of youth: "Dear God: Please teach the leaders of our country that needless poverty isn't justice."

Social Justice labeled Roosevelt the American Kerensky because, it said, he was trying to create the conditions which would allow the communists to take over the country. It was never clear whether *Social Justice* viewed Roosevelt as the dupe of the communists or as their leader. When Roosevelt was reelected in 1936,

Father Coughlin stated that this was proof that democracy could be dangerous because an unintelligent, careless, selfish citizenry could elect chiselers and racketeers to even the highest elective office.[41] Coughlin had no doubts that the electorate had failed its crucial test and that democracy had failed. He was certain that by 1940 Roosevelt, afraid of holding a presidential election because of an outraged electorate, would install himself as dictator; that the President would resort to any means to insure his continued maintenance in office, even purposely creating an economic breakdown that could be solved only with greater executive powers.[42]

Roosevelt's attempt to "pack" the Supreme Court simply confirmed Coughlin's belief that he wanted to make himself a dictator, even if it meant that a coup d'etat would have to be carried out.[43] Readers of *Social Justice* were urged to write letters opposing the Supreme Court "packing" bill to their congressmen and were also urged to get at least ten friends to do the same. It warned that if Roosevelt were successful, the Constitution would be abrogated by 1940. When the bill was finally defeated, *Social Justice* attributed this to the steadfastness of Father Coughlin's followers, who, by letting their opinions be known, had given congressmen the backbone to stand up to President Roosevelt.

During the first year of its publication, *Social Justice* had very little to say about United States involvement in European affairs. But with the rising tensions in Europe in early 1937, it became evident that there was some sentiment in the United States for American involvement in foreign affairs. On March 15, 1937, in an effort to combat such sentiment, *Social Justice* took a vigorously isolationist position:

Instead of avoiding foreign entanglements, the administration in Washington is actually inviting them. . . .

Let us stay at home and mind our own business. Let us insist on a America self-sustained and self-contained, free from foreign entanglements and foreign influence. Let us be ready for the defense of our country and homes from alien aggressions, but never again be the aggressor.

The journal urged the government to construct naval and air forces that would be sufficiently strong to protect the Western Hemisphere but would not be used beyond the natural limitation of Pan-America. Readers were warned that the cost of any future war would be shocking in terms of heartache resulting from the slaughter of innocent women and children, depression, disease and famine — a situation from which only the munitions makers and the bankers would profit. These bankers, *Social Justice* claimed, were acting with the endorsement and cooperation of the New Dealers in fermenting such a war.[44] In order to avoid any possibility of United States involvement in a war, *Social Justice* urged the support of the Ludlow Amendment, which called for a national referendum prior to a declaration of war on any country. When the Ludlow Amendment failed, it laid the blame on President Roosevelt's determination to get the United States involved in a war.

The journal dramatized its opposition to foreign involvement by carrying pictures and illustrations depicting the horrors of war. In the March 6, 1939, issue an illustration of a fallen doughboy bore the caption:

Whose boy is this, sprawled in the mire of our new frontier on the Rhine? Perhaps only a few kilometers away his father lies where he fell when international ghouls established the outposts of America on the same river in 1918.

Never forget, Mr. and Mrs. America, that YOUR BOY is being counted today. The international warmongers, footing up the man-strength of the United States, are figuring on YOUR BOY for the guns.

In the April 3, 1939, issue, under a picture of a father saying good-bye to his son, the caption described how the father had struggled to bring up his son and, although a loyal American, he wondered if democracy was worth saving if American boys had to fight in Europe for it. On September 25, 1939, a picture of a dead American doughboy with an accompanying caption that attributed his death to the "international ghouls" urged parents to make known that they would not let their sons die in a foreign war. On October 14, 1939, the journal depicted a wounded American soldier, bleeding profusely, with the following caption:

Under the shell-shot sky of Europe an American boy is dying. His life blood slowly ebbs into the filth and mire of a foreign land. . . . The boy from New Hampshire stares blindly towards the West and, in the way of all dying soldiers, moans — MOTHER.

Illustrations such as these played on the fears of tens of thousands of American parents — people who thoroughly disliked Hitler, but were not willing to sacrifice their sons to destroy him. Many Americans thought Hitler, Mussolini and the Spanish civil war too far removed to ever have an effect on their lives.

By 1939 *Social Justice* had pinpointed President Roosevelt as the man most responsible for efforts to discard the traditional United States policy of isolationism. In a May 18, 1939, article, the President was sarcastically congratulated for having put America into a war that had yet to begin. When the Roosevelt administration threw its support behind the passage of a measure permitting the sale of war materials on a "cash and carry" basis, legislation obviously favoring England, *Social Justice* viewed it as the act of a small group of war-minded legislators intent on making the United States a satellite of Britain. When this legislation received a temporary setback because of an outpouring of mail against it to congressmen, Father Coughlin wrote a letter to one of his supporters:

May I also thank you from the bottom of my heart for the fine cooperation which you and your friends have extended in stopping the lifting of the embargo. It was our greatest victory, all things considered.[45]

From the outbreak of World War II on September 1, 1939, to America's involvement in it on December 7, 1941, *Social Justice* emphasized hostility to Great Britain and support of most of Germany's policies. Page after page of the weekly now commented on and criticized British policies and actions. Such criticism may be partly attributed to the hostile attitude of many militant Irishmen — an attitude that had been shared by both Coughlin and Bishop Gallagher.[46] Britain's motive in going to war, *Social Justice* claimed on September 25, 1939, was neither to fulfill its treaty obligations nor to defend democracy, but rather to save its financial and economic investments which were being jeopardized by Hitler.

The journal's stories about the war being waged on the Atlantic Ocean reflected its anti-British bias. When the British ship *Athenia* was sunk by a German U-boat, resulting in the loss of American as well as British lives, *Social Justice*, on October 30, 1939, accused the British of having sunk the ship to stir up anti-German feeling in the United States. It chastised Great Britain for the search and seizure of American ships in the war zone and wondered why State Department officials did not vociferously protest these actions. The sinking of the *Graff Spee* by three British cruisers was viewed as a violation of America's territorial waters and Britain's actions in this affair were described as "high-handed."[47]

Social Justice constantly predicted the imminent defeat of Great Britain. It said that communism was making large gains among the lower classes in Britain, which were bearing the brunt of the German bombings. These communist gains were regarded as significant enough to bring Britain to the verge of revolution. The journal even implied that Churchill, Bevan and other British leaders were imposing communism on their people by stressing discipline and uniform standards of existence. It attacked Britain for its stupidity in not surrendering to Germany, because it was "a foregone conclusion that Germany will capture Britain." Therefore, "it might be sensible for Britain to lay down her arms and save a useless and fruitless destruction."[48]

When the British refused to capitulate and the Battle of Britain was begun, *Social Justice* characterized the people of London as potential hostages, predicting that Britain would be in German hands by August 15, 1940. Even when Goering called a halt to the daytime bombing of Britain because of high plane losses, *Social Justice* ridiculed the idea that Germany was losing the Battle of Britain.[49]

By April 7, 1941, *Social Justice* was forced to admit that Germany could not conquer Britain, but it continued to extol the virtues and power of the German war machine. On April 14, 1941, the journal denied that Britain's war was important to the future of the United States and voiced the belief that Britain, not Germany, was the world's most aggressive nation. On June 16, 1941, it pointed out how fortunate it was that the United States was not on Britain's side, because then its soldiers, too, would be corpses and its honor tarnished by defeat.

Social Justice termed German air raids on British population centers reprisals for British air raids on German cities. It accused Britain of causing the starvation of noncombatants in central Europe by her blockade of the continent, and it chastised the British for dropping bombs on "eighty-eight million German Christians and forty million Italian Christians."[50]

A September 25, 1939, article on the invasion of Poland pointed out that the Poles were betrayed by their French and British allies, who had failed to send them men, ships, planes and equipment. While admitting in this article that Poland "had been overrun by the un-Christian force of the Hitlerites and Stalinites," the October 9, 1939, issue stated that it was Russia that had devoured Poland, and there was no longer any mention of Germany's role.

Social Justice appeared to be in a dilemma on how to view the destruction of Poland: many of its readers were of Polish ancestry and would resent criticism of that country. The problem was resolved in its February 19, 1940, issue by publishing two letters from readers, one condemning Germany and the other condemning Poland. Both writers claimed to be Poles. The letter condemning Poland claimed that Poland was led by Jews and concluded with the statement: "I would rather be a German-Pole, which I am, and fight for eventual autonomy, than be a Jewish-owned Polish serf doing his bidding."

Social Justice claimed that Germany's move into Norway was to prevent Britain from seizing that country after she had violated Norwegian sovereignty by sending her warships into Norway's neutral waters. Such British aggression was justification for Germany's invasion of Denmark as well as Norway. When Germany invaded the Netherlands and Belgium, *Social Justice* saw this as an act no more aggressive than the British occupation of Iceland.[51]

When France was faced with imminent collapse, readers of *Social Justice* were told on June 17, 1940, not to be concerned because very few Catholics had gained prominent positions in the French government, which was controlled by Marxists, atheists and anti-Christians. When France finally did capitulate, *Social Justice* stated that the Third French Republic was guilty of anti-clericalism and of following a consistently anti-Christian policy. The journal concluded that a fascist France "will afford better opportunities for the mental, spiritual and social development of its people than did the France that was ruled by the spirit of the atheist Voltaire."[52]

According to *Social Justice*, the old social order, identified with capitalism and European imperialism, would be replaced under the Nazis by a new social order in which all the people of Europe would share in the benefits of society. Hitlerism was the personification of the national forces behind the anti-Comintern axis formed by Germany, Italy and Japan, and their victory would release the internal forces of Christianity to transform Nazism into something better.[53] On July 1, 1940, *Social Justice* pointed out that the Nazi regime had eradicated pornographic literature, obscene theatrical performances and many social crimes from Germany. A superior financial system had been instituted and subversive societies and politicians had been banished from the scene. It stated:

Had we Christians enforced the discipline and produced the good accomplished by the Nazis for a good end, we would not be weeping at the wailing wall, fearful lest totalitarianism is about to engulf America.

Another reason for its support of Hitler was that the German people had only two choices, Nazism or communism. There was no mention of a third, the democratic choice inherent in the Weimar Constitution.

When Germany invaded the Soviet Union on June 22, 1941,

Social Justice facetiously congratulated Churchill for having "persuaded Stalin to dagger Hitler in the back," and somehow neglected to mention that it was Germany that was doing the invading. Instead, the emphasis was on Soviet aggression toward Germany, which, if not halted, would lead to the communization of every country in Europe. The journal predicted a quick German victory on the Eastern Front because "when the going gets really tough a great many of the Red soldiers will quit and go home."[54] When Soviet resistance stiffened around the city of Smolensk, the journal pointed out that the German armies had freed more territory from Soviet domination than they had won in their campaigns in Western Europe. When Smolensk finally fell, *Social Justice* lauded this German victory by highlighting the story of the first celebration of an Orthodox Catholic Mass in the city "since Stalin's communists outlawed the Christian religion in the Soviet Union."[55]

Many Americans were surprised by the intensity and capability of Soviet resistance, but *Social Justice* called such news "propaganda": "Russia is whipped — just as much as Belgium and France and Greece were whipped; just as surely as Britain will be whipped."[56] A week later, on September 22, 1940, readers were told that if the Soviets could stop the greatest military machine of modern times, the Red army would certainly move on to world conquest and world revolution.

While the war was being waged in Europe, *Social Justice* kept urging the United States to keep out of it and permit Germany to crush Great Britain and the Soviet Union. The United States, it said, could remain a mighty bulwark of Christianity and civilization if it remained aloof from the war.

Social Justice consistently emphasized how poorly prepared the United States was for war, and used this approach to develop an anti-war sentiment based on fear. The United States Army, it stressed, was smaller than Switzerland's; the country was bridled with "a shop-worn democracy, compromising leaders and a one ocean navy."[57] It agreed with Charles Lindbergh that the Nazis were too strong to be defeated on the battlefield and that it would therefore be prudent for America to avoid a war with Germany.

The journal also suggested Lindbergh as an excellent candidate for President on the Republican ticket.[58]

While stressing Germany's armed might, *Social Justice* claimed that Hitler could not invade the United States because he lacked the necessary transports. But it also believed that Hitler could be trusted in his pledge that he had no designs upon North America.[59] When conscription was introduced and the United States began to prepare for war, *Social Justice* ran items which could have led to the belief that our armed forces were riddled with hopeless incompetents. The loss of pilots in crashes were attributed to poor training and inferior planes. The new United States Army was described as obsolete, untrained, ill equipped and facing certain defeat by Nazi Germany. Conditions in army camps were described as so shocking that no paper would dare to print the number of deserters per week, the number of suicides per week and the rapid breakdown of morale. The journal did not, however, provide its readers with the facts and figures; instead, it highlighted stories emphasizing the disenchantment of servicemen with their duties in army camps. Much of what the journal said had a factual basis, but its aim was to create a fear of becoming involved in war rather than a desire to prepare for it.[60]

Social Justice accused Roosevelt of stirring up hatred against Hitler and Mussolini and encouraging anti-Semitism because "he packed Washington with Jews far beyond the dictates of reason and prudence."[61] It pointed to Felix Frankfurter, Louis Brandeis, Bernard Baruch and Henry Morgenthau as some of the Jews who formed the moving spirits behind an invisible government in Washington.

When Roosevelt was nominated for a third term in July, 1940, *Social Justice* said that democracy had ceased to exist and the country was "careening downgrade into the valley of dictatorship."[62] But after Roosevelt's reelection, the journal, on November 18, 1940, offered to forgive him for his past errors and to praise him if his future actions merited praise. Apparently they did not because criticism of his administration resumed shortly thereafter. The weekly again attacked Roosevelt for giving assistance to Britain in its war against Germany, and continued to associate the

President with communism, specifically accusing him of "coddling the murderous, anti-Christian regime of Stalin" by extending United States friendship to the Soviet Union.[63]

The Japanese attack on Pearl Harbor on December 7, 1941, caught *Social Justice* between issues, since the December 8 edition was already on its way to the newsstands. When reporters tried to get Father Coughlin's reaction to the attack, a spokesman replied that there would be no comment.

The December 15 issue of the weekly proclaimed, "We're at War!" and went on to state its new policy:

It does mean we submit to the will of the government. It does mean we will discountenance all intellectual or physical sabotage. It does mean we will be no obstructionists in the pursuit of this war. However, we are no Stephen Decaturs. While the Government of our country is right we will applaud the Government. When the Government of our country is definitely wrong, we reserve the right to say so.

From this issue through the final issue on April 20, 1942, *Social Justice* bitterly criticized the government. It stated that the war had resulted in the end of individual liberties and the beginning of national regimentation, censorship of pen, voice and assembly. It expressed the belief that the war was "a lash God is using to sting us for social sins," and held that the war was deliberately planned by President Roosevelt.[64] Its attacks on the Roosevelt administration were relentless. "God bless the admirals, sailors and marines of the navy. God rid us of the politicians who endanger them and victory."[65]

Father Coughlin maintains that his criticisms of the war effort and the purchase of $25,000 worth of Defense Bonds by the Social Justice Publishing Company were not incongruous.

I'm an American. I wanted our boys to win the war, but I knew that the politicians were bunglers and manipulators. Somebody had to criticize them and keep them honest. . . . I never felt that my *Social Justice* impeded the war effort. We were certainly striving to keep the country out of war. I knew what was being planned. I knew that war was inevitable, in spite of my efforts. The big boys wanted that war.[66]

On February 2, 1942, *Social Justice* again cited American Jews as having played a large role in promoting the war, but continued to deny having an anti-Semitic viewpoint. On March 16, 1942, *Social Justice* commented that Jews in Germany had been persecuted as far back as 1933 because they had declared a sacred war against Hitler, his two million Nazis and the fifty million Catholics, Protestants and other German Gentiles who were not Nazis. It further stated that because one goal of the Jews was to involve the United States in a war against Germany, Hitler's persecution of the Jews in Europe was justified.[67]

The journal devoted considerable space to emphasizing the strengths of the Axis powers in contrast to the glaring weaknesses of the Allies. America's enemies were described as powerful, well trained and well officered, and possessing great natural resources. To defeat them would require that United States citizens make momentous personal sacrifices — sacrifices which the journal doubted many Americans were ready to make. It did say, however, on January 19, 1942, that all Americans should serve in the war and that those who refused to do so were imprudent and unpatriotic, for if the United States lost the war, everything would be taken by the invaders. This comment was one of the few statements, and certainly the most substantial, made by the weekly to support the United States war effort.

Social Justice warned its readers of the dangers of the United States alliance with the "sleazy Britishers."[68] Americans were told to be alert against giving material to Britain before the needs of this country were satisfied. There was no recognition that Britain was fighting for survival in a common cause with the United States. In spite of the bleak situation in Britain in the winter of 1941–1942, *Social Justice*, on December 22, 1941, commented that there was plenty of food available there and that it was being sent from the United States at a time when many American children did not have enough to eat. The article concluded with the question, "Is it too 'pro-Nazi' to demand that American school children be adequately fed *before we give billions of dollars worth of food and war materials to Great Britain and the Communist U.S.S.R.?*"

The journal chastised Americans who now considered the Soviet Union an ally; only a short time ago, it pointed out, Russia was allied with Hitler. It went on to accuse the Soviet Union of being part of a secret alliance with Japan and Germany against the United States — this at a time when some of the bloodiest, most decisive battles of the war were being fought at Stalingrad and Leningrad.[69] When the Japanese were inflicting serious losses on the American-Filipino forces in the Philippines, the journal accused Washington of abandoning General MacArthur by sending to Britain military assistance that could have helped him. It stated that MacArthur had to overcome not only the enemy on the battlefield, but also the incompetents in Washington.[70]

On March 2, 1942, *Social Justice* told its readers that a fifteen-year war was now possible because of the failure of American military and naval policy. Three weeks later it stated that the war would be concluded in 1942 — in favor of the enemy. The news from the European and Pacific fronts at this time was grim, to say the least. Nevertheless, Coughlin's *Social Justice* continued its unremitting attacks on America's leaders and the war effort. In recalling his attitude toward the war, Father Coughlin explains:

we were going to lose that war eventually. . . . I regarded Marxism as the parent of both Nazism and communism. One was the left wing and the other the right wing of the same bird of prey. And no matter which one of them came out victorious, they would start to undermine us. That day arrived and they have been doing it very cleverly as Joseph Stalin promised he would do it — getting us to spend ourselves into destruction. He meant morally spend ourselves. He is the father of pornographic literature in this country. He is the father of dissension on the campuses of this country. He is the father of disruption in our courts in this country. He is the father of the turmoil we are suffering. The dollar miscarriage we have suffered here is minimal. The moral miscarriage is maximal.[71]

As a result of his attacks on the war effort, criticism of Coughlin and *Social Justice* intensified. Many people called for his arrest on charges of sedition, while others thought he should be tried for treason. His enemies accused him of undermining the morale of members of the armed forces and of workers on the home front. For example, the March 31, 1942, issue of the left-wing New York daily *P.M.* devoted nine pages to attempting to prove that Father Coughlin was a danger to the nation. *P.M.* concluded that *Social Justice* was a "direct and unmistakable threat to both the man in the front lines of our fighting forces and to the men on the home front of our factories. It cannot be ignored as 'silly' or 'unimportant' or simply 'repulsive' or as an organ that spreads its sedition only to the crackpot fringe that would be seditious anyway." *P.M.* denounced Father Coughlin for having "openly advocated resort to violence . . . openly attacked democracy as a form of government . . . carrying out the techniques of Nazi psychological warfare — using ammunition made in Germany . . . actively influencing the men and women on whom our lives depend — in the armed forces of the United States and on the production lines which make our weapons."

This issue of *P.M.* also carried a cartoon by Dr. Seuss depicting Hitler reading *Social Justice* while talking to Father Coughlin on the phone and saying, "Not bad, Coughlin . . . but when are you going to start printing it in German?"

Columnists Drew Pearson and Robert S. Allen claimed that President Roosevelt, after reading several issues of *Social Justice*, sent for Attorney General Francis Biddle and ordered him to get tough on Coughlin and to do so immediately.[72]

Social Justice responded that such attacks as these were aimed at suppressing the truth, and it compared the crucifixion of Christ by the Jews to the latter-day attempt to silence Father Coughlin.[73] It maintained that it would continue to print the truth and let the government prosecute its editors if they were truly guilty of sedition.[74] It became apparent to Coughlin that the government was preparing to do something about him:

I knew that all the uproar about my writing was a planned effort to give the government a chance to silence me one way or another. The people who controlled the world had given poor Roosevelt his orders. They had decreed that Father Coughlin must go. I knew that my silencing was imminent. The only thing I was not sure about was how my silence was to be achieved.[75]

9

To Cease and Desist

In fact, the government was considering a course of action to silence Father Coughlin. In the late winter of 1942, FBI men, accompanied by moving vans, pulled up to the Shrine of the Little Flower and served the priest with papers authorizing the seizure of the records of all the corporations he had established, along with his personal papers.[1] A federal grand jury was already investigating certain people and publications for possible seditious activities. Evidence against Coughlin was being accumulated by the office of the Attorney General, which viewed Coughlin's crusade as an effort to exhort the nation to failure during the terrible months of war. Some such evidence was discussed by O. John Rogge, an assistant United States attorney general, working on the case. Rogge stated that in early 1939 Father Coughlin had sent his associate Leo Reardon to Berlin as his personal emissary to see if he could get Hitler to make a public statement to the effect that Nazis were supporters of Christianity. Reardon met with Foreign Minister Joachim Von Ribbentrop, who refused to commit himself on this matter but did praise Father Coughlin. Later in the year, Father Coughlin sent a letter to Fritz Hailer, the German honorary consul in Detroit, which repeated the request and also criticized Roosevelt and the Jews. Hailer forwarded his letter to

Berlin. Rogge stated that "a copy of Coughlin's letter is in the files of the German Foreign Office, together with a memorandum under the date of August 11, 1939, signed by one Herr Woerman, head of the political department of the German Foreign Office."[2]

Evidence of Coughlin's ties to Axis propaganda which was probably uncovered by the grand jury became public in 1946. *In Fact* printed, from the Department of Justice files, the sworn statement of Aleksi Pelypenko, a secret agent of the United States government, who had posed as an Axis agent. Pelypenko's testimony for the government had been crucial in the conviction of Nazi agent Anastase Vonsiatsky. In his statement, Pelypenko said that in early 1941 he had met the German consul in Detroit, a man named Hailer, who told him, "It is imperative that you confer with Father Coughlin; he is one of our collaborators." He also affirmed that Coughlin was working for Germany at that time in carrying out the dissemination of anti-Semitic and anti-British propaganda. Pelypenko claimed to have arranged a meeting which took place in the priest's home. Pelypenko spoke mainly in German, which was translated into English for Coughlin by another priest. Coughlin said that he wished to receive as much anti-Semitic and anti-communist material as possible, material "which I can use against them in this country." During their conversation, Coughlin described Roosevelt as a "war-monger . . . a hireling of the Jews." The statement also alleged that later, Pelypenko met with a secretary in the German embassy by the name of von Heyden, and told him of his conversations with Coughlin. Von Heyden said of Coughlin ". . . he is our man, we help him financially and we give him material to use." Pelypenko said he was told that by cooperating with Coughlin he had helped Germany.[3]

Coughlin denies that he was ever a German agent or that he had contact with German agents, but he does admit that Leo Reardon did meet with Von Ribbentrop. "But he did this on his own, not on instructions from me."[4]

While the grand jury was gathering evidence, Attorney General Francis Biddle took additional action against Coughlin. On April 14, 1942, he wrote a letter to Postmaster General Frank Walker, in which he pointed out the similarity between Cough-

The hearing in May 1942 to decide whether *Social Justice* magazine should lose its second-class mailing privilege as a consequence of printing seditious material (United Press International Photo)

lin's statements and enemy broadcasts and stated that *Social Justice* had reproduced

in this country the lines of enemy propaganda warfare being waged against this country from abroad. . . . Furthermore a study of ten major themes which have been broadcast by our enemies since December 1, 1941, as reported by the foreign broadcast monitoring service of the FCC, shows a close relation of material contained in *Social Justice* to those themes during approximately the same period. . . . Some of the themes emphasized by both *Social Justice* and by enemy propaganda are: pride in the achievement of the Axis powers and sympathy with their aims; disparagement of the intention and motives of the government of the U.S.; blame for the war on international bankers and their control of or influence in the present national administration and in the government of the Allies; creation of racial hatred and distrust; constant and frequent attacks upon the war policies of the present government; and doubt as to the ability of the United Nations to end the war.

Biddle inquired about the possibility of revoking the second-class mailing privilege of *Social Justice* on the grounds that it had violated Section 3 of Title I of the Espionage Act of 1917, which calls for penalties for obstruction of the United States war effort by conveying false information in aid to the enemies of the United States. Section 1, Title XII of the same act declares that any matter in violation of this statute is "non-mailable matter and shall not be conveyed in the mails or delivered from any post office or by any letter carrier." The Attorney General further claimed that *Social Justice* "has engaged over a period of time in a sustained and systematic attack on certain of our activities directly related to the war effort, as well as upon public morale generally." He also stated that *Social Justice* was creating disunity and doubts about the Allied war effort through the "deliberate and intentional distortion of the truth." Biddle was very explicit in citing specific instances of what he considered to be statements justifying the revocation of *Social Justice*'s second-class mailing privilege:

I now call your attention to the following statements made since our entry into the war, as a few of the many statements establishing in my opinion that the necessary elements constituting a violation of the Espionage Act are present and denial of second class mailing privileges is proper. [The date at the beginning of each quotation is the date on which it appeared in *Social Justice*.]

February 23, 1942: "Was Pearl Harbor an accident? Was the scuttling of the Normandie an accident?

"Was the diabolical program of governmental muddling an accident?

"Or was all this planned that way? — Planned from within; planned by men who prayed for democracy while blue-printing chaos . . ."

December 15, 1941: "The famous words — 'We planned it that way' — uttered by Mr. Roosevelt are as applicable in this world war as to anything he has accomplished during his three terms as President."

March 23, 1942: "We have been out looking for a war with the Orient for a good many years. Now we've got it. It's time we realized something of what we're up against."

March 9, 1942: "We are practical enough to ask ourselves the leading question: 'Why attempt the hopeless?' The question is more pertinent when we remember that a Japanese submarine was bombing the coast of California; that Nazi submarines were devastating cargo bottoms in the Caribbean at the moment the President was arguing in defense of his case. . . ."

March 23, 1942: "How long will this war be pursued in America? Will Americans graciously bow down to all the totalitarian decrees which will restrict their sugar, their motor cars, their oil, their apparel, their way of life and their pocket books simply to satisfy the ambitions of those who translate victory by the complete overthrow of their enemies? Or will the American people want to listen to reason and terminate a war which now no one can win completely, and which Americans can lose completely?"

March 23, 1942: "Many taxpayers already are asking themselves: Are we getting what we pay for?

"Many parents whose sons are serving in the army for a mere pittance are souring because the soldiers are not better equipped and because the political army goes marching on in prosperity."

January 5, 1942: "Hence, our foreign policy, devoid of all fine phrases, was one blueprinted to defend international capitalism and British imperialism no matter what the cost might be in tradition, in dollars and in blood to the citizens of our country."

December 8, 1941: "The United States and Great Britain are planning a post-war program. Vitally related to that program is the confiscation and control of all the raw materials of the world."

January 19, 1942: "This Malayan fight is not just another battle in a World War to the Kuhn, Loeb crowd. It is a battle for their investments in the Malayan and Far East Section. . . .

"Billions of American dollars will be spent to preserve these privately owned investments. Hundreds of thousands of American and English boys, possibly, will sacrifice their lives to save Malaya — and incidentally to preserve the investment from which profits are wrenched from the natives of Malaya to swell the purses of international bankers."

January 26, 1942: "Before we proceed further, let it be bluntly stated that besides fighting for liberty, our American boys will be expected to fight to regain the Malayan Peninsula not for the people of Malaya or Great Britain but for Sir John Hay and his legalized gangsters who own or control the Malayan Peninsula and the rubber racket throughout the world."

January 16, 1942: "Our engaging in war against Japan will initiate a long, bitter, gruesome, destructive period which will witness the abandoning of our *Constitution*, the destruction of private property and the adoption of a totalitarian form of government which will level off all families and persons."

January 12, 1942: "At the moment it is useless to remonstrate with public officials who played politics with commodities, supplies and preparedness to such an extent that a sinful shortage exists — a shortage of war materials which could have been averted.

"Perhaps the shortage was intentional to create an opportunity for confiscating the wealth of America."

March 9, 1942: "At present we lack the ships to launch a successful offensive. Without ships, a great percentage of the guns, tanks, munitions and the airplanes we manufacture will find their way to the docks of Boston, New York, Jersey, Hoboken, Baltimore, Philadelphia, Norfolk, New Orleans, Galveston, San Diego, San Francisco and Seattle only to be piled there to deteriorate."

March 16, 1942: "In fact, we are becoming more and more convinced that the radicals who have seized our Federal Government care not one whit about driving Hitler from the face of the earth."

December 15, 1941: "All in all, the Tribune's revelations, based on documents which its publishers claim to have in hand, force us to examine our national sanity for even entertaining such tactical and theoretical ideas of sending 5 million men to fight on foreign fields, at the expense of wrecking the last vestige of our constitutional rights, our property rights, and our children's rights. Upon these latter — the children — imponderable burdens will be placed for centuries to come because we, their parents, were engaged in saving the economic system of international capitalism and the imperial regime of the British empire."

March 2, 1942: "We have reminded the American people time and time again of Britain's propensity for deserting her allies because of her unwillingness or inability to fight her own battles. We have enumerated Britain's long list of unfulfilled promises of aid not only to her allies but also to her own beleaguered armies in the field."

Walker immediately informed Biddle that a hearing would be given the publisher of *Social Justice* at the Postmaster General's office on April 29, 1942, at which time the publisher would have to show cause why the second-class privilege of the journal should not be suspended, annulled and revoked. Walker then notified the postmaster at Royal Oak to withhold dispatch of any future issues of *Social Justice* and to refer copies to the solicitor for the Post Office Department to determine their mailability. Walker also informed E. Perrin Schwartz (Coughlin by his own admission was no longer publisher) that he or a duly authorized representative was to be present at the hearing. The registered letter stated: "The matter will be heard and disposed of at a time stated whether or not appearance is made." In the meantime the grand jury gathering evidence on sedition was directed to investigate *Social Justice*'s ownership.

Father Coughlin reacted strongly to the move against *Social Justice*. He accused "Jews and Communists and New Dealers" of being responsible for the government's actions.[5] He also informed Biddle that he was ready to appear before the grand jury at any time, and that if any criminal laws had been violated, he alone was responsible for the weekly.

Coughlin openly admitted his role in its publication:

Time and again I have said and here repeat that I am neither the editor, publisher nor owner of *Social Justice* Magazine. However, I do here and now publicly state that I, Father Charles E. Coughlin alone am responsible for and do control the magazine, its policies and contents.[6]

Recalling Biddle's investigation of his activities, Father Coughlin says that he would have welcomed an indictment. He remembers meeting with the Attorney General in Washington, D.C., and demanding that he either be allowed to continue publication of *Social Justice* or be indicted for sedition. Coughlin told Biddle: "You are nothing but a God damn coward! You should have been a street cleaner. . . . You have no courage. You were born a coward and you're still one!"[7]

Biddle, however, was not about to rush into an indictment for he was quite aware that such an act would have given Father Coughlin a priceless opportunity to portray himself as the innocent victim of persecution before a nationwide audience and to solidify support for his beliefs. He was not about to have the many Catholics who were critical of the priest turn about in his defense. Nor would he give the pro-Coughlin New York *Daily News* and *Chicago Tribune* the opportunity of espousing his cause. No. The role of martyr was not one that Biddle wished to see Coughlin play. The priest would relish it and this image would rapidly spread with the vastness of publicity.

Already the press was rallying around a cry for its freedom. The *New York Times*, disturbed by events in Washington, on April 16, 1942, decried the views of *Social Justice* while defending its right to speak:

Ninety percent of America's population would feel that the air was purer if this publication [*Social Justice*] were to disappear. . . . *Social Justice* . . . has uttered . . . views, if generally accepted would impair the unity of the American people, spread distrust of our leaders and their motives, and assist the cause of our enemies. If they were to prevail, we would lose this war, and with it our liberties — including the liberty of the press and of speech. It is perfectly natural, therefore, that most Americans should experience a sense of relief at the news that Postmaster General Walker, on the initiative of Attorney-General Biddle, has suspended the Coughlin magazine mailing privileges. The provocation has been outrageous.

At the same time we must remember that the American people in the past have had a way of answering lies with truth, hate with tolerance, incitements to civil strife by a united front to the enemy of mankind. They have never strayed far or long from the principles of the Declaration, the Bill of Rights and the Gettysburg Address.

In these circumstances we must ask ourselves how far we can go in the direction of the suppression of opinion, even opinion as filthy as that expressed in *Social Justice*, unless the facts of the case warrant the direct charge of sedition and prosecution on that ground. When we suppress or hamstring opinion on any other ground, we set a dangerous precedent.

Biddle decided on a course of action that he hoped would silence Coughlin quickly and quietly. He met with Leo T. Crowley, a friend of the President, a Catholic, chairman of the board of the Federal Deposit Insurance Corporation and a man with a flair for smoothing out very difficult situations. Biddle informed Crowley of the history of the case, pointing out that should a grand jury indict Coughlin, further division among the people might occur doing great harm to the war effort. He asked Crowley to appeal to the Church hierarchy not to force the government into such a fight. Crowley, who was also a close friend of Archbishop Mooney, volunteered to fly to Detroit immediately to discuss with him the possibility of silencing Father Coughlin. Crowley was confident of his ability to succeed: "I'll bring it back tied up — then we can tell the President."[8]

Crowley went to Detroit, and told Mooney of the government's willingness to deal with Coughlin in a restrained manner if he would order Coughlin to cease his public activities. Mooney seemed pleased with the opportunity to silence Father Coughlin, for he had already been in contact with the Vatican and had also consulted some of America's leading Catholic prelates on how to deal with Father Coughlin.[9] On May 1, 1942, Mooney sent for Coughlin and ordered him to cease his writings and nonreligious activities or be defrocked. Confronted with this hard choice, Coughlin agreed to cease publication of *Social Justice* and make no attempt to resume his broadcasts.

Father Coughlin is now quite reticent about what transpired at that meeting with Mooney, blaming Pope Pius XII more than he does Mooney.

Mooney was always a gentleman. . . . Not necessarily a friend of mine, but a gentleman. . . . He was very regretful that he had to do to me what was done. I have kept my voice silent regarding Mooney, the gentleman, who was doing as he was instructed to do. He, too, was a soldier in the army.

It was, indeed, a pleased President who received word from Archbishop Mooney that Father Coughlin would at last be silent.[10] The only matter to be resolved was that of *Social Justice*'s mailing privilege. E. Prewitt Semmes asked the Post Office Department for a postponement of the April 29 hearing date. The new date was set for May 4, 1942. The April 27, 1942, issue of *Social Justice* did not appear, nor did the issue of May 4, 1942. No representative of the publisher of the journal appeared on May 4, and the second-class mailing privilege of *Social Justice* was revoked on the grounds that the journal contained seditious material. Prior to the hearing, Postmaster General Walker had received a notice from the publisher-owner of the Social Justice Publishing Company, E. Perrin Schwartz, stating that *Social Justice* would no longer be published and thus was abandoning its second-class mailing privilege. Walker also received a telegram from Father Coughlin. It said:

I approve the action of the publisher owner of *Social Justice* abandoning the second class mail privilege accorded to it under the Act of March 3, 1879, as amended.[11]

Of Roosevelt's role in his silencing, Coughlin says that "the President was only taking orders." In response to the question of who could give orders to the President of the United States, Coughlin chastised this writer for his naïveté and lack of sophistication in not knowing the existence of "that small group of people who run the world." Coughlin insists that Roosevelt was still his friend, but that a personal appeal to him over Biddle's head would have been futile. "Biddle was taking his orders from the real big boys, so it would have been useless to ask Roosevelt for help. The big boys wanted me out of the way."[12]

P.M. reacted to rumors of a deal involving Coughlin, the Catholic Church and the government. On May 26, 1942, it stated: "Releasing Charles Coughlin — staying the hand of justice in his interest — could have only one effect on national morale: it would strengthen the heart and hand of every enemy this country has within its borders and without."

Grand jury proceedings against Father Coughlin were quietly dropped.

According to George Seldes, O. John Rogge was eager to indict Father Coughlin for sedition, but his view did not prevail. Rogge says: "I wasn't told not to indict. It was rather in the form of an impression I received from my superiors."[13] At a press conference, newsman Robert Allen asked Biddle why Father Coughlin, if he were guilty of sedition, was being treated differently from anyone else guilty of such an act. But regardless of the ethics involved, the silencing of Father Coughlin had been accomplished.

In a letter to subscribers mailed in June, 1942, Cora Quinlin, secretary-treasurer of the Social Justice Publishing Company, explained the demise of the journal, and promised to refund unused subscription money, upon request, even though available funds were low. She wrote that on April 16, the Social Justice Publishing Company had received a letter from Postmaster General Walker calling for a hearing on the possible revocation of the second-class mailing privilege which *Social Justice* enjoyed. The staff planned to continue issuance of the journal, as the second-class mailing privilege could not be revoked without a hearing. The contents were prepared in manuscript and sent to Arnold Powers, Inc., for typesetting and mat making. Upon completion, the material was sent to Cuneo Press, which supplied the paper, the printing, the binding and the general operations preparatory to the distribution of *Social Justice*. Cuneo Press, however, refused to fulfill its obligations. A Detroit printer was found and a few hundred copies of the journal were published and submitted to the postmaster at Royal Oak for consideration. The Postmaster General in Washington ruled that the April 27 edition was unmailable, as was the previous issue, although the second-class mailing privilege had not been revoked. The May 4 issue was then prepared and sent on to Arnold Powers, Inc., which refused to do the typesetting. Thus, even before the scheduled Post Office Department hearing, *Social Justice* had found publication impossible.

On August 20, 1942, Cora Quinlan wrote letters of thanks to *Social Justice* readers who agreed not to have their remaining subscription money returned to them. She also indicated that Father Coughlin was restrained by the Church from involvement in nonreligious activities; nor could he answer correspondence that was not sent directly to him. To this point Miss Quinlan stated:

> Some persons have been laboring under the false impression that Father Coughlin can neither receive letters nor answer them. This untruth was spread in many quarters and affected many innocent persons. Let me hasten to assure that Father Coughlin most definitely can receive and answer any letters sent to him directly. . . . And I encourage you to write to him directly with the assurance that your missive will be promptly answered.

In October of 1942, Miss Quinlan again sent letters to subscribers who had not yet given instructions as to what the company should do with the subscription money owed them. The letter pointed out that silence on the part of the subscriber did not give the Social Justice Publishing Company the right to do as it pleased with the money. To expedite the subscriber's response, a self-addressed envelope and a checklist indicating what other subscribers had done with their subscription money were enclosed.

Persons were also urged to join a Coughlin-sponsored organization called the League of the Little Flower, with the promise that membership contributions would be "used to help Father Coughlin promote his religious activities." The League was simply a revival of an earlier organization dissolved by Father Coughlin in 1928. Its stated purpose was to lead people back to God and thus *Social Justice* subscribers were urged to join and enlist their friends as well.

Father Coughlin also asked former *Social Justice* subscribers to enroll their friends in the League of the Little Flower.[14] He wrote to them that the world was involved in the war as a punishment inflicted by God for its social sins. The United States committed many such social sins: the legality of divorce, the sale of birth control devices and the separation of church and state were cited as examples. Christianity and authoritarianism were to be preferred to democracy with its majoritarianism. Coughlin said, however, that this view was being rejected by too many Americans, and as a result, Americans were suffering. Social penance had to be carried out to avoid God's wrath. This could be done by participating in a novena with him at the Shrine of the Little Flower, beginning September 26 and ending October 4, 1942. Father Coughlin's continued activities were not being overlooked.

On September 27, 1942, *P.M.* accused him of "attempting to resume his writings. But the response to Father Coughlin's pleas must have been poor; there were no further communications from him after October, 1942. Some of his followers were now too busy with the war, while others had become dismayed at his lack of frenzy. It is also possible that Archbishop Mooney ordered a complete halt to his activities.

There can be little doubt that the dominant factor in the silencing of Coughlin was the entry of the United States into World War II. Once the war had begun, the government could not tolerate Coughlin's anti-government propaganda. Involvement in the war eventually brought unity and prosperity to the country and made Coughlin irrelevant to many of his former followers and vulnerable to government actions in a time of crisis. His days as a national figure were over. He was destined to be a simple parish priest.

Adjusting to such a life was not easy for him. Any thought of rising through the Church hierarchy was out of the question; his public activities had made that impossible. Still, from 1942 on, Father Coughlin lived a full life, though it lacked the flamboyancy that characterized his life as a public figure. He did, however, make the news from time to time.

In 1943, a postal clerk, alerted by a ticking noise, discovered a bomb in a package addressed to Father Coughlin. A Newark police captain commented that the bomb was "either a scare bomb or dud . . . prepared by a religious fanatic."[15]

In March, 1944, the columnist Victor Reisel wrote that Father Coughlin had been uttering fiery words from his pulpit, attacking England, Russia and the war effort, and was once again preparing to assume his leadership of the Far Right.[16] On July 13, 1944, *P.M.* said that Coughlin was plotting to assume his public activities at the conclusion of World War II. The newspaper stated that Coughlin had told his plans to Joe McWilliams, the former leader of the Christian Mobilizers, when they met at Father Coughlin's church. At that time, McWilliams was being tried by the government for sedition.

In the spring of 1944, Father Coughlin surprised his worshippers at the Shrine of the Little Flower by declaring that Joseph Stalin had been "an ordained deacon in the Catholic Church." (In fact, Stalin had studied to be a priest in the Greek Orthodox Church.) The priest went on to declare that in the last three years Stalin had moved to wipe out the curse of communism, and he forecast that after the war Stalin would allow religious freedom.[17]

On May 19, 1947, Gerald L. K. Smith's publication, *The Letter*, stated that Father Coughlin had attended and addressed an assemblage celebrating a wedding anniversary of Mr. and Mrs. Dick Richards. Others attending the party were Kim Sigler, governor of Michigan; Eddie Rickenbacker; members of the Fisher family; K. T. Keller, president of Chrysler; and J. Edgar Hoover.

In 1949, Father Coughlin became the center of yet another controversy. Testifying at the income tax evasion case of Dr. Bernard Gariepy, Thomas J. Whitfield, a tax consultant, said that Dr. Gariepy had told him that Father Coughlin had paid him $68,000 in the three-year period from 1942 through 1944 as payment for "taking liberties with Gariepy's wife."[18] Testifying under oath before Federal Judge Frank A. Picard, Coughlin denied ever having paid Gariepy a penny for anything other than professional reasons. Gariepy was later found guilty of evading tax payments.

This was not the first time that questions had arisen about Father

Coughlin's sexual morality. It had been rumored that Father Coughlin, as a young priest, was caught in the act of pederasty with another priest, who was defrocked. But the author could locate only an Anti-Defamation League memo entitled *Structure of Charles E. Coughlin's Organization* to attest to this. The memo was neither signed nor dated and is in itself inadequate evidence.

He continued to say mass every Sunday at his church, attracting from 8,000 to 10,000 worshippers weekly. He stood behind a small pulpit on a balcony, microphone in hand, and addressed his flock. His voice retained its richness and was as electric as it had been when he attracted millions of listeners to his Sunday broadcasts.

Every morning he awakened at 6:30 A.M. and was at his desk by 8:30 A.M. He loved sports and he usually devoted his afternoons to watching the Detroit Tigers, going to the race track or following the fortunes of the Detroit Lions. During the winter, he would head for the warmer climates of Florida, California or Arizona.

In 1966, Father Coughlin celebrated his fiftieth year as a priest. He was praised by Richard Cardinal Cushing as a "man ahead of his time" and a "giant of his generation among the committed priests of America."[19] He was as mentally alert as ever. Physically, he resembled a man of sixty rather than of seventy-five.

But on May 27, 1966, Archbishop John F. Dearden announced that Father Charles E. Coughlin, "acting on his own initiative, requested a meeting today at which he asked to be freed of his responsibilities as pastor of the Shrine of the Little Flower because of impaired health."[20] Archbishop Dearden agreed to "grant Father Coughlin's request" as soon as a successor could be found. A day later Father Coughlin denied his wish to retire but pointed out that "if Archbishop Dearden wants me to retire, I'll leave."[21] Obviously the archbishop so desired. On August 15, 1966, Coughlin left his beloved Shrine of the Little Flower. He is still bitter about his enforced retirement.

Coughlin had accumulated a considerable amount of money from the profits of his corporations and investments. He used some of it to purchase a house in Birmingham, Michigan, close to the residence of George Romney. Every morning he said mass in its lovely chapel. Even in his eighties he still took pleasure in driving his own car.

In 1969, he published a book entitled *Bishops Versus the Pope*, much of which centers on the activities of dissident clergy, whom Coughlin characterizes as "loud-mouthed clerical advocates of arson, riot and draft-card burning. They are swingers who suffer so terribly from an inferiority complex that they reach madly for the brass ring of popular recognition which dangles on the merry-go-round of secularism."[22]

Father Coughlin tries hard to keep abreast of current affairs. He says that he tremendously admires the youth of today, even the Chicago Seven, one of whom, Tom Hayden, had attended the Shrine of the Little Flower elementary school run by Father Coughlin. On the other hand, in the same interview, Father Coughlin said that the man he admires the most on the contemporary scene is Judge Julius H. Hoffman, the presiding judge in the Chicago Seven trial.

In a column that appeared on the Op Ed page of the *New York Times* on January 12, 1972, Father Coughlin voiced his opinion on contemporary domestic problems, a subject which now occupies much of his thought and energy.

Henceforth unrestricted liberties and impolitic freedoms cannot be tolerated; those able and capable of contributing to production and the common welfare will either cooperate with their fellow citizens or be penalized; all indigents, aged, infirm, incapable citizens shall be the common concern of the nation as will be child-orphans.

The present society of libertarian democracy wherein minority rights take precedence over those of the majority must be suppressed, otherwise it will be impossible to establish an operative economy.

Father Coughlin says that he sees Israel as a bulwark against communism. He even purchased $500 worth of Israel bonds on January 6, 1955.[23] But he remains certain that the editorial policies expressed in *Social Justice* concerning the entry of the United States into World War II were correct. He also does not believe that the Jews were singled out as a group for persecution under Nazi rule.

If we had stayed out of the war we could have conquered the conqueror in Europe. We could have joined the decent people of Germany and France and Holland and Belgium and Italy and the rest of those who opposed the persecution of the Christians and the Jews.

We could have starved the victor into submission. We could have punished the victor for having done what he did to Germany, to France, to the Jews, to the Christians. It was the greatest faux pas in the whole history of civilization, from the days of Adam and Eve down to the present.

He has become philosophic and contemplative about his demise as a public figure.

I didn't succeed because I could not get bishops to support me. Bishops with their sanctified collars have been my bane all through my life. I knew the futility of the whole thing. I knew that my days as a prophet had come to an end. My days as a leader had come to an end. I had the whole government against me. I had the whole Church against me and I was under the stricture of obedience from my archbishop. A priest is of no value whatsoever unless he's first of all obedient to his superiors; no more valuable to the Church than is a soldier to his general unless he obeys the orders given to him. Consequently, because my superior, Archbishop Mooney, told me to cease and desist, I obeyed him. Obedience comes before sacrifice and comes long, long before self. Any jackass can be a disobedient servant. But sometimes it takes a little bit of courage to be obedient.

He regrets little of his past:

I am at peace with my own conscience and am serene in the knowledge that those whose opinion I care for have confidence in me.[24]

10

A View from the '70s

FATHER Coughlin, like many men who became public figures, owed his prominence to his abilities and to chance. It was his ability, drive, charisma and well suited voice that ingratiated him at a young age to Bishop Gallagher and enabled him to start his own radio show in 1926. Even then he understood the potential of this untapped medium in communicating with millions of people. He was the first American to utilize the radio to advocate a political, social or economic doctrine. In the early 1930s Roosevelt developed his fireside chats and Hitler and Goebbels spread the Nazi gospel over the airwaves. But Father Coughlin preceded them. As a result of his Sunday broadcasts on the crucial social and economic problems of the day, Father Coughlin attracted a regular nationwide listening audience numbering in the millions by 1930. By the time of the Great Depression, Father Coughlin had been on the radio for three years perfecting his delivery, sharpening his words and developing a sizable following. The depression, resulting in great misfortune for tens of millions of Americans, presented him with the opportunity to become the most powerful figure, outside of government, in the United States in the 1930s.

In the early 1930s, when Coughlin attacked the economic evils of capitalism and the menace of communism, his audience cut across religious lines. He was a trail blazer in a time when most clergymen closed their eyes to the injustice, poverty and frustration of this world, and spoke instead of the joys awaiting true believers in the next. Father Coughlin preached about the problems in this world. Whatever his motives, he addressed himself to the problems of the day. In this sense, he was the forerunner of the concerned clergy who actively participated in the civil rights and student movements of the 1960s and 1970s.

His expressed concern for the plight of the masses, however, is open to question, for his private actions were at considerable variance with his public utterances. He denounced bankers and Wall Street machinations, yet he was a large silver speculator, invested heavily in the stock market, and boasted of his friendships with the most influential bankers in the Detroit area, who, the priest said, still constantly seek his advice on fiscal matters.[1] He denounced those who grew rich from speculative and business ventures, but he himself became wealthy and today still lives in one of the most exclusive areas of suburban Detroit.

Father Coughlin was able to finance his activities through his control of a network of corporations and their boards of directors. His financial manipulations may have been legal, but at the very least, they misled much of the public. He used a tax-exempt church for the headquarters of his profit-seeking corporations. People sent him money on the premise that he was using it for the specific purpose which he announced. For example, he asked for money for the League of the Little Flower and the Radio League of the Little Flower to finance the construction of a new church and to finance his broadcasts. A substantial part of this money was then utilized to purchase real estate, and stocks, provide for a loan for his father, and establish a profit-making corporation which published a newspaper. He organized the political National Union for Social Justice with money that had been contributed by his supporters for the ostensible purpose of performing charitable deeds. Over $99,000 was given the NUSJ by the Radio League. (See the Appendices A-F.) He created the Social Justice Poor Society for the stated purpose of assisting the poor. Yet it never did any such thing nor did he ever mean it to.

The Shrine of the Little Flower Church, Royal Oak, Michigan (Photo by Joyce Marcus)

In the early 1930s, when he was beginning his career as a public figure, Father Coughlin stated his personal philosophy:

Do you know how I would live if I renounced religion and was illogical enough to disbelieve in a life beyond — in the real life? Why, if I threw away and denounced my faith, I would surround myself with the most adroit hi-jackers, learn every trick of the highest banking and stock manipulations, avail myself of the laws under which to hide my own crimes, create a smoke screen to throw into the eyes of men, and — believe me, I would become the world's champion crook. If I didn't believe in religion and in a happy beyond, I would get everything for myself that I could lay my hands on in this world.[2]

Coughlin's attacks on Roosevelt stemmed from his feeling that the President had double-crossed him and had merely used him in the effort to attract his supporters to the New Deal. Coughlin never understood that Roosevelt, as a consummate politician, was doing everything possible to perform the prime function of every political candidate — winning elections. Roosevelt was charming and full of flattery, but it is doubtful that he more than implied to Coughlin that the priest would be one of his close advisers. More likely, it was Coughlin's own inflated ego, coupled with Roosevelt's charm, that led him to believe that he would be a power during the first Roosevelt administration. When he realized that he was merely one of many who could talk to the President, Father Coughlin's feeling of betrayal surfaced and took the form of vituperative criticism of the President, criticism which increased in intensity after the 1936 presidential election.

Although never an astute politician, Father Coughlin realized that the results of the 1936 election proved that the political center and left of center had been preempted by the President and that it would be foolish to compete with him for support on this political spectrum. He thought that the only chance of attaining power was in moving to the Right and later attracting millions of other supporters from the Center and Left who would soon become disenchanted with the failure of Roosevelt's economic policies. In that free, open election in which the electorate turned from him, he was left convinced that only a dictatorship could effectively supplant the imperfections of the democratic political system. He saw Hitler and Mussolini as leaders able to terminate depressions in their countries and as the only leaders to understand the menace of communism. His advocacy of a corporate state would provide the people an alternative to the threats posed by communism, the Jews, Roosevelt and Great Britain.

It was easy for Father Coughlin to change political directions. He had few firm convictions beyond his admiration for strong, dictatorial rule, his hatred of communism and a rather traditional feeling of anti-Semitism which in the early part of the twentieth century was more condoned than criticized by the Church. His early exposure to anti-Semitism in the Church circles in which he had received his training left its mark on him and, perhaps, on many other churchmen as evidenced by their silence when confronted with it.

This early exposure to anti-Semitic views and his later bitterness toward Roosevelt and the men around him, many of whom were Jewish, brought Coughlin's anti-Semitism to the surface. Thus, by the late 1930s it was relatively easy for Coughlin to try to associate the Jews with a worldwide communist revolutionary movement. By this time he knew that Hitler had profited immensely from damning the Jews. He also knew that many Americans were still bitter and frustrated — possibly enough to enable him to recoup what he thought to be his declining appeal if he could show that the Jews were tied in with the communists on the one hand and the international bankers on the other and that the Jews were influencing the decision-making process of governments throughout the world. Undoubtedly, Coughlin was also angry that so many American liberals were sympathetic to the plight of the Jews in Europe, but seemed completely indifferent to the plight of the Church in Spain, Mexico and the Soviet Union.

Although never more than a parish priest in the hierarchy, the support he received in the early years of his public career from his ecclesiastical superior, Bishop Michael Gallagher, enabled him to speak without fear of ecclesiastical retaliation from any American prelate. Only the Pope could order him to be silent. Yet, it was not until Gallagher was replaced by Archbishop Mooney, a man who thoroughly disapproved of Coughlin, that the priest embarked on the most controversial and vitriolic aspect of his career. When Mooney moved against Coughlin, he found himself overruled and embarrassed by the intervention of Vatican officials on behalf of Father Coughlin. Even when Eugenio Pacelli, who vigorously disliked Coughlin, became Pope Pius XII, the priest continued his controversial public career, thus illustrating his influence inside the Vatican. For by this time, Coughlin had impressed on many Church notables that he was the man leading the crusade against communism, the deadly enemy of the Catholic Church. Because of Coughlin's outspoken criticisms of communism, by 1937 the Vatican was willing to tolerate the priest's more virulent attacks against Roosevelt and other well-known figures on the world scene. And more than occasionally, Coughlin's attacks on such individuals could even be viewed by the Vatican as serving notice that no coddling of communists would be tolerated by the Church. Thus, not even Archbishop Mooney could exercise control over the priest until the participation of the United States in World War II and the possibility of a public trial made Coughlin's utterances more of an embarrassment than an asset to the Church.

While many churchmen openly supported Coughlin, most aided him by simply remaining silent and in so doing put the stamp of approval on his activities and, in fact, made it seem to many that he was the spokesman for the Catholic Church in the United States.

What were the results of Father Coughlin's activities? In a time of great frustration, he spawned discord, hate and violence. Using his tremendous energy and great talents, he achieved a position from which he was able to disseminate his credo to millions and destroy the confidence of men in their countrymen and arouse them against one another. He was a propagandist on behalf of fascism. He weakened the will and numbed the understanding of millions of Americans. What made his pronouncements even more dangerous was that his diatribes were delivered under the guise of religion and piety. He was a man of the cloth, but he stands as an illustration of how bigotry can emanate from religion. He used the media successfully and his bluster frightened many people. Powerful men in government and in the Church feared him because they assumed his following was larger than it actually was. Thus, many good people stood by and said nothing — a precedent that was followed in the McCarthy era. Father Coughlin's success provides evidence that the power a man is thought to wield may be more potent than the power he actually does wield.

An analysis of his career can help trace the ideological antecedents of McCarthyism in the 1950s and the radical Left and radical Right of the 1960s and early 1970s. They, too, shared a strong belief that the federal government was not dealing properly with the internal and external problems facing this country. Coughlin, McCarthy, those on the radical Left and radical Right, realized that democracy ends when the persecution of minorities and the suspension of individual rights begin. Toward that end they represented a threat to the political stability and the continuation of a cohesive democratic society in the United States.

One Sunday afternoon, not long ago, my family and I had dinner with Father Coughlin at his magnificent home. His love of children was evident as he fussed over Beth and Jonathan, telling her of her beauty and him of the latest baseball news. During the fascinating conversation with the priest, a time during which he radiated warmth, charm and energy, one could easily understand what is meant by "charisma."

Prompted by his expressed concern for improving the lot of the workingman, my wife asked if he had been a socialist. "My God, no!" was his reply. In discussing the youth of today, he had these words to say:

I have sympathy for the young people of this nation. Why should they be packed up and sent to war in Korea or Viet Nam with no hope of winning? We are not even trying to win. No one on the face of the earth has ever won a defensive war. War is won by taking the offensive. All we are doing is waiting for these guerrillas to attack us. And we call that war; that's not war, that's slaughter. . . . Why should our young men go over there? — If I were forty years younger I would be out there leading today's youth.[3]

Today, as he looks back on his life he has few regrets for his past activities. "If I had to do it all over again, I would do it the same way."

The parish school that Coughlin built is still open. The school yard rings with sounds of children at play as the elderly priest watches them from his parked car. His gaze wanders across the street. There, on Woodward Avenue and Twelve Mile Road, stands a house of God. It stands as an architectural jewel nestled in the clasp of Progress. It stands as a monument to its creator. If Father Coughlin's legacy to mankind is one of discord and hate this, at least, is a gift of beauty.

The basement of his beloved Shrine of the Little Flower where his employees worked has been converted into a nursery school. The tower of the church, which served as his center of operations, is in a state of demise and decay. The office, from which he delivered most of his broadcasts, is covered with the feathers and droppings of pigeons that make their home in the crevices of the room's broken windows. Coughlin's adjoining private bathroom bears the same legacy of time — the shower, sink and toilet bowl rusted, with their waters flowing orange rot.

Here, amidst the fallen plaster of the tower, one hears echoes of the past, and the musty smell of things long dead permeates the air.

Sometimes it is difficult to tell the difference between heroes and villains. Sometimes it is difficult to perceive the evil cloaked in righteousness.

Perhaps, after all, the means a nation uses in achieving the ends she strives for are the ends in themselves.

CHAPTER NOTES

BIBLIOGRAPHY

Chapter Notes

1. INTRODUCTION

1. *Iron Age*, CXXX (1932), p. 31; *Historical Statistics of the United States*, p. 379; Sidney Leuchtenberg, *Franklin D. Roosevelt and the New Deal, 1932–1940*, pp. 1–17; H. C. Allen, *The United States of America*, pp. 224–228.

2. Gary T. Marx, in *The Social Basis of the Support of a Depression Era Extremist: Father Coughlin*, p. 119, estimates that Coughlin's listening audience was three and one-half million people. Charles Tull, in *Father Coughlin and the New Deal*, p. 20, estimates the Coughlin listening audience at thirty million. Father Coughlin in an interview with the author estimated it at forty-five million.

3. Interview with Father Edward Clark, Chaplain of Fordham University, November 14, 1969.

4. Interview with Manny Makufka, May 1, 1970.

5. Interview with Dr. Harry N. Rivlin, March 1, 1970. Dr. Rivlin was present at the rally.

6. Interview with John Constable, April 15, 1970.

7. Statement of Receipts and Disbursements and Assets and Liabilities, of the Radio League of the Little Flower, Year Ended September 30, 1939. Father Flanagan made the $100 contribution on August 11, 1939.

2. EARLY LIFE

1. Interview with Father Coughlin, April 11, 1970.

2. *Detroit Times*, April 9, 1933.

3. Interview with Father Coughlin, April 11, 1970.

4. Earlier pro-Coughlin biographies by Louis Ward, *Father Coughlin: An Authorized Biography*, and Ruth Mugglebee, *Father Coughlin of the Shrine of the Little Flower*, attributed his year in Texas to poor health, but did not specify what illness affected him. If he was ill, it certainly did not deter him from continuing his participation in athletics.

5. Interview with Father Coughlin, April 11, 1970.

6. *Ibid.*

7. Memorandum from Malone Prevost to the *Detroit Free Press*, March 28, 1933.

8. Interview with Father Coughlin, April 11, 1970.

9. Mugglebee, p. 155.

10. *Ibid.*

11. *Ibid.*

12. Interview with Father Coughlin, April 11, 1970.

13. Mugglebee, p. 160.

14. *Detroit News*, November 15, 1936.
15. Mugglebee, pp. 162–163.
16. Interview with Father Coughlin, April 11, 1970.

3. GROWING FAME

1. Interview with Father Coughlin, April 11, 1970.
2. *Detroit Free Press*, January 17, 1927.
3. *Ibid.*
4. Interview with Father Coughlin, April 11, 1970.
5. *Ibid.*
6. *Ibid.*
7. *Detroit News*, June 5, 1966.
8. Interview with Father Coughlin, April 11, 1970.
9. *Ibid.*
10. Ruth Mugglebee, *Father Coughlin of the Shrine of the Little Flower*, p. 183.
11. *Ibid.*, p. 186.
12. *Detroit Free Press*, July 26, 1930.
13. Interview with Father Coughlin, April 11, 1970.
14. Mugglebee, p. 210; Interview with Father Coughlin, April 11, 1970.
15. Interview with Father Coughlin, April 11, 1970.
16. Louis Ward, *Father Coughlin: An Authorized Biography*, pp. 33–86. Ward, in his adoring pro-Coughlin biography, claimed that 1,250,000 letters were received by the priest (p. 86). A spokesman for CBS, who wished to remain anonymous, informed me that Father Coughlin's claims were supported by totally inaccurate statistics.
17. As quoted in Ward, pp. 86–87.
18. *New York Times*, March 21, 22, 1934. This was admitted by NBC President Merlin Ayesworth in testimony before the House Merchant Marine and Fisheries Committee.
19. Interview with Father Coughlin, April 11, 1970.
20. Ward, pp. 97–98.
21. Father Charles E. Coughlin, *Radio Discourses, 1931–1932*, p. 19.
22. Interview with Father Coughlin, April 11, 1970; Ward, pp. 20–21.
23. *Detroit News*, December 2, 1931.
24. Coughlin, *Radio Discourses*, pp. 149–153; *Detroit News*, April 12, 1932.
25. Interview with Father Coughlin, April 11, 1970.
26. *Detroit News*, April 12, 1932.
27. *New York Times*, June 10, 1932, and August 10, 1932.
28. *Detroit Free Press*, April 14, 1932.
29. *The Pilot*, April 18, 1932.
30. Ward, pp. 269–270.
31. *Ibid.*
32. *Detroit News*, December 10, 1934.
33. Mugglebee, pp. 239–243.
34. *Detroit News*, May 22, 1932.
35. Interview with Father Coughlin, April 11, 1970.

4. HIGH FINANCE

1. G. Hall Roosevelt to Franklin D. Roosevelt, May 5, 1931, Roosevelt Papers.

2. Interview with Father Coughlin, April 11, 1970.

3. *Ibid.*

4. *Ibid.; Detroit News*, July 11, 1936.

5. Interview with Father Coughlin, April 11, 1970.

6. Father Coughlin to Franklin Delano Roosevelt, August 12, 1932, Roosevelt Papers.

7. Roosevelt to Coughlin, August 21, 1932, Roosevelt Papers.

8. Coughlin to Roosevelt, September 16, 1932, Roosevelt Papers.

9. Louis Ward, *Father Coughlin: An Authorized Biography*, p. 113.

10. Interview with Father Coughlin, April 11, 1970.

11. Rexford Guy Tugwell, *The Democratic Roosevelt*, p. 350.

12. Eleanor Roosevelt to Charles Tull, March 16, 1960.

13. Interview with Father Coughlin, April 11, 1970.

14. Telephone conversation with James Farley, February 26, 1970; Eleanor Roosevelt to Charles Tull, March 16, 1960; Raymond Moley to Charles Tull, March 17, 1960.

15. Interview with Father Coughlin, April 12, 1970.

16. Memo for Marvin McIntyre, March 23, 1933, Roosevelt Papers.

17. Ward, p. 177.

18. Interview with Father Coughlin, April 11, 1970.

19. Marvin McIntyre to Louis Howe, March 27, 1933, Roosevelt Papers.

20. *Detroit Free Press*, March 29, 1933.

21. *Ibid.*

22. Ward, p. 211.

23. Fred Cook to Marvin McIntyre, April 6, 1933, Roosevelt Papers.

24. *Articles of Association, League of the Little Flower*, January 10, 1928, p. 1.

25. Amy Collins to John S. Haggerty, Michigan secretary of state, July 29, 1930.

26. *1930 Annual Report, League of the Little Flower*, p. 2. For a more complete financial picture of the corporation, see Appendix A.

27. William L. Slattery to James Farley, March 19, 1935, Roosevelt Papers.

28. For more detailed financial information, see Appendices A-G.

29. Father Coughlin to Jesse Jones, June 30, 1933; Father Coughlin to William Julian, June 30, 1933, Roosevelt Papers.

30. Father Coughlin to Marvin McIntyre, June 30, 1933, Roosevelt Papers.

31. Letter from an unidentified individual to Miss Margaret Lehand, March 23, 1934, Roosevelt Papers.

32. *Detroit News*, August 24, 1933.

33. *Ibid.*, August 25, 1933.

34. *Detroit Free Press*, September 7, 1933.

35. Telephone conversation with James Farley, February 26, 1970.

36. Franklin Roosevelt to Father Coughlin, July 11, 1933, Roosevelt Papers.

37. Father Coughlin to Franklin Roosevelt, July 21, 1933, Roosevelt Papers.

38. Franklin Roosevelt to Marvin McIntyre, August 7, 1933, Roosevelt Papers.

39. Marvin McIntyre to Father Coughlin, August, 1933, Roosevelt Papers.

40. Steve Early to Father Coughlin, September 22, 1933, Roosevelt Papers.

41. Interview with Father Coughlin, April 12, 1970.

42. Father Coughlin to Franklin Roosevelt, August 5, 1933, Roosevelt Papers.

43. Father Coughlin to Marvin McIntyre, September 22, 1933, Roosevelt Papers; Father Coughlin to Franklin Roosevelt, September 23, 1933, Roosevelt Papers.

44. Father Coughlin to Marvin McIntyre, August 12, 1933, Roosevelt Papers.

45. Father Coughlin to Franklin Roosevelt, September 24, 1933, Roosevelt Papers.

46. Interview with Father Joseph Fitzpatrick, S.J., Chairman Sociology Department, Fordham University, November 3, 1970.

47. Memo for Marvin McIntyre, November 23, 1933, Roosevelt Papers.

48. Telephone conversation with James Farley, February 26, 1970.

49. Father Coughlin to Franklin Roosevelt, November 24, 1933, Roosevelt Papers.

50. *Detroit News*, November 29, 1933.

51. *New York Times*, November 29, 1933.

52. *Ibid.*, December 3, 1933.

53. *Ibid.*

54. Interview with Father Coughlin, April 11, 1970.

55. *Detroit News*, January 5, 1934.

56. *Ibid.*, January 15, 1934.

57. *Ibid.*, January 17, 1934.

58. Interview with Father Coughlin, April 11, 1970.

59. *Detroit News*, February 5, 1934.

60. Interview with Father Coughlin, April 12, 1970.

61. *Detroit News*, April 16, 1934.

62. Interview with Father Coughlin, April 12, 1970.

63. *Detroit Free Press*, April 29, 1934.

64. *Ibid.*; *Cleveland Press*, May 2, 1934.

65. Interview with Father Coughlin, April 12, 1970.

66. *Ibid.*

5. ENTERING POLITICS: THE NATIONAL UNION FOR SOCIAL JUSTICE

1. Charles E. Coughlin, *A Series of Lectures*, p. 16.

2. *Ibid.*, pp. 17–18. A shortened version of these principles was to appear on the editorial page of virtually every issue of *Social Justice*. (See Appendix J).

3. Interview with Father Coughlin, April 11, 1970. Father Coughlin still feels so strongly about the sixteen principles that his only request concerning the preparation of this biography was that the author mention how vital he regarded these principles and that they be reproduced in the book.

4. Ruth Mugglebee, *Father Coughlin of the Shrine of the Little Flower*, p. 335.

5. *Ibid.*, p. 21.

6. *Ibid.*

7. *Ibid.*, p. 80.

8. Charles E. Coughlin, *Money, Questions and Answers*, p. 16.

9. Coughlin, *A Series of Lectures*, pp. 43–45.

10. *New Republic*, April 24, 1935, p. 300.

11. *Detroit News*, December 17, 1934.

12. From an address by Rabbi Ferdinand M. Isserman of Temple Israel, St. Louis, Missouri, at an NUSJ meeting in Detroit, April 24, 1935.

13. *Articles of Association, National Union for Social Justice*, December 11, 1934.

14. Father Coughlin to John M. Feigh, January 25, 1935.

15. Interview with Father Coughlin, April 11, 1970.

16. *New York Times*, April 21, 1936. *Articles of Association, Radio League of the Little Flower*, August 9, 1930, p. 1.

17. *New York Times*, June 23, 1935.

18. Coughlin, *A Series of Lectures*, January 27, 1935.

19. *Ibid.*, p. 125.

20. Mugglebee, p. 341.

21. Phone conversation with James Farley, March 9, 1970.

22. Interview with Father Coughlin, April 11, 1970; T. Harry Williams, *Huey Long*, p. 801; Mrs. Jean Perrin Donahue in an interview with the author, January 27, 1970. Mrs. Donahue is the daughter of the editor of *Social Justice*, E. Perrin Schwartz. She also wrote a number of articles for the journal.

23. Benjamin Stolberg, "Dr. Huey and Mr. Long," *Nation*, September 25, 1935, p. 344.

24. Interview with Father Coughlin, April 11, 1970.

25. Gerald L. K. Smith to the author, February 16, 1970.

26. *Detroit Free Press*, May 13, 1935.

27. *Detroit Times*, September 9, 1935.

28. Interview with Father Coughlin, April 11, 1970.

29. *Ibid.*

30. Coughlin, *A Series of Lectures*, pp. 193–196.

31. *New York Times*, March 5, 1935.

32. "Clergy and Politics," *Commonweal*, March 22, 1935, pp. 579–580.

33. *Detroit News*, March 8, 1935.

34. *Ibid.*

35. *Ibid.*, March 12, 1935.

36. *Ibid.*

37. *New York Times*, March 12, 1935.

38. *Ibid.*

39. *Ibid.*, March 31, 1935.

40. *Detroit News*, March 31, 1935.

41. *Ibid.*, April 23, 1935.

42. Interview with Father Coughlin, April 12, 1970.

43. James Farley, *Jim Farley's Story*, p. 52.

44. Interview with Father Coughlin, April 11, 1970.

45. *Ibid.*, April 12, 1970.
46. *Detroit News*, April 22, 1935.
47. *Ibid.*, April 25, 1935.
48. *New York Times*, May 15, 1935.
49. *Detroit News*, May 8, 1935.
50. *Ibid.*, May 23, 1935; Interview with Father Coughlin, April 11, 1970.
51. Interview with Father Coughlin, April 11, 1970; *Detroit News*, June 3, 1935.
52. *Detroit Times*, May 29, 1935.
53. *Detroit News*, August 12, 1935.
54. *Ibid.*, September 10, 1935.
55. Interview with Father Coughlin, April 11, 1970.
56. *Ibid.*
57. *Ibid.*
58. *Ibid.*
59. *Ibid.*

6. THE ELECTION OF 1936

1. *Detroit News*, September 15, 1935.
2. *Ibid.*, September 22, 1935.
3. *New York Times*, November 4, 1933.
4. Interview with Father Coughlin, April 11, 1970.
5. *Detroit News*, December 23, 1935.
6. Gerald L. K. Smith to the author, February 6, 1970.
7. H. L. Mencken, "Why Not Gerald?," *Baltimore Evening Sun*, September 7, 1936.
8. Interview with Father Coughlin, April 11, 1970.
9. *New York Times*, January 6, 1936.
10. Interview with Father Coughlin, April 11, 1970.
11. *Detroit News*, February 23, 1936.
12. Interview with Father Coughlin, April 11, 1970.
13. *Social Justice*, March 13, 1936.
14. General Records of the Department of State from the Decimal Files, 1930–1944, relating to Father Charles E. Coughlin, RG59 500 C 114 1627. Dispatch dated February 21, 1935.
15. Memo from files of Marvin McIntyre, January 18, 1936, Roosevelt Papers.
16. Interview with Father Coughlin, April 11, 1970.
17. *New York Times*, February 17, 1936.
18. *Ibid.*, February 18, 1936.
19. *Social Justice*, March 13, 1936.
20. *Ibid.*, May 29, 1936.
21. Interview with Father Coughlin, April 11, 1970.
22. *Ibid.*
23. *Social Justice*, April 24, 1936.
24. *Ibid.*, June 29, 1936.
25. Phone conversation with James Farley, March 9, 1970.

26. *Social Justice*, June 22, 1950.
27. *Detroit Free Press*, June 17, 1936.
28. *New York World Telegram*, June 20, 1936.
29. Gerald L. K. Smith to the author, February 6, 1970.
30. Interview with Father Coughlin, April 11, 1970.
31. *Ibid.*
32. Gerald L. K. Smith to the author, February 17, 1970. Townsend was later cited for contempt of Congress and was sentenced to thirty days in jail. He was pardoned by President Roosevelt in March, 1937, just prior to the time he was to start serving his sentence.
33. H. L. Mencken, "Why Not Gerald?," *Baltimore Evening Sun*, September 7, 1936.
34. *Detroit News*, July 16, 1936.
35. *Ibid.*, July 17, 1936.
36. *New York Times*, July 21, 1936.
37. *Detroit News*, June 23, 1936.
38. *Ibid.*, July 18, 1936.
39. *Ibid.*, July 23, 1936.
40. *Ibid.*, July 25, 1936.
41. Interview with Father Coughlin, April 11, 1970.
42. *Ibid.*
43. *New York Times*, July 25, 1936.
44. *Detroit News*, July 26, 1936.
45. *Ibid.*, July 27, 1936.
46. *Detroit Free Press*, August 13, 1936.
47. Interview with Father Coughlin, April 12, 1970.
48. *Detroit Free Press*, August 17, 1936, estimated the crowd at 25,000. Charles Tull in *Father Coughlin and the New Deal* estimated the crowd at 42,000.
49. *Detroit Free Press*, August 17, 1936.
50. *Ibid.*
51. *New York Times*, August 18, 1936.
52. *Detroit News*, August 17, 1936.
53. *Ibid.*
54. See Chapter 7 for further details on the activities of Pelley and Jung.
55. *Detroit Free Press*, August 28, 1936.
56. *Detroit News*, August 28, 1936.
57. *Detroit Jewish Chronicle*, August 21, 1936.
58. *Detroit News*, August 28, 1936.
59. *Detroit Jewish Chronicle*, August 21, 1936.
60. *New York Times*, September 3, 1936.
61. *Newsweek*, September 12, 1936.
62. Interview with Philip Johnson, October 21, 1970.
63. *Detroit News*, September 13, 1936; *New York Times*, September 14, 1936.
64. *Detroit News*, September 23, 1936.
65. Interview with Father Coughlin, April 11, 1970.
66. *Ibid.*
67. *Ibid.*

68. Gerald L. K. Smith to the author, December 12, 1969, and February 6, 1970.

69. Interview with Father Coughlin, April 11, 1970.

70. *Detroit Free Press*, October 9, 1936.

71. *Ibid.*, October 14, 1936.

72. *Ibid.*, October 17, 1936.

73. *Detroit Times*, October 17, 1936.

74. *Detroit News*, October 18, 1936.

75. Affidavit from Richard Lobenthal and Annette Ron, May 25, 1970. The permit was issued by the Royal Oak Police Department.

76. *New York Times*, October 18, 1936.

77. *Detroit Free Press*, November 1, 1936.

78. *Detroit News*, November 2, 1936.

79. James Farley to Franklin Roosevelt, November 2, 1936, Roosevelt Papers.

80. Interview with Father Coughlin, April 11, 1970.

81. *Ibid.*

82. *Social Justice*, November 16, 1936.

83. Interview with Father Coughlin, April 11, 1970.

7. THE RETURN TO ACTION

1. *Social Justice*, February 1, 1937.

2. Interview with Father Coughlin, April 11, 1970. Mooney was designated a cardinal on December 23, 1945.

3. *Ibid.*

4. *Detroit News*, October 10, 1937.

5. *Ibid.*, November 8, 1937. In a phone conversation the author had with Mr. Semmes in April, 1968, he said that he did not remember who had drafted the letter.

6. Phone conversation with E. Prewitt Semmes, April, 1968.

7. *New York Times*, October 10, 1937.

8. *Ibid.*, November 23, 1937.

9. Phone conversation with E. Prewitt Semmes, April, 1968.

10. *New York Times*, December 5, 1937.

11. Interview with Father Coughlin, April 11, 1970.

12. *Detroit News*, April 23, 1945.

13. Donald Strong, *Organized Anti-Semitism in America: The Rise of Group Prejudice*, 1939-1940, p. 14.

14. William Dudley Pelley, *The Door to Revelation*, p. 1. Pelley's views are clearly stated in some of his other books: *Editorials by Pelley*, published in 1936 in *Pelley's Weekly*, and *No More Hunger*.

15. United States Congress, *Investigation of Nazi and Other Propaganda*. House Report 153, 74th Congress, First Session, hereafter referred to as *McCormack Hearings*. June 7, 1934, pp. 281-283.

16. O. John Rogge, *The Official German Report*, pp. 192-194. Rogge was Assistant United States Attorney General, 1942-1943. He had access to classified files which he utilized in his book.

17. *Pelley's Weekly*, November 18, 1936.
18. *Liberation*, December 30, 1933.
19. *Pelley's Weekly*, November 18, 1936.
20. *Liberation*, June 14, 1938.
21. *Ibid.*, June 21, 1938.
22. *Defender*, August, 1935. For more information on Winrod's views, refer to the following books by him: *Adam Weishaupt, A Human Devil*; *Europe at This Moment*; *Hitler in Prophecy*; *The Present International Crisis*; *The Truth about the Protocols*.
23. *Ibid.*, September, 1935.
24. Rogge, p. 216. Miss Dilling's views of the Jewish-communist menace to this country can also be noted in *The Roosevelt Red Menace and Its Background*.
25. *McCormack Hearings*, pp. 5–8.
26. *The International Jew* was a compilation of articles that appeared in the *Dearborn Independent*. The first published version of the "Protocols" appeared in serial form between August 28, 1903, and September 7, 1903, in a newspaper called *Moldavanian*, published by the czarist Russian minister Kruschevan, who had organized a pogrom against Jews in Kishinev that same year.

V. L. Burtzev, a Russian historian and an expert in the workings of the czar's secret police and Russian revolutionary organizations, stated unequivocally that the "Protocols" were a forgery drawn up by the secret police of Czar Nicholas II. Research bears this out. The "Protocols" first appeared in book form in 1905 in Sergei Nilus's *The Great and the Small and the Anti Christ as a Near Political Possibility*, which told of a secret session of the Jewish Zionist Congress held in Basel, Switzerland, in 1897, to plan a Jewish take-over of the world. According to Nilus, a czarist spy, present at the Congress, smuggled out a copy of what transpired at this secret meeting. This is nonsense. Actually the real basis for Nilus's thesis was predicted in an essay written in 1864 by a French lawyer, Maurice Joly, called *Dialogue in Hell Between Machiavelli and Montesquieu*, a copy of which is available in the Royal Library of Brussels. In writing this book, Joly hoped to ridicule the regime of Napoleon III.

A comparison of the "Protocols" and *Dialogue* shows that the "Protocols" are a copy of *Dialogue*, with some additional clumsy reediting. In 1919, the "Protocols" were issued in a German edition called *The Secrets of the Wise Men of Zion* and within a few years, editions appeared in Poland, France, England, Italy, and the United States.

These facts are recounted by Father Michael Ahern in *The Pilot*, a Catholic weekly of the Boston archdiocese, on October 23, 1938, pp. 1–10, and by Philip Slomovitz in *Social Justice*, September 26, 1938, pp. 10–11. Slomovitz was editor of the *Detroit Jewish Chronicle* and is now the publisher and editor of the *Detroit Jewish News*. Father Coughlin gave Slomovitz the opportunity to reply to the publication of the "Protocols," in *Social Justice*.

27. *History and Organization of the German-American Bund*, State of New York, Joint Legislative Committee, 1939 Legislative Document No. 98, p. 306.
28. *Ibid.*, pp. 227–228.
29. Rogge, pp. 176–178, 182–184.
30. *Anti-Nazi Bulletin*, July, August, 1944.

31. Strong, p. 196.
32. Gustavus Myers, *History of Bigotry in the United States*, pp. 416–417.
33. Rogge, pp. 204–207. See the following publications by Edmondson for more information about his views: his monthly publication *X-Ray, Move to Destroy Free Speech*, and *The Edmondson Case: Jews vs. Christians in Court*.
34. At the time, copies of this circular could be purchased for one cent each by writing to Edmondson.
35. Rogge, p. 487. Sanctuary was a prolific writer. He wrote the following books, after Hitler's rise to power: *An Answer to the Voice for Human Rights*; *Alfred E. Smith*; *A Foundation of Sand*; *Revolution and the Real Fifth Column*; *Roosevelt Warming the Serpent*; *War Guilt and War Mongers*.
36. *Social Justice*, December 12, 1939.
37. *Ibid.*, June 13, 1938.
38. *Ibid.*, July 25, 1938.
39. Phone conversation with Elliott Shapiro, September 18, 1970.
40. Harold Tietz to Father Coughlin, July 10, 1939.
41. Father Coughlin to Harold Tietz, August 3, 1939.
42. James Wechsler, "The Coughlin Terror," *Nation*, July 22, 1939.
43. *Voice for Human Rights*, September, 1939.
44. *New York Times*, September 26, 1939.
45. *Ibid.*, September 4, 1939.
46. *Commonweal*, January 26, 1940, p. 293.
47. Memorandum from J. Edgar Hoover to Attorney General Jackson, January 25, 1940.
48. Charles E. Coughlin, *Am I an Anti-Semite?*, pp. 35, 37.
49. *New York Times*, November 27, 1938.
50. *Detroit News*, December 4, 1938.
51. *Ibid.*, December 12, 1938; Radio Address by Frank J. Hogan, "An American Catholic Speaks on Intolerance," December 11, 1938.
52. *Detroit Jewish Chronicle*, December 16, 1938. Cardinal Mundelein's statement was read over NBC by Bishop Bernard J. Sheil, Vicar General and Senior Auxiliary Bishop of Chicago.
53. Monsignor John Ryan, "Anti-Semitism on the Air," *Commonweal*, December 30, 1938, p. 261; George Shuster, "The Jew and Two Revolutions," *Commonweal*, December 30, 1938, p. 262.
54. *Detroit Jewish Chronicle*, December 17, 1938.
55. *Detroit News*, November 27, 1938.
56. *Detroit Jewish Chronicle*, December 16, 1938.
57. Rev. William Kernan, *The Ghost of Royal Oak*, p. 22.
58. Coughlin, *Am I an Anti-Semite?*, p. 71. From his broadcast of December 4, 1938.
59. Father Coughlin to Lecia M. Paas, December 27, 1938.
60. Letter from unknown person to Father Coughlin, December 28, 1938.
61. Richard A. Mann to WJJD, November 27, 1938.
62. Coughlin, *Am I an Anti-Semite?*, from a December 4, 1938, broadcast.
63. *Am I an Anti-Semite?*, pp. 86–87.
64. Keith Sward, *The Legend of Henry Ford*, p. 456.
65. Interview with Father Coughlin, April 11, 1970.
66. *Detroit News*, January 9, 1939.
67. *Detroit Times*, March 3, 1939.

68. *Detroit News*, March 6, 1939.
69. Interview with Father Coughlin, April 11, 1970.
70. *Detroit News*, January 17, 1939.
71. *Ibid.*, February 13, 1939.
72. *Ibid.*, February 26, 1939.
73. Address entitled "Hitler's Hatchet Man," by the Reverend Father James R. Cox of Old 'St. Patrick's Catholic Church, delivered before the Dormont Rotary Club in the Dormont Methodist Episcopal Church.
74. Interview with Father Coughlin, April 12, 1970.
75. *An Answer to Father Coughlin's Critics*, p. 128.
76. *Detroit Times*, June 5, 1939. These constant squabbles were having their physical and emotional effects on Coughlin. His efforts had resulted in "the strain on my nerves and strength taxed doubly this year." (Letter from Father Coughlin to *Social Justice* subscriber, June 6, 1939.)
77. On April 15, 1967, a priest who wished to remain anonymous told the author that he had been outside Cardinal Hayes's office when he held a meeting with Father Coughlin in the late 1930s. The priest maintains that he clearly heard Coughlin yelling and using foul language which was directed toward the cardinal. The cardinal did not respond in kind.
78. Father Edward Lodge Curran, *A Reply to Elliott Roosevelt*. No publisher was noted for this publication but Father Coughlin had the copyright to it.
79. *Detroit News*, July 17, 1939.
80. *New York Times*, August 17, 1939.
81. Letter from Frank X. Martel to Martin A. Sillmon, editor of the *St. Louis Union Labor Advocate*, July 10, 1939.
82. *Detroit News*, August 28, 1939.
83. *Ibid.*, September 4, 1939, September 11, 1939.
84. *Ibid.*, October 4, 1939.
85. *Ibid.*, October 5, 1939.
86. Father Coughlin to J. H. Williams, March 28, 1940.
87. V. Robinson, an employee of the Social Justice Publishing Company, to F. Gordoni, October 21, 1940.
88. Distributed at a meeting of Social Justice Distributors. December 5, 1940.
89. *New York Times*, May 19, 1940.
90. Interview with Father Coughlin, April 11, 1970.
91. *Detroit News*, August 27, 1940.
92. Interview with Father Coughlin, April 11, 1970.

8. *SOCIAL JUSTICE*

1. Interview with Father Coughlin, April 11, 1970. *Social Justice* was published by the Social Justice Publishing Company, which in turn was owned by the Radio League of the Little Flower. During 1938 and 1939, the Social Justice Poor Society listed ownership of the only ten shares of stock issued by the Social Justice Publishing Company. The Social Justice Poor Society was also owned by the Radio League of the Little Flower.

Father Coughlin, in the midst of his controversy with Archbishop

Mooney over the contents of *Social Justice*, tried to ensure his control over the journal by forming the Social Justice Poor Society on December 22, 1937. The names of the incorporators were Ben Beckham, Jr., Josephine Arnold and Elva Bleach, all of whom were associated with the law firm of E. Prewitt Semmes. The purpose of the corporation was to perform charitable works. The corporation was to be financed by voluntary contributions and dues from members. Only the board of trustees, which consisted of Father Coughlin, Eugenia Burke and Marie Rhodes, had the power to make, alter, amend or repeal the corporation bylaws. The corporation's address was Father Coughlin's parish church.

An examination of financial statements of the Social Justice Poor Society does not indicate that any charitable works were ever performed. The 1938 Annual Report listed no assets and no liabilities. This was puzzling in view of the fact that the Social Justice Poor Society had listed $1,000 in assets as of December 22, 1937, although in a report stating the company's assets as of December 31, 1937, no assets were listed. Further investigation, however, reveals that there was an amended Annual Statement filed on July 11, 1939, for the Social Justice Poor Society, which listed as an asset ownership of all the outstanding stock of the Social Justice Publishing Company, which had assets valued at $1,000. The 1939 Annual Report continued to list as an asset ownership of all the outstanding shares in the Social Justice Publishing Company. After tentative peace was established between Father Coughlin and Archbishop Mooney, the existence of the Social Justice Poor Society was terminated on August 30, 1940.

When formed in 1936, the Social Justice Publishing Company was a profit-making organization, which issued ten shares of no-par stock to finance its endeavors. Each share had a par value of one hundred dollars and all shares were owned by Charles E. Coughlin. In February, 1936, the Social Justice Publishing Company was in debt to the Radio League of the Little Flower for the sum of $116,528.88. During the year ending September 30, 1936, the Radio League of the Little Flower gave $1,000 to the Social Justice Publishing Company. This sum was the total par value of the stock issued by the Social Justice Publishing Company. Thus, Father Coughlin was president of the Radio League of the Little Flower at the same time that he was president and sole owner of the Social Justice Publishing Company. In this manner, he was able to take money donated to a nonprofit organization and use it to take personal control of the Social Justice Publishing Company.

2. Through the July 20, 1936, issue, *Social Justice* resembled a standard newspaper, with four columns to each of its sixteen pages. With the July 27, 1936, issue the journal carried five columns on each of its sixteen pages, although the size of the page remained constant. With the February 28, 1938, issue the journal appeared with a new, more attractive format. It had a colorful picture of an important person on its front page, along with a small picture of Father Coughlin. The journal now published articles with by-lines. The quality of the paper stock was superior; the pages were stitched together; and the size of the printing type was larger, giving *Social Justice* the overall appearance of a *Life* magazine rather than a newspaper. The number of pages was increased from sixteen to twenty.

The May 2, 1938, issue of *Social Justice* was not published, a fact Father Coughlin attributed to "publication difficulties." Morris Steinberg, president and treasurer of Morris Press, which was printing this attractive version of *Social Justice*, said that the priest had told him that the printing of the magazine was costing too much money and that its publication would have to be discontinued. Steinberg knew that the circulation of *Social Justice* was declining, but he was upset when he discovered that Coughlin was negotiating with Cuneo Press, the original printers of the journal, to resume publication. Coughlin told Steinberg that he could no longer honor the contract he had signed with Morris Press on February 23, 1938, to print the magazine. On the basis of this contract Steinberg had spent a considerable amount of money on expanding plant facilities and in hiring additional employees. Faced with financial ruin, Steinberg brought a $200,000 suit against Coughlin for breach of contract. Coughlin's Social Justice Publishing Company promptly filed a countersuit for $200,000 against Steinberg, also for breach of contract. The legal wrangle that followed was finally settled when the Social Justice Publishing Company agreed to pay the Morris Press $12,500.

The May 9, 1938, issue, printed by Cuneo Press, utilized the less expensive paper used prior to the March 1, 1938, issue. This less expensive paper was used until the demise of the journal. The number of pages was increased to twenty-four, although by September 5, 1938, *Social Justice* contained only twenty pages.

Beginning with the March 11, 1940, issue, the number of columns was reduced from five to four per page, and Father Coughlin's name no longer appeared on page one. With the April 8, 1940, issue, the number of columns per page was three and the print was much larger than previously. Each column was headed with the word "Comment." By this time articles with the names of their authors ceased to appear in the journal.

On May 20, 1940, Father Coughlin's name appeared above "A Page of Comment," but by the following week his name did not appear over this column. Father Coughlin's name never again appeared above articles in *Social Justice*. The use of a three-column page continued until the demise of the journal. Although his name did not appear as the author of articles, he did write for the journal, which continued to laud his activities. The March 30, 1942, edition of the journal contained only sixteen pages. This remained the length of the journal until its expiration.

3. John L. Spivak, "Coughlin's Frenzied Finances," *New Masses*, XXXIII, November 28, 1939, p. 6.

An examination of the changing masthead of *Social Justice* is an excellent indicator of Father Coughlin's relations with his Church superior. When the journal was published in 1936, and Bishop Gallagher was alive, the masthead of the journal described it as "Father Coughlin's Weekly Review." Father Coughlin was also listed as editor and publisher. When Archbishop Mooney and Father Coughlin were in the midst of their dispute, the masthead changed. The November 1, 1937, issue of *Social Justice* stated that the journal printed "The Suppressed Truth." Even when it seemed that the dispute between them had been resolved, the archbishop must have asserted his authority over Coughlin to a certain degree, for the December 27, 1937, issue of the journal described Father Coughlin as "editorial counsel," rather than editor.

In the fall of 1938, *Social Justice* encountered further difficulties with Archbishop Mooney as a result of the journal's publication of the "Protocols of the Elders of Zion." As a consequence of these difficulties, the journal was no longer described as "Father Coughlin's Weekly Review," but rather as "*Social Justice*, National Weekly Review." Father Coughlin remained the editorial counsel but only "by permission of his Ecclesiastical Superior." Despite this, the journal continued to be controversial, and remained completely under Father Coughlin's control.

The September 11, 1939, issue listed E. Perrin Schwartz as editor. It was now described as the "National Weekly Founded by Father Coughlin." By the end of 1939, however, *Social Justice* listed Louis Ward as editorial director; his name appeared over the name of Schwartz, who was listed as editor. Ward was one of the early biographers of Coughlin, and his rise can be attributed to Father Coughlin's anger at Schwartz for having granted an interview to John L. Spivak, a reporter for *New Masses*. This interview was the integral part of a series of articles by Spivak that were hostile to Father Coughlin. The masthead now remained constant until the demise of the journal in April, 1942.

4. Gary Marx uses a circulation figure of one million in *The Social Basis of the Support of a Depression Era Extremist: Father Coughlin*, p. 119; Frank Knesset, of N. W. Ayer and Son, Inc., to the author, May 16, 1968.

5. Throughout the publication of the journal the Radio League of the Little Flower, which showed large profits, had to appropriate funds to the Social Justice Publishing Company to keep it operating. In spite of the substantial deficits which it consistently incurred, *Social Justice* was published for more than six years, which is a prime indicator of the importance Father Coughlin placed on the journal's continued publication.

Father Coughlin's financial problems were further complicated when the Internal Revenue Department ruled that the Radio League of the Little Flower was not exempt from federal income taxes or other taxation:

> It is the view of the Bureau that the question of whether a substantial part of the activities of an organization is intended to influence legislation must be determined by the ends toward which the activities of the organization are conducted. Where, as in the instant case, the activities of an organization have for their purpose the creation of public sentiment favorable to purposes which can be accomplished principally through legislation, the organization is engaged in a substantial measure, in attempting to influence legislation.
>
> It is clear from the evidence presented that your activities to a large extent consist of giving publicity to the views of Father Coughlin on social and economic questions and it is the opinion of the Bureau that a substantial part of your activities consists of attempting to influence legislation.

In appeal of this ruling, entitled "A Memorandum for the Radio League of the Little Flower in Support of Exemption from Income, Excess Profits and Other Taxes," which contended that the activities of the Radio League did not, to any appreciable extent, consist of giving publicity to the views of Father Coughlin on social and economic questions, E. Prewitt Semmes, Coughlin's lawyer, emphasized that the major function of the Radio League of the Little Flower was to support the Shrine of the Little Flower Parish.

Available data indicate that *Social Justice* was a consistent money loser. The weekly publication costs for *Social Justice* were approximately $12,500. For the year ending September 30, 1936, the Social Justice Publishing Company lost $116,528.88, the exact sum the Radio League of the Little Flower then loaned the company. In this same period Father Coughlin was given a loan of $2,506.68 by the Radio League. In the period ending September 30, 1937, the Radio League made a loan of $83,009.78 to the Social Justice Publishing Company. The net loss of the Social Justice Publishing Company for that year was $33,519.10. The 1938 Annual Report of the Social Justice Publishing Company showed a net operating loss of $75,958.42. There was also a liability listed for subscriptions paid in advance for the sum of $37,406.80. Since the annual subscription at the time cost two dollars, the number of subscribers to *Social Justice* can be estimated to have been 18,700. In addition, the 1938 Annual Report of the Social Justice Publishing Company listed Walter Baertschi as president, Edward Kinsky, a Brooklyn lawyer, vice-president, and Catherine Wilson, secretary and treasurer. These three individuals also formed the company's board of directors. Father Coughlin was the resident agent for the company.

By December 31, 1938, Walter Baertschi, who had replaced Coughlin as president of the Social Justice Publishing Company during the priest's 1937 confrontation with Archbishop Mooney, was himself replaced by E. Perrin Schwartz, who was also listed as the editor of *Social Justice*. In addition, Baertschi was no longer listed as a member of the board of trustees of the company and his name ceased to be associated with any of Father Coughlin's activities. It is possible that Father Coughlin parted with Mr. Baertschi to appease Archbishop Mooney. It should be remembered that the archbishop was the recipient of some very strong criticism from *Social Justice* during the period that Baertschi was supposedly operating it.

The 1939 Annual Report listed losses of the Social Justice Publishing Company to be $130,658.14. This is an indication that the circulation of *Social Justice* was declining. In its 1940 Annual Report, the Social Justice Publishing Company showed a loss of $136,402.18. The amount of cash available was $93,272.89, an increase of approximately $28,000.00 over the previous year. This increase could be explained by the absence of capital assets in the form of land. In the 1939 Annual Report, the Social Justice Publishing Company showed capital assets in the form of land valued at $14,222.16. The 1940 Annual Report showed a sharp increase in liabilities for subscriptions paid in advance, which amounted to $115,190.62. This was an increase of over $30,000.00 for the same item in the 1939 Annual Report. E. Perrin Schwartz remained as president and member of the board of trustees. There was no vice-president listed for the company. The secretary and the treasurer, Cora Quinlan and Alberta Ward, were members of the board of trustees replacing Edward Kinsky and Catherine Wilson.

On February 23, 1940, the Social Justice Publishing Company changed its business address from Woodward Avenue at Twelve Mile Road, Royal Oak, Michigan, to 3425 Woodward Avenue, Royal Oak, Michigan. On that date Cora Quinlan became the appointed resident agent of the Social Justice Publishing Company.

By September 30, 1940, holdings of the Radio League of the Little Flower in the Social Justice Publishing Company were liquidated for $40,000. For the one-year period ending September 30, 1940, the Radio League listed the Social Justice Publishing Company as an asset worth $71,383.13.

The 1941 Annual Report of the Social Justice Publishing Company listed losses for the one-year period ending December 31, 1940, as $48,614.53. This was a decrease from the $136,402.18 loss stated on the 1940 Michigan Annual Report. In the 1941 Annual Report an asset of $35,209.10 was listed for deferred broadcasting expense. Liabilities increased to $127,490.69 from the $95,934.22 in liabilities listed in the 1940 Annual Report. Subscriptions paid in advance totaled $73,172.61, down from $115,190.62 listed in the 1940 Annual Report, thus indicating the declining circulation of *Social Justice*. Federal income tax payments were $20,895.99, which was considerably more than the $732.62 in federal taxes paid the previous year.

The 1942 Annual Report of the Social Justice Publishing Company showed that the company lost $20,188.33 for the one-year period ending December 31, 1941. Federal income taxes amounted to $32,335.54. Subscriptions paid in advance were $72,992.06, about the same as the previous year. Notes and accounts payable dropped to $7,469.83 from $80,742.67 in the 1941 Annual Report, indicating a continuous decline in the number of subscribers to *Social Justice*. The Social Justice Publishing Company listed as an asset $25,000.00 worth of defense bonds it purchased shortly after the outbreak of World War II.

The 1943 Annual Report of the Social Justice Publishing Company, the last one during the existence of *Social Justice*, showed a profit of $57,971.01. The cash assets of the company were $846.72, down from $64,219.88 listed in the 1942 Annual Report. Federal taxes on income dropped to $1,588.42 from $32,335.54. Notes and accounts payable increased to $82,225.00 from the $7,489.83 listed in the 1942 Annual Report. Obviously, Father Coughlin needed substantial financial support to carry on his activities.

6. Father Coughlin to Lecia M. Paas, Winnetka, Illinois, December 27, 1938, and February, 1939.

7. Father Coughlin to unknown person residing in Brooklyn, New York, April, 1939.

In a January 24, 1940, form letter to Morris Kobacher, who was tardy in renewing his subscription to *Social Justice*, Coughlin enclosed a religious medal which he said had been touched to the relic of the True Cross. He urged Kobacher to join him in the fight to "crush the serpent's head of communism and start America back to Christ." In a similar letter to A. Maltin, dated January 4, 1949, Father Coughlin enclosed yet another medal that had "touched the relic of the True Cross," with a request that Maltin contact a neighborhood boy who would agree to sell from ten to twenty-five copies of *Social Justice* weekly. The commission for each weekly sale of *Social Justice* was to be three and one-half cents. By this time the price of the journal had been raised from five cents to ten cents.

In a letter to the Michigan Unemployment Commission dated March 5, 1937, which sought the exemption of its employees from coverage by the state unemployment law, Amy Collins, treasurer of the Social Justice Publishing Company, stated, in a letter which attempted to justify in regard to the Social Justice Publishing Company and the Radio League of the Little Flower that "the income of neither inures to the benefit of any individual or individuals, directly or indirectly." Yet, when the Social Justice Publishing Company was finally dissolved on October 29, 1943, all assets were turned over to Amelia F. Coughlin and Thomas J. Coughlin, Father Coughlin's parents, who were listed as holding all the capital stock issued and outstanding. The 1943 Annual Report of the Social Justice Publishing Company listed assets of $227,225.01, including $152,914.13 in investments. Even if the debts amounting to $86,029.00 were paid off, this still left a considerable sum of money for Father Coughlin's parents. When the priest's parents died they left him quite well-to-do. This fact disputes the statement made to the Michigan Unemployment Compensation Commission that the income of the Social Justice Publishing Company and the Radio League of the Little Flower did not accrue to the benefit of any individuals.

8. In a form letter mailed December 16, 1938, Father Coughlin urged his friends to purchase copies of *The Kingship of Christ* and *The Mystical Body of Christ in the Modern World*, both written by Father Dennis Fahey.

In the process of praising the merits of Father Fahey's *Rulers of Russia*, Father Coughlin urged his readers not to be anti-Semitic, but on the other hand, he reminded F. Rethna of Chicago that some Jews were associated with "Carl Marx" and Freemasonry. A March, 1940, letter requested readers to purchase Father Fahey's books and also to ask for contributions on a monthly basis to support Father Coughlin's radio shows.

9. John Roy Carlson, *Undercover*, pp. 32–33.

10. *Social Justice*, February 14, 1938.

11. *Ibid.*, November 20, 1939.

12. Francis Yockey, *Imperium* (New York: The Truth Seeker Company, Inc., 1963).

Imperium can be considered to be in a similar vein to Spengler's *The Decline of the West*. Yockey saw his book as "the first blow in the gigantic war for the liberation of Europe [p. vii]." The main enemy of this liberation was what Yockey labeled the "Cultural Distorter," which was actually a synonym for the Jews. Below are examples of Yockey's views:

> Native American movements like the second Ku-Klux-Klan, formed in 1915, as an expression of the reaction of the American organism to the presence of the foreign matter, were more or less successfully called "un-American" by the propaganda organs in America, which even by that time had come under strong Culture-distorting influences [p. 497].

He further labeled as propaganda the fact

> that 6,000,000 members of the Jewish Culture-Nation-State-Church-People-Race had been killed in European camps, as well as an indeterminant number of other people. The propaganda was on a worldwide scale, and was of a mendacity that was perhaps adapted to a uniformized mass, but was simply disgusting to discriminating Europeans. The propaganda was technically quite complete. "Photographs" were supplied in millions of copies. . . . Hundreds of thousands more made fortunes in post-war black-markets. "Gas-chambers" that did not exist were photographed, and a "gasmobile" was invented to titilate the mechanically-minded [p. 533].

Yockey's characterization of black people gives ample evidence of his ignorance and bigoted thinking.

> The soul of the Negro remains primitive and child like in comparison with the nervous and complicated soul of Western man, accustomed to thinking in terms of money and civilization. The result is that the Negro has become a charge of white society. Marriage is almost unknown among the Negroes, and the women raise the large families. In the large cities, the Negro population supplies approximately ten times as many criminals as its numbers would indicate to be its proportion. Social diseases are general among this race, and the hospitals as well as the penitentiaries deal with highly disproportionate numbers of Negroes. Primitive violence is natural in the Negro, and the sense of social disgrace is lacking in him in connection with crimes. Negro sections of the Northern cities are dangerous to the life of white persons [p. 515].

William Clancy, Jr., Assistant United States Attorney General, said that Yockey had frequently visited Germany before the war and again in the 1950s and that he appeared to be involved in "a systematic and well planned operation in passports, the purpose of which we do not know [*New York Times*, June 18, 1960]."

13. Arthur Schlesinger, Jr., said the following of Johnson and his close friend Alan Blackburn:

> In December, 1934, Philip Johnson, a brilliant architect, and Alan Blackburn, announced that they were quitting their jobs at the Museum of Art, to go to Louisiana and study Huey Long. Long and his associates did not take to the Harvard men and they soon left Louisiana. Johnson and Blackburn planned to form a National Party inspired by the writing of Lawrence Dennis. . . . Blackburn and Johnson turned up later as associates of Father Coughlin [*The Age of Roosevelt: The Politics of Upheaval*, p. 62].

14. Interview with Father Coughlin, April 11, 1970.

15. The October 3, 1938, issue of *Social Justice* contained an article by a Ben Marcin which cited the works of Samuel Roth, a Jew convicted of pornography, to prove the veracity of the "Protocols." Marcin incorrectly claimed to be quoting from Roth's book *Now and Forever*.

> As they appear in history, Jews are a tribe of deadly persecutors, and not a persecuted minority as they pretend to be. Through propaganda, they have tried to convince public opinion to the contrary, but facts and history stand as their accusers, even their own authors and publications.

This quotation was actually from another book of Roth's entitled *Jews Must Live*. Sigmund Livingston, then chairman of the Anti-Defamation League, in a letter to Archbishop Mooney dated October 10, 1938, described this book as "one of the most disgraceful books ever written." Marcin's article went on to ask:

But what do three Jewish Rabbis themselves say? In 1901, Rabbi Rudolf Fleischman of the Polish city of Schocken, now called Skoki, stated: "The Protocols really did exist, and they were no forgery. However, they were positively of Jewish origin." In 1906, Rabbi Grunfeld of the Polish city of Swarzdodz gave the following characteristically Jewish answer: "My dear questioner, you are too curious, and want to know too much. We are not permitted to talk about these things. I am not allowed to say anything, *and you are not supposed to know anything about the Protocols.* For God's sake be careful, or you will be putting your life in danger." In 1924, Dr. Ehrenpreis, at one time Chief Rabbi of Sweden, later banished from Soviet Russia (who became disgusted with the cruelty of the Jews, and joined the Greek Orthodox Church), said: "*Long have I been well acquainted with the contents of the Protocols, indeed for many years before they were ever published in the Christian press.* The Protocols of the Elders of Zion were in point of fact not the original Protocols at all, but a compressed extract of the same. Of the 70 Elders of Zion, in the matter of the origin and of the existence of the original Protocols, there are only ten men in the entire world who know."

In another letter dated October 19, 1938, Livingston informed Archbishop Mooney that there was no evidence that Rabbis Grunfeld and Fleischman ever existed. Evidence to the contrary came to the Anti-Defamation League on December 16, 1938, in a letter from Rabbi Chaim C. Grodzinsky, who was rabbi of the largest congregation in Vilna, Poland (Vilna is in the immediate vicinity of Swarzdodz and Skoki). Rabbi Grodzinsky stated:

I know no Rabbi Rudolph Fleischman of Skoki and likewise no Rabbi Grunfeld of Swarzdodz, and I did not know them in the past. Then, I took information from the Central Bureau of the Agudas Horabbonim (Union of Rabbis) in Warsaw. To them also the two above mentioned names are fully unknown either for the present time or for the past.

Rabbi Ehrenpreis said that the statements he was quoted as making were "pure invention" and denied ever visiting Russia. In response to Marcin's statement that Rabbi Ehrenpreis had joined the Greek Orthodox Church because he had become disgusted with the cruelty of the Jews, Rabbi Ehrenpreis stated (in an undated telegram to the Anti-Defamation League thought to have been sent in late 1938) that he had never joined the Greek Orthodox Church and that he was still a rabbi in Stockholm.

The *Social Justice* article maintained that at the Berne trial of the two book dealers selling the "Protocols," the presiding Judge Mayer was a Jew and that only Jewish witnesses had been given the opportunity to testify. Yet the record of the trial was public and newspaper accounts of the trial show that witnesses from both sides were given the opportunity to testify. A postal telegraph from the Jewish Telegraphic Agency to the Anti-Defamation League, sent from Berne, Switzerland, on October 6, 1938, confirmed that Judge Mayer was a Protestant, not a Jew.

Social Justice in addition took Philip Slomovitz, editor of the *Detroit Jewish Chronicle*, whom it allowed to publish in its pages an article rebutting the authenticity of the "Protocols."

> In his article, "The Truth About the Protocols," Mr. Slomovitz refers to one of his authorities, "Count Heinrich Coudenhove-Kalergi," an eminent Catholic thinker. In the first place this gentleman is not a Catholic, but a 33rd-degree Mason and is married to a Jewess.

Actually, a memorandum from the Anti-Defamation League dated October 3, 1938, states that Count Coudenhove-Kalergi was a devout Catholic who evidenced respect for Judaism.

"Ben Marcin" was by far the most controversial contributor of articles to *Social Justice*. It was "Marcin's" articles which strongly attacked the Jews and it was he who responded to Philip Slomovitz's articles repudiating the "Protocols of the Elders of Zion."

Father Coughlin had emphasized in 1938 that Ben Marcin, the author of the articles defaming Jews, was himself Jewish. In April of 1970, however, Father Coughlin told the author that he did not recall knowing a Ben Marcin and admitted to the possibility that the articles appearing under the Marcin by-line may have been ghost written. He maintains that he does not know who could have written the Marcin articles. "Mr. Schwartz would know and he is dead. I have no idea. It could have been Mr. Schwartz. It could have been Mr. Reardon or Mr. Wright. But to my knowledge there was never such a person. I never knew such a person." In fact, there was no Ben Marcin. The name was apparently derived from the first six letters of the last name of Bernice Marcinkiewicz, who was a stenographer, corporation officer and trustee in Father Coughlin's corporate ventures. The articles that were published under Marcin's name were written by various staff members of the Social Justice Publishing Company. The articles concerning the validity of the "Protocols of the Elders of Zion" were written by E. Perrin Schwartz, editor of *Social Justice*, and Joseph Wright, a staff member.

Schwartz told this to Mr. H. Lodge Robertson, plant superintendent for Arnold Power, Inc., which did the art work and general layout for *Social Justice*. Mr. Robertson swore to the veracity of these facts in a notarized statement. This statement was corroborated by a phone conversation with Bernice Buchta (née Marcinkiewicz), April 8, 1970.

Joseph Wright was a regular staff member of *Social Justice*. His article attacked the regimentation of the New Deal, praised Neville Chamberlain, and attacked the Soviet Union (*Social Justice*, March 7, 1938; August 15, 1938; October 17, 1938; February 13, 1939). Wright now resides in Grosse Pointe, Michigan, and considers his association with Father Coughlin a bad memory from the past. Wright, in a phone conversation with the author, vehemently denied that he had anything to do with the "Protocols" series; he claims that Father Coughlin and Schwartz wrote these articles.

Leo Reardon was an adviser to Father Coughlin and by the late 1930s his personal representative on political affairs. After the demise of *Social*

Justice, Reardon became associated with Upton Close, and later became business manager of the Mannion Forum.

E. Perrin Schwartz was editor of *Social Justice* from its inception in 1936 to its demise in 1942. A onetime lawyer, he was editor of the *Milwaukee Journal* from 1920 to 1936, with the exception of the years 1921 to 1922, when he was editor of the *Chicago Daily News*. When *Social Justice* ceased publication he became editor of the Elkhart *Indiana Daily Truth*. By 1939 Schwartz had been relegated to a position of secondary importance to Father Coughlin's chief adviser, Leo Reardon. There can be little doubt that Father Coughlin grew disenchanted with Schwartz after he displayed a propensity to talk too much.

Philip Slomovitz was angered enough by "Marcin's" articles to protest their contents to Father Coughlin. In a letter dated April 11, 1938, Slomovitz asked:

Where does Mr. Marcin get such information? Why does he revive the stupid lie about "policy" in Jewish matters and about "control" of such policy? And why do you publish such references which may tend to incite people against us? It is so easy to avoid raising false issues that I hope there will be a closer watch on such matters in future issues of *Social Justice*. . . .

It was to be a forlorn hope.

16. In the August 8, 1938, issue of *Social Justice*, Coughlin used as proof for this belief a White Paper issued by the English government, which allegedly stated that the Jews were "responsible for the bolshevik take-over of Russia and are the real rulers of Russia," and that Jewish banking houses had financed the Russian Revolution and that twenty-four of the twenty-five most important communist leaders were Jewish.

The allegations made by *Social Justice* and Coughlin about the official British White Paper were repudiated in a study entitled "Anti-Semitism in the Air" (*Commonweal*, vol. XXIX, December 30, 1938, pp. 260–262), conducted by Monsignor John Ryan. Monsignor Ryan pointed out that Coughlin's information was drawn from *The Mystical Body of Christ in the Modern World* by Father Denis Fahey, whom he cited as an "anti-Semite." Fahey's material was, in fact, based on an article which had appeared in an anti-Semitic London weekly called *The Patriot*, which based its facts on material that had appeared March 6, 1920, in a French publication called *Documentation Catholique*. The latter publication claimed to have received its information from an alleged report made by the "American Secret Service" to the French High Commissioner.

An examination of the "Official British White Paper" referred to by Coughlin reveals no reference to the banking firm of Kuhn-Loeb and Company, which *Social Justice* said helped finance the bolshevik revolution. The unabridged White Paper that *Social Justice* cited was not even an official British government report concerning bolshevism, but rather a letter based on a report which was the result of the observations of a Mr. Oudendyke, a Dutch representative to the court at St. Petersburg. His statement was the sole basis for the report that Jews perpetrated the bolshevik take-over.

See *Social Justice*, August 8, 1938; see also *A Collection of Reports on Bol-shevism in Russia, No. 1* (London: His Majesty's Stationery Office, 1919).

The claim that the Jews financed the bolshevik revolution also appeared in an article in the Nazi publication *World Service*, on February 15, 1936, from which *Social Justice* quoted almost verbatim. According to Father Fahey the source for the information about Jewish domination of the bolshevik government in 1917 was Robert Wilton, the Russian correspondent for the London *Times*, who was an eyewitness to the event.

In response to Coughlin's and *Social Justice*'s statement about the existence of an "American Secret Service" report stating that international Jewish bankers financed the bolshevik revolution, the chief of the United States Secret Service, Frank Wilson, issued a statement to the press which said:

> The only United States governmental agency having the name of "Secret Service" is the United States Secret Service, which is a division of the Treasury Department. I have investigated our records and questioned members of the service who were on duty from 1916 to 1920, including my predecessor, William H. Moran, with respect to the statements made and quoted by Father Coughlin. They know of no such investigation or report as that which Father Coughlin discussed, and it is quite certain that no such report was ever made by the United States Secret Service. [See the *New York Times*, November 29, 1938.]

In the November 28, 1938, issue of *Social Justice*, he claimed that fifty-six of fifty-nine members of the Soviet Central Committee in 1935 were Jews. He also stated that the three non-Jews were married to Jewish women. An examination of these claims and one stating that twenty-four out of twenty-five quasi-cabinet ministers of the Soviet Union in 1917 were Jewish refutes the available evidence. (Frank Alfred Golder, *Documents in Russian History, 1914–1917*, p. 619; *Statesman's Yearbook*, 1935, pp. 1260–1261, and 1938, pp. 1272–1273).

Documents in Russian History lists only one Jew, Leon Trotsky, as being a member of the Soviet of People's Commissars in 1917. It cannot be determined with certainty what *Social Justice* meant by "quasi-cabinet," since there was no such designation made by the Soviet Union. However, the *Statesman's Yearbook* for the years 1935 and 1938 shows that the claims of *Social Justice* that fifty-six of fifty-nine members of the Central Committee of the Soviet Communist Party were Jewish is totally inaccurate.

Further refutation of Coughlin's statements resulted from a conference between Sigmund Livingston and Alexander Kerensky on November 26, 1938, at which time Kerensky unequivocally disputed *Social Justice*'s characterizing the leading bolsheviks as Jews, stating that bolshevism was not a Jewish idea and that most Jews had vigorously opposed bolshevism. Kerensky maintained that Trotsky had said he would sacrifice eight-ninths of the Jewish people for acceptance of his international ideas and that the Jewish people as well as all other Russian national groups had suffered from the bolshevik take-over. (See the notes of the Livingston-Kerensky conference.)

When several Nazi agents were arrested in the United States, primarily due to the efforts of undercover agent Leon Turrou who posed as a pro-Nazi, *Social Justice*, on December 19, 1938, carried an article under the Ben Marcin by-line labeling Turrou "an O.G.P.U. agent long employed by Soviet Russia to spy upon the United States government." The article further charged that Turrou was in the service of influential Jews who were using him to create strain and ill-will in German-American relations. The December 26, 1938, issue of *Social Justice* carried a full page retraction of the charges against Turrou.

17. *Social Justice*, August 8, 1938.
18. *Ibid.*, May 1, 1936.
19. E. Perrin Schwartz to George Seldes, n.d.
20. *Social Justice*, April 3, 1939.
21. *Ibid.*, April 11, 1938.
22. *Ibid.*, December 7, 1936.
23. *Ibid.*, April 4, 1938.
24. *Ibid.*, September 19, 1938.
25. *Ibid.*, May 8, 1936; November 30, 1936; November 23, 1936; March 15, 1937; February 27, 1939.
26. *Ibid.*, April 25, 1938.
27. *Ibid.*, August 1, 1938.
28. *Ibid.*, October 24, 1938.
29. *Ibid.*, March 13, 1939.
30. *Ibid.*, July 16, 1936.
31. *Ibid.*, June 13, 1938.
32. *Ibid.*, October 5, 1936.
33. *Ibid.*, October 26, 1936.
34. *Ibid.*, July 12, 1937.
35. *Ibid.*
36. *Ibid.*, July 19, 1937.
37. *Ibid.*, January 17, 1938.
38. *Ibid.*, October 4, 1937.
39. *Ibid.*, August 10, 1936.
40. *Ibid.*, April 24, 1936.
41. *Ibid.*, March 27, 1936.
42. *Ibid.*, June 6, 1938.
43. *Ibid.*, February 22, 1937.
44. *Ibid.*, January 10, 1938.
45. Father Coughlin to Lecia Paas, February, 1939.
46. General Records of the Department of State from the Decimal Files, 1930–1944, relating to Father Charles E. Coughlin, RG 59, 500 C 114 1627, dispatch dated February 21, 1935, state that Bishop Gallagher's "whole career has been an example of rabid anti-British feeling."
47. *Social Justice*, December 25, 1939.
48. *Ibid.*, July 8, 1940.
49. *Ibid.*, June 17, 1940; July 1, 1940; September 16, 1940.
50. *Ibid.*, July 29, 1940.
51. *Ibid.*, April 29, 1940; June 10, 1940.
52. *Ibid.*, July 22, 1940.
53. *Ibid.*, November 25, 1940; March 18, 1940.
54. *Ibid.*, August 11, 1941.
55. *Ibid.*, August 25, 1941.
56. *Ibid.*, September 15, 1941.

57. *Ibid.*, June 24, 1940.
58. *Ibid.*, June 3, 1940; April 28, 1941; September 22, 1941.
59. *Ibid.*, May 19, 1941.
60. *Ibid.*, April 21, 1941; June 23, 1941; August 18, 1941; August 25, 1941.
61. *Ibid.*, July 1, 1940.
62. *Ibid.*, August 12, 1940.
63. *Ibid.*, June 16, 1941; November 4, 1940.
64. *Ibid.*, December 15, 1941.
65. *Ibid.*, December 22, 1941.
66. Interview with Father Coughlin, April 11, 1970.
67. *Ibid.*, March 16, 1942.
68. *Ibid.*, January 19, 1942.
69. *Ibid.*, February 2, 1942; February 23, 1942.
70. *Ibid.*, February 23, 1942.
71. Interview with Father Coughlin, April 11, 1970.
72. *Washington Post*, March 26, 1942.
73. *Social Justice*, March 30, 1942.
74. *Ibid.*, April 20, 1942.
75. Interview with Father Coughlin, April 11, 1970.

9. TO CEASE AND DESIST

1. Interview with Father Coughlin, April 11, 1970.
2. O. John Rogge, *The Official German Report*, pp. 303–304. Also see the *Detroit Free Press*, October 23, 1946.
3. Sworn statement by Aleksi Pelypenko before Herman L. Isler, notary public, Kings County, New York, as it appeared in *In Fact*, February 11, 1946.
4. Interview with Father Coughlin, April 11, 1970; Biddle to Walker, April 14, 1942, Walker Papers, Notre Dame University; Walker to the Postmaster at Royal Oak, Michigan, April 14, 1942, Walker Papers; Walker to the Publisher of *Social Justice*, April 14, 1942, Walker Papers.
5. *Detroit News*, April 15, 1942.
6. *New York Times*, April 21, 1942.
7. Interview with Father Coughlin, April 11, 1970.
8. Francis Biddle, *In Brief Authority*, p. 247.
9. Francis Cardinal Spellman to Frank Walker, March 31, 1942, Walker Papers.
10. Biddle, pp. 247–248.
11. Post Office Department Order Number 17558, May 4, 1942.
12. Interview with Father Coughlin, April 11, 1970.
13. George Seldes to the author, November 30, 1968; telephone conversation with Mr. Rogge on December 5, 1968.
14. Father Coughlin to William Pinsley, September 10, 1942. This letter contained many inducements to join the League of the Little Flower. The mailing contained a wallet-sized picture of St. Theresa, to whom the Shrine of the Little Flower was dedicated, a wallet-size prayer dedicated to St. Theresa, petitions for the safe return of loved ones from the armed services and a membership application for the League of the Little Flower.
15. *Detroit News*, May 1, 1943.

16. *New York Post*, March 18, 1944.
17. *Detroit News*, April 4, 1944.
18. *Ibid.*, November 1, 1949.
19. *Ibid.*, June 9, 1966.
20. *New York Times*, May 28, 1966.
21. *Ibid.*
22. Charles E. Coughlin, *Bishops Versus the Pope*, p. iii.
23. In a telephone conversation on April 3, 1972, with Meyer Steinglass, director of public relations of the Israel Bond Organization, it was confirmed that Father Coughlin purchased $500 worth of State of Israel bonds on January 6, 1955.
24. Father Coughlin to a Mr. Borok, March 12, 1946.

10. A VIEW FROM THE '70s

1. Interview with Father Coughlin, April 11, 1970.
2. Ruth Mugglebee, *Father Coughlin of the Shrine of the Little Flower*, p. 127.
3. Interview with Father Coughlin, April 11, 1970.

Bibliography

BOOKS

Aaron, Daniel, ed. *America in Crisis*. New York: Knopf, 1952.

Allen, Frederick. *Since Yesterday*. New York: Harper, 1940.

Allen, H. C. *The United States of America*. New York: Praeger, 1965.

Archambault, Alberic. *The Samsons*. Boston: Humphries, 1941.

Belloc, Hilaire. *The Jews*. 3rd ed. Boston: Houghton Mifflin, 1937.

Bennett, David. *Demagogues in the Depression: American Radicals and the Union Party, 1932–1936*. New Brunswick, N. J.: Rutgers University Press, 1969.

Biddle, Francis. *In Brief Authority*. Garden City, N. Y.: Doubleday, 1962.

Blanchard, William. *Racial Nationalism: Principles and Purposes*. Live Oak, Fla.: White Front Publishing Corp., 1938.

Brophy, Edward F. *The Christian Front*. New York: privately printed, n.d.

Browder, Earl. *Fighting for Peace*. New York: International Publishers, 1939.

Brusher, Joseph. *Popes Through the Ages*. Rev. ed. Princeton, N. J.: Van Nostrand, 1964.

Buell, Leslie. *Isolated America*. New York: Knopf, 1940.

Burns, James. *Roosevelt: The Lion and the Fox*. New York: Harcourt, Brace, 1956.

Carlson, John Roy. *Undercover*. New York: Dutton, 1943.

Carter, John. *American Messiahs*. New York: Simon & Schuster, 1955.

Cole, Wayne. *America First*. Madison, Wisconsin: University of Wisconsin Press, 1953.

A Collection of Reports on Bolshevism in Russia. No. 1. London: His Majesty's Printing Office, 1919.

Conner, Jacob. *Christ Was Not a Jew*. New York: privately printed, 1936.

Coughlin, Charles E. *Am I an Anti-Semite?* Detroit: The Condon Printing Company, 1939.

————. *Bishops Versus the Pope*. Bloomfield Hills, Michigan: Helmet and Sword, 1969.

————. *By the Sweat of Thy Brow*. Detroit: Radio League of Little Flower, 1931.

————. *Eight Discourses on the Gold Standard*. Detroit: Radio League of the Little Flower, 1933.

————. *Eight Lectures on Labor, Capital and Social Justice*. Royal Oak, Michigan: Radio League of the Little Flower, 1934.

————. *Money, Questions and Answers*. Royal Oak, Michigan: National Union for Social Justice, 1936.

————. *Radio Addresses, January 12, 1936–April 21, 1940*. Royal Oak, Michigan: Radio League of the Little Flower, 1940.

————. *Radio Discourses, 1931–1932*. Royal Oak, Michigan: Radio League of the Little Flower, 1932.

————. *A Series of Lectures.* Royal Oak, Michigan: Radio League of the Little Flower, 1935.

————. *A Series of Lectures on Social Justice, 1935–1936.* Royal Oak, Michigan: The Radio League of the Little Flower, 1936.

————. *Sixteen Radio Lectures: 1938 Series.* Royal Oak, Michigan: Published by Charles E. Coughlin, 1938.

————. *Why Leave Our Own.* Detroit: Radio League of the Little Flower, 1939.

Creutz, W. *New Light on the Protocols.* Chicago: Right Cause Publishing Company, 1935.

Cronin, John. *Catholic Social Principles.* Milwaukee: Bruce Publishing Company, 1950.

Curley, James. *I'd Do It Again.* Englewood Cliffs, New Jersey: Prentice-Hall, 1957.

Curran, Edward Lodge. *A Reply to Elliott Roosevelt.* Royal Oak, Michigan: 1939.

Decter, Moshe. *A Review of the Historical Background of Contemporary American Reactionary Politics.* New York: Bureau of Applied Research, Columbia University, 1954.

DeJong, Louis. *The German Fifth Columns in World War II.* Chicago: University of Chicago Press, 1956.

Dennis, Lawrence. *Coming American Fascism.* New York: Harper Brothers, 1936.

————. *The Dynamics of War and Revolution.* New York: Weekly Foreign Letter, 1940.

Dilling, Elizabeth. *The Octopus.* Chicago: privately printed, 1938.

————. *The Red Network.* Chicago: privately printed, 1934.

————. *The Roosevelt Red Menace and Its Background.* Chicago: privately printed, 1936.

Ebenstein, William. *The Nazi State.* New York: Farrar and Rinehart, 1943.

Edmonson, Robert Edward. *Bulletins 1934–1940.* New York: privately printed, 1940.

————. *The Edmonson Case: Jews vs. Christians in Court.* New York: Edmonson Service, 1936.

————. *Move to Destroy Free Speech.* New York: privately printed, 1937.

Ehler, Sidney, and John Morrall, eds. *Church and State Thru the Centuries.* London: Burns and Oates, 1954.

Fahey, Denis. *The Kingship of Christ.* Royal Oak, Michigan: Social Justice Publishing Company, 1940.

————. *The Mystical Body of Christ in the Modern World.* Royal Oak, Michigan: Social Justice Publishing Company, 1940.

————. *The Rulers of Russia.* 3rd ed. Detroit: Condon Publishing Company, 1940.

Farley, James. *Jim Farley's Story: The Roosevelt Years.* New York: Whittlesey House, 1948.

Father Coughlin's Friends. *An Answer to Father Coughlin's Critics.* Royal Oak: Radio League of the Little Flower, 1940.

Fichte Bund. "What Do You Know About Czechoslovakia?" Pamphlet Number 1102, 1938.

Forster, Arnold. *Danger on the Right*. New York: Random House, 1964.
———. *A Measure of Freedom*. Garden City, New York: Doubleday and Company, 1950.
———. *The Radical Right: Report on the John Birch Society and Its Allies*. New York: Vintage Books, 1967.
———. *The Trouble Makers*. New York: Doubleday and Company, 1952.
Forster, Arnold, and Benjamin Epstein. *Cross Currents*. New York: Doubleday and Company, 1956.
Fry, Leslie (pseudonym). *An Analysis of Zionism*, by Paquita Louise de Shishmareff. London: MCP Publications, 1938 (?).
Fuchs, Lawrence. *The Political Behavior of American Jews*. Glencoe, Illinois: Free Press, 1956.
Gaebelein, Arno C. *The Conflict of the Ages*. New York: Our Hope, 1933.
Gallagher, Michael. *On the Position of Reverend Charles E. Coughlin*. Royal Oak, Michigan: Radio League of the Little Flower, 1935.
General Jewish Council. *Father Coughlin: His "Facts" and Arguments*. New York, 1939.
Greeley, Father Andrew. *The Catholic Experience*. New York: Doubleday and Company, 1967.
Goldberg, David. *Perish the Jew: A Clinical Treatment of Anti-Semitism*. New York: Bloch Publishing Company, 1939.
Golder, Frank. *Documents in Russian History, 1914–1917*. New York: The Century Company, 1929.
Hadley, Edwin Marshall. *Facing the Facts*. Elgin, Illinois: Brandt Publication Company, 1939.
Hamilton, William. *Salute the Jew!* Chicago: privately printed, 1935.
Handlin, Oscar. *Race and Nationality in American Life*. Boston: Little, Brown and Company, 1957.
Historical Statistics of the United States. Washington, D. C.: U. S. Government Printing Office, 1960.
Hoffer, Eric. *The True Believer: Thoughts on the Nature of Mass Movements*. New York: Frederick Praeger, 1954.
Hofstadter, Richard. *The Age of Reform*. New York: Alfred Knopf, 1955.
Hughes, Ingram. *Anti-Semitism: A World Survey*. Los Angeles: American Nationalist Publications, 1934.
Ickes, Harold. *The First Thousand Days*. New York: Simon and Schuster, 1936.
The International Jew. Dearborn, Michigan: Dearborn Publishing Company, 1922.
Irwin, Theodore. *Inside the Christian Front*. Washington, D. C.: American Council on Public Affairs, 1940.
Jager, Henry. *Father Coughlin: Promise or Menace*. New York: privately printed, 1935.
Jenkins, Newton. *Republic Reclaimed*. Chicago: privately printed, 1938.
Kayville, Victor de. *Downfall of Russia: Bolshevism and Judaism*. Chicago: Chicago Rights Cause Publications Company, 1936.
———. *Is the Orthodox Jew Harmless?* Chicago: Chicago Rights Cause Publications Company, 1935.
Kernan, William. *The Ghost of Royal Oak*. New York: Free Speech Forum, 1940.

Lee, Alfred, and Elizabeth Lee, eds. *The Fine Art of Propaganda*. New York: Harcourt, Brace and Company, 1939.

Leuchtenberg, Sidney. *Franklin D. Roosevelt and the New Deal, 1932-1940*. New York: Harper and Row, 1963.

Lippman, Walter. *Public Opinion*. New York: Harcourt, Brace and Company, 1922.

Lowenthal, Leo, and Norbert Guterman. *Studies in Prejudice: Prophets of Deceit*. New York: Harper and Brothers, 1949.

Lutmin, Reinhard. *American Demagogues of the Twentieth Century*. Boston: Beacon Press, 1954.

Madigan, Edward John. *Think It Over: A Fundamental Discussion of the Questions of the Day*. Portland, Oregon: privately printed, 1939.

Magil, A. B. *The Real Father Coughlin*. New York: Workers Library Publishers, Inc., 1939.

Marcus, Sheldon. *Social Justice: The History of a Weekly Journal, 1936-1942*. Doctoral dissertation, Yeshiva University, 1970.

Marx, Gary. *The Social Basis of the Support of a Depression Era Extremist: Father Coughlin*. Monograph 7. Berkeley, California: Survey Research Center, University of California, 1962.

Master, Nick. "Father Coughlin and Social Justice." Master's thesis, University of Wisconsin, 1955.

McCoy, Donald. *Angry Voices: Left of Center Politics in the New Deal Era*. Lawrence, Kansas: University of Kansas Press, 1958.

Mitchell, Broadus. *Depression Decade: From New Era Through New Deal*. New York: Farrar and Rinehart, 1947.

Moley, Raymond. *After Seven Years*. New York: Harper and Brothers, 1939.

Moody, Joseph. *Why Jews Are Persecuted*. St. Louis: The Queen's Work Publishers, 1938.

Moseley, George Van Horn. *Addresses*. Compiled by N. W. Rogers. New York: Nationalist Press Association, 1940.

Mote, Carl. *The New Deal Goose Step*. New York: Daniel Ryerson, 1939.

Mugglebee, Ruth. *Father Coughlin of the Shrine of the Little Flower*. Garden City, New York: Garden City Publications, 1933.

Myers, Gustavus. *History of Bigotry in the United States*. New York: Random House, 1943.

Nevins, Allan. *The Evening Post: A Century of Journalism*. New York: Boni and Liveright, 1922.

Newman, Edwin S. *The Hate Reader: A Collection of Material on the Impact of Hate Movements in American Society*. Dobbs Ferry, New York: Oceana Publications, 1964.

Parker, Frank. *Christian Communism Is Satanism*. Riverdale on Hudson, New York: Oceana Publications, 1964.

Pelley, William Dudley. *The Door to Revelation*. Asheville, North Carolina: Pelley Publishers, 1939.

———. *Editorials by Pelley*. Asheville, North Carolina: Pelley Publishers, 1936.

———. *No More Hunger*. Asheville, North Carolina: Pelley Publishers, 1936.

Poynter, J. W. *The Popes and Social Problems*. London: Watts Publishing Company, 1949.

Robinson, Edgar. *The Roosevelt Leadership, 1933–1945*. Philadelphia: Lippincott and Company, 1955.

Rogers, N. W. *Are All Jews Liars?* New York: Nationalist Press Association, 1940.

Rogge, O. John. *The Official German Report*. New York: Thomas Yoseloff, 1961.

Rollins, Richard. *I Find Treason: The Story of an American Nazi Agent*. New York: William Morrow and Company, 1941.

Roy, Ralph Lord. *Apostles of Discord: A Study of Organized Bigotry and Disruption on the Fringes of Protestantism*. Boston: Beacon Press, 1953.

Roosevelt, Franklin Delano. *F.D.R. — His Personal Letters*. Edited by Elliott Roosevelt. 2 vols. New York: Duell, Sloan and Pearce, 1947.

Sanctuary, Eugene. *An Answer to the Voice for Human Rights: Alfred E. Smith*. New York: privately printed, 1940.

————. *Are These Things So?* New York: World Alliance Against Jewish Aggressiveness, 1934.

————. *A Foundation of Sand*. New York: privately printed, 1935.

————. *Revolution and the Real Fifth Column*. New York: privately printed, 1940.

————. *Roosevelt Warning the Serpent*. New York: privately printed, 1935.

————. *War Guilt and War Mongers*. New York: privately printed, 1941.

Schapiro, J. Salwyn. *Anticlericalism*. Princeton, New Jersey: Van Nostrand Company, 1967.

————. *Movements of Social Dissent in Modern Europe*. Princeton, New Jersey: Van Nostrand Company, 1962.

Schlesinger, Arthur. *The Age of Roosevelt: The Coming of the New Deal*. Boston: Houghton Mifflin Company, 1958.

————. *The Age of Roosevelt: The Crises of the Old Order*. Boston: Houghton Mifflin Company, 1957.

————. *The Age of Roosevelt: The Politics of Upheaval*. Boston: Houghton Mifflin Company, 1960.

Schoomaker, Edwin. *Democracy and World Dominion*. New York: Richard R. Smith, 1939.

Shirer, William. *Berlin Diary*. New York: Alfred Knopf, 1941.

The Shifting Balance of World Forces: 1898–1945. Vol. XII of *The New Cambridge Modern World History*. Edited by C. L. Wombat. Cambridge, England: Cambridge University Press, 1968.

Smith, Gerald L. K. *The Hoop of Steel*. Detroit: Committee of One Million, 1942.

Soddy, Frederick. *Wealth, Virtual Wealth and Debt*. London: Allen and Unwin, 1926.

Soltin, J. *The Struggle Against Anti-Semitism: A Program of Action for American Jewry*. New York: Jewish Bureau of the National Communist Party, 1938.

Sparling, Harold. *Why I Am Running for Congress*. Los Angeles: privately printed, 1940.

Spivak, John. *Anti-Semitism Exposed! Plotting America's Pogroms*. New York: The New Masses, 1934.

————. *A Pattern for American Fascism*. New York: New Century Publishers, 1947.

——. *Secret Armies: The New Techniques of Nazi Warfare.* New York: Modern Age Books, 1939.

——. *Shrine of the Silver Dollar.* New York Modern Age Books, 1940.

Springer, Harvey H. *Termites.* Wichita, Kansas: Defender Publishers, 1940.

Statesman's Yearbook. 1935, 1938. New York: St. Martin's Press.

Stearns, Harold, ed. *America Now.* New York: Charles Scribner's Sons, 1938.

Stegner, Wallace. "The Radio Priest and His Flock," in *The Aspirin Age*, edited by Isabel Leighton. New York: Simon and Schuster, 1949.

Strong, Donald. *Organized Anti-Semitism in America: The Rise of Group Prejudice, 1930–1940.* Washington, D. C.: American Council on Public Affairs, 1941.

Sullivan, George E. *Wolves in Sheep's Clothing.* Washington, D. C.: The Sodality Union, 1937.

Sward, Keith. *The Legend of Henry Ford.* New York: Rinehart and Company, 1948.

Swing, Raymond Gram. *Forerunners of American Fascism.* New York: Julian Messner, 1935.

Thomas, Norman. *After the New Deal, What?* New York: The Macmillan Company, 1936.

Thorkelson, Jacob. *Rescue the Republic.* Asheville, North Carolina: Pelley Publishers, 1939.

Tugwell, Rexford. *The Democratic Roosevelt.* Garden City, New York: Doubleday and Company, 1957.

Tull, Charles. *Father Coughlin and the New Deal.* Syracuse: Syracuse University Press, 1965.

Ward, Louis. *Father Coughlin: An Authorized Biography.* Detroit, Michigan: Tower Publications, Inc., 1933.

Wechter, Dixon. *The Age of the Great Depression, 1929–1941.* New York: The Macmillan Company, 1948.

Weintraub, Ruth. *How Secure These Rights? Anti-Semitism in the United States.* Garden City, New York: Doubleday and Company, 1949.

Who's Who. 1936, 1937, 1938, 1939, 1940, 1941, 1942. New York: The Macmillan Company.

Who's Who in America. 1936–1937, 1938–1939, 1940–1941, 1942–1943, 1944–1945. Chicago: The A. N. Marquis Company.

Williams, T. Harry. *Huey Long.* New York: Alfred Knopf, 1969.

Winrod, Gerald L. *Adam Weishaupt: A Human Devil.* Wichita, Kansas: Defender Publishers, 1935.

——. *Europe at This Moment.* Wichita, Kansas: Defender Publishers, 1935.

——. *Hitler in Prophecy.* Wichita, Kansas: Defender Publishers, 1937.

——. *The Present International Crisis.* Wichita, Kansas: Defender Publishers, 1939.

——. *The Truth About the Protocols.* Wichita, Kansas: Defender Publishers, 1935.

Yockey, Francis. *Imperium.* New York: The Truth Seeker Company, 1963.

ARTICLES

Ahern, Father Michael. "The Protocols of the Elders of Zion." *The Pilot*, October 23, 1938.
Broun, Heywood Hale. "Enough Is Enough." *New Republic*, December 9, 1938.
"Clergy and Politics." *Commonweal*, March 22, 1935.
Iron Age, CXXX, 1932.
Kernan, William. "Coughlin, the Jews, and Communism." *Nation*, December 17, 1938.
Look, September 26, 1936.
Nation, November 28, 1936.
New Republic, April 24, 1935.
Newsweek, September 12, 1936.
New Yorker, The, August, 1940.
Patman, Wright. "Curbing the Chain Store." *Nation*, November 28, 1936.
Pilot, The, April 18, 1932.
Ryan, John. "Anti-Semitism in the Air." *Commonweal*, December 30, 1938.
Shenton, James. "Fascism and Father Coughlin." *Wisconsin Magazine of History*, Autumn, 1960.
———. "The Coughlin Movement and the New Deal." *Political Science Quarterly*, Fall, 1958.
Shuster, George. "The Jew and Two Revolutions." *Commonweal*, December 30, 1958.
Spivak, John L. "The Coughlin Racket." *New Masses*, November 21, 1939.
———. "Coughlin's Frenzied Finance." *New Masses*, November 28, 1939.
———. "Coughlin's Lawyer Speaks." *New Masses*, December 5, 1939.
———. "Coughlin and Ford." *New Masses*, December 12, 1939.
———. "Coughlin and the Nazis." *New Masses*, December 19, 1939.
Stolberg, Benjamin. "Dr. Huey and Mr. Long." *Nation*, September 25, 1935.
Swing, Raymond Gram. "Father Coughlin: The Wonder of Self Discovery." *Nation*, January 2, 1935.
Tonjoroff, Svetozar. "Jews in World Reconstruction." *The American Hebrew*, September 10, 1920.
Vairo, Philip D. "The Italian Immigrant in the United States." *Indian Sociological Bulletin*, July, 1965.
Wechsler, James. "The Coughlin Terror." *Nation*, July 22, 1939.

LETTERS, TELEGRAMS, MEMORANDA, FORMS AND ORGANIZATION FILES

Anti-Defamation League files on Barnes, James Strachey; Blackburn, Alan; Curran, Father Edward Lodge; Deisz, Reverend Joseph; Dondero, Representative George; Johnson, Philip; Matthews, J. B.; Scanlan, Patrick; Sullivan, George Edward; Thomas, Senator Elmer; Wise, Jennings.
Anti-Defamation League Memorandum *re* the "Protocols of the Elders of Zion," October 3, 1938.

Anti-Defamation League Memorandum entitled "Structure of Charles E. Coughlin's Organization," undated.
Application for Membership in the National Union for Social Justice.
Berler, Mrs. Permelia, and Family to Radio Station WJJD, November 25, 1938.
Biddle, Attorney General Francis, to Postmaster General Frank Walker, April 14, 1942.
Birkhead, Leon, National Director of Friends of Democracy, Memorandum and Protest to the Federal Communications Commission and the National Association of Broadcasters, Fall, 1939.
Brands, Eilzabeth Christine, Secretary to the National Union for Social Justice, to Franklin Delano Roosevelt, June 22, 1936, Roosevelt Papers. Roosevelt Library, Hyde Park, New York.
Campbell, William J., United States Attorney, Northern District of Illinois, to O. John Rogge, Assistant Attorney General, April 8, 1940.
Coffey, Father J. Edward, to the author, October 18, 1968.
Collins, Amy, to John S. Haggerty, Secretary of the State of Michigan, July 29, 1930.
——— to Michigan Unemployment Compensation Commission, March 8, 1937.
Cook, Fred, to Marvin McIntyre, April 6, 1933, Roosevelt Papers.
Coughlin, Charles E., to:
Mr. Borok, March 12, 1946.
Bernice Brandy, April 20, 1940.
John Feigh, January 25, 1935.
C. O. Griffin, Lindsay, California, January, 1937.
Jesse Jones, June 30, 1933, Roosevelt Papers.
William Julian, June 30, 1933, Roosevelt Papers.
Joseph Kennedy, January 29, 1936, Roosevelt Papers.
Morris Kobocher, Toledo, Ohio, January 24, 1940.
Murray Lauer, Chicago, December 19, 1938.
Samuel Lustgarten, Chicago, January 9, 1939.
A. Maltin, Chicago, January 4, 1940.
Marvin McIntyre, April 10, 1933, Roosevelt Papers.
Marvin McIntyre, August 6, 1933, Roosevelt Papers.
Marvin McIntyre, August 12, 1933, Roosevelt Papers.
Marvin McIntyre, Spetember 22, 1933, Roosevelt Papers.
Marvin McIntyre, November 14, 1933, Roosevelt Papers.
Marvin McIntyre, March 21, 1934, Roosevelt Papers.
Lecia Paas, Chicago, December 16, 1938.
Lecia Paas, Winnetka, Illinois, December 27, 1938.
Lecia Paas, Winnetka, Illinois, January, 1939.
Lecia Paas, Winnetka, Illinois, February, 1939.
Mrs. D. Pearce, DeWitt, Michigan, April 1, 1932.
William Pinsley, Chicago, September 12, 1942.
Lester Plotkin, Chicago, March 18, 1940.
Miss F. Rethna, Chicago, January 30, 1940.
Franklin Delano Roosevelt, August 12, 1932, Roosevelt Papers.
Franklin Delano Roosevelt, July 21, 1933, Roosevelt Papers.
Franklin Delano Roosevelt, September 23, 1933, Roosevelt Papers.

Franklin Delano Roosevelt, September 24, 1933, Roosevelt Papers.
Franklin Delano Roosevelt, November 24, 1933, Roosevelt Papers.
Franklin Delano Roosevelt, March 5, 1934, Roosevelt Papers.
Albur Shepard, Chicago, January 30, 1940.
Social Justice subscribers, September 10, 1942.
Harold Tietz, July 10, 1939.
Harold Tietz, August 3, 1939.
Unidentified person, February 19, 1940.
Unidentified person, March 8, 1940.
Unknown person residing in Brooklyn, New York. No date.
Mildred White, February, 1940.
J. H. Williams, March 28, 1940.
Curran, Rev. Edward Lodge, to Attorney General Robert Jackson, July 2, 1940.
Early, Steve, to Father Coughlin, September 22, 1933, Roosevelt Papers.
────── to Franklin Delano Roosevelt, June 22, 1936; September 30, 1936, Roosevelt Papers.
Ehrenpreis, Rabbi, telegram to the Anti-Defamation League. No exact date known. Thought to be sent in late 1938.
Farley, James, to Franklin Delano Roosevelt, November 2, 1936, Roosevelt Papers.
Form letter distributed at a meeting of Social Justice Distributors, December 5, 1940.
Gitlin, Hilda, sworn notarized statement, September, 1939, Cook County, Illinois.
Grodzinsky, Rabbi, telegram to the Anti-Defamation League, December 16, 1938.
Hoover, J. Edgar, to Attorney General Robert Jackson, January 25, 1940.
Kenesset, Frank, of N. W. Ayer and Son, to the author, May 16, 1968.
Larrabee, P. T., assistant to Margaret LeHand, to Rev. Maurice S. Sheehy, October 15, 1936.
Liberson, David, to Attorney General Robert Jackson, July 11, 1940.
Livingston, Sigmund, to Archbishop Edward Mooney, October 10, 1938; October 19, 1938.
────── and Alexander Kerensky, notes from conference of November 26, 1938.
Lobenthal, Richard, and Annette Ron, affidavit, May 25, 1970, Anti-Defamation League Files.
Lustgarten, Samuel, to Father Coughlin, December 29, 1938.
Malin, Richard A., to Radio Station WJJD, November 27, 1938.
Martel, Frank X., to Martin A. Dillmon, July 10, 1939.
Matthews, J. B., to Father Coughlin, August 10, 1939.
McCormack, Representative John W. (D. Mass.), to Franklin Delano Roosevelt, September 26, 1936, Roosevelt Papers.
McEvoy, James, of the law firm of Milburn and Semmes, attorneys for Father Coughlin, to the Michigan Unemployment Compensation Commission, October 1, 1941.
McIntyre, Marvin, to:
  Father Coughlin, August 8, 1933, Roosevelt Papers.
  Eddie Donovan, July 21, 1933, Roosevelt Papers.

Louis Howe, March 27, 1933, Roosevelt Papers.
Louis Howe, November 28, 1933, Roosevelt Papers.
Henry Morgenthau, Secretary of the Treasury, May 23, 1935, Roosevelt Papers.
Memorandum from files, January 18, 1936, Roosevelt Papers.
Moley, Raymond, to Charles Tull, March 17, 1960.
O'Toole, Rev. Vincent, to Marvin McIntyre, December 4, 1933, Roosevelt Papers.
Pelypenko, Aleksi, sworn statement before Herman Isler, Notary Public, Kings County, New York, as it appeared in *In Fact*, February 11, 1946.
Jewish Telegraphic Agency, telegram to the Anti-Defamation League concerning the "Protocols of the Elders of Zion." Sent from Berne, Switzerland, October 6, 1938.
Prevost, Malone, to *Detroit Free Press*, March 28, 1933.
Quinlan, Cora, to:
F. Gordoni, Chicago, April 1, 1941.
M. Levin, Chicago, January 6, 1942.
A. Maltin, Chicago, September 12, 1940.
Social Justice subscribers, June, 1942.
Social Justice subscribers, October, 1942.
Unidentified person, August 20, 1942.
Radio League of the Little Flower, memorandum in support of exemption from income, excess profits, and other taxes, October 1, 1941. Drafted by E. Prewitt Semmes.
Rhodes, Marie, to Marvin McIntyre, January 25, 1934, Roosevelt Papers.
Robertson, H. Lodge, sworn notarized statement, September 29, 1939.
Robinson, V., an employee of the Social Justice Publishing Company, to Lyle Hills, San Francisco, July 12, 1940.
—— to F. Gordoni, Chicago, October 21, 1940.
Rogge, O. John, to Harold M. Kennedy, United States Attorney, Brooklyn, New York, January 20, 1940.
Roosevelt, Eleanor, to Charles Tull, March 16, 1960.
Roosevelt, Franklin Delano, to Rev. Charles E. Coughlin, August 21, 1932; September 16, 1932; July 11, 1933, Roosevelt Papers.
—— to Marvin McIntyre, August 7, 1933; August, 1933; October 7, 1936, Roosevelt Papers.
Roosevelt, G. Hall, to Franklin Roosevelt, April 3, 1933; May 5, 1931, Roosevelt Papers.
Schafer, Rep. John C. (Dem. Wisc.), to Leon Birkhead, March 25, 1940.
Schrembs, Archbishop Joseph, to Father Coughlin, November 24, 1939.
—— to George Furth, November 24, 1939.
Schwartz, E. Perrin, to George Seldes (not dated).
Seldes, George, to the author, November 30, 1968.
Semmes, E. Prewitt, to the author, May 3, 1968.
Sheehy, Rev. Maurice S., assistant to the Rector of The Catholic University of America, to Margaret LeHand, July 18, 1936; October 5, 1936, Roosevelt Papers.
Speer, Robert, Guy Shipler, Rev. John Paul Jones, Franz Boaz, Rev. John Holmes Haynes, Richard Cox, A. Philip Randolph, Rev. A. Clayton Powell, Clyde Miller, Paul Brissendon, Benjamin Harrow, Wesley Mit-

chell, Christian Gauss, Robert Lynd, Harold Urey, Rev. William Imes, telegram to Attorney General Robert Jackson, January 18, 1940.

Slattery, William, to James Farley, March 19, 1935, Roosevelt Papers.

Slavin, John H., of the Internal Revenue Service, District of Michigan, to Franklin Roosevelt, April 5, 1938, Roosevelt Papers.

Slomovitz, Philip, to the author, October 30, 1968.

—— to Father Coughlin, April 11, 1938.

Smith, Gerald L. K., to the author, December 12, 1969; February 6, 1970; February 17, 1970.

Spellman, Francis Cardinal, to Frank Walker, March 31, 1942, Walker Papers, Notre Dame University.

Spivak, John L., to the author, February 26, 1968; March 16, 1968; May 9, 1968.

Stair, E. D., to Franklin Roosevelt, March 27, 1933, Roosevelt Papers.

Unknown person to Father Coughlin, December 28, 1938.

Unknown person to Margaret LeHand, March 23, 1934, Roosevelt Papers.

Unsigned memoranda to Marvin McIntyre, March 23, 1933; November 23, 1933, Roosevelt Papers.

Walker, Postmaster General Frank, to the postmaster at Royal Oak, Michigan, April 14, 1942, Walker Papers, Notre Dame University.

—— to the publisher of *Social Justice*, April 14, 1942, Walker Papers, Notre Dame University.

Wayne, Robert, chairman of the Committee on Public Relations, Knights of the Ku Klux Klan, Philadelphia, to Franklin Roosevelt, March 27, 1934, Roosevelt Papers.

Wise, Jennings, to Mr. Thompson, November 28, 1955.

Wise, Rabbi Stephen, to Jennings Wise, February 1, 1938.

STATE AND FEDERAL GOVERNMENT DOCUMENTS

General Records of the Department of State from the Decimal Files, 1930–1944, relating to Father Charles E. Coughlin, RG 59, 500 C 114/1627. Dispatch dated February 21, 1935.

History and Organization of the German-American Bund. State of New York, Report of Joint Legislative Committee, 1939.

League of the Little Flower. Articles of Association, January 10, 1928; Certificate of Amendment to the Articles of Association, July 21, 1930; Notice of Dissolution, July 24, 1930; Annual Financial Statements, 1929, 1930.

National Union for Social Justice. Articles of Association, December 11, 1934; Annual Reports, 1935–1943; Certificate of Dissolution, August 9, 1944.

Radio League of the Little Flower. Articles of Association. August 9, 1930; Annual Reports, 1930–1943; Annual Statement of Receipts and Disbursements and Assets and Liabilities. Years Ending September 30, 1936–1940.

Social Justice Poor Society. Articles of Incorporation, December 22, 1937; Annual Reports, 1938, 1939; Amended Michigan Annual Statement, July 11, 1939; Certificate of Dissolution, September 6, 1940.

Social Justice Publishing Company. Articles of Incorporation, February 4, 1936; Appointment of a Resident Agent, February 4, 1936; Notice of Change of Resident Agent, February 23, 1940; Annual Reports, 1937–1943; Certificate of Dissolution, November 30, 1943; Payroll, Social Justice Publishing Company, First Quarter, 1939.

United States Congress, *Investigation of Nazi and Other Propaganda.* Washington, D. C.: Government Printing Office, 1938–1943. 10 volumes and appendices.

APPENDICES

Appendix A

LEAGUE OF THE LITTLE FLOWER, INCORPORATED
BALANCE SHEET, June 1, 1930

Assets

Balance in bank, commercial	$ 3,297.37
Balance in bank, savings	27,423.91
Furniture & fixtures, office	4,029.05
Furniture & fixtures, household	1,024.82

Accounts Receivable

E. O. Lardie	52.08
L. Conley	252.06
W. E. Tighe	208.05
T. J. Coughlin	3,904.87
Sorority	3.83
O. Border	650.00
Fr. Lynch	98.18
Total Assets	$30,944.22

Liabilities

Reserve for depreciation		
Office furniture	$ 283.33	
Household furniture	75.67	
Accounts Payable		
Rev. Chas. E. Coughlin	187.16	
Total Liabilities	546.16	
Gain	30,398.06	
		$30,944.22

The League of the Little Flower books were audited on December 31, 1928

Appendix B

RADIO LEAGUE OF THE LITTLE FLOWER, INCORPORATED
ANNUAL REPORTS, 1930-1941[a]
(AS OF DECEMBER 31 OF PRECEDING YEAR)

	1930	*1933*	*1934*	*1935*
Assets				
Real estate	$	$	$	$
Goods, chattels, merchandise, material and other tangible property	5,282.95	9,104.91	9,646.91	
Cash on hand	34,045.27	58.85	34,654.33	5,753.61
Value of credits owing to the corporation	5,156.16	332.48	100.00	545.12
All other property (specify kinds) Office furniture and fixtures				
Library				
Total	$ 44,484.38	$ 9,496.24	$ 44,401.24	$ 6,298.73
Liabilities				
Liability on real estate mortgage				
Liability on chattel mortgage				
Liability on all other secured indebtedness	5,579.61	None		
Liability on all unsecured indebtedness			13,613.07	
Other liabilities Outstanding bills			25,756.33	
Total	$ 5,579.61	None	$ 39,369.40	None

[a]Figures for 1931 and 1932 not available.
[b]Note that the total is off by a penny.

1936	1937	1938	1939	1940	1941
$	$ 14,260.25	$ 49,514.66	$ 99,317.58	$ 99,317.58	$ 99,419.91
45,500.00	54,406.64	7,775.73	64,389.95	9,000.00	9,000.00
7,705.39	12,002.71	22,671.59	190,680.63	77,375.09	44,951.75
26,153.33	125,117.77	116,355.51	118,151.49	217,481.49	188,768.13
				842.72	1,368.46
					14,500.00
$ 79,358.72	$205,787.37	$196,297.49	$472,539.65	$404,016.89[b]	$358,008.25
	5,672.17	4,532.20			
		1,742.44	3,557.18	2,790.00	4,716.72
None	$ 5,672.17	$ 6,274.64	$ 3,557.18	$ 2,790.00	$ 4,716.72

Appendix C

RADIO LEAGUE OF THE LITTLE FLOWER, INCORPORATED
BALANCE SHEETS, SEPTEMBER 30, 1935-1940

	1935	*1936*
Assets		
Cash and bank	$ 23,443.56	$ 26,678.79
Investments	54,406.64	54,406.64
Real estate	7,263.65	8,368.15
Stock–Social Justice Pub. Co.		1,000.00
Social Justice Poor Society		
Social Justice Pub. Co.		(116,528.88)
Notes receivable		
Chas. F. Coughlin	(442.27)	2,545.85
Nat. Union for Social Justice	4,413.22	(86.78)
R. Moynahan		
H. Roll		14.75
C. Guthvere	145.00	35.00
A. Mathews	125.00	
Condon Printing Co.		
Cuneo Press		
Rev. J. Contway	100.00	100.00
St. Therese Parish	23.43	
Mass account	40.00	(70.00)
Office furniture and fixtures		
Choir	1,277.50	
Checks returned		
Bondy Library		
	$ 90,795.73	$ (23,536.48)
Liabilities		
H. & H. Taylor		
Bondy		
Total		
Balance	90,795.73	(23,536.48)
	$ 90,795.73	$ (23,536.48)

1937	1938	1939	1940
$ 22,606.49	$ 74,277.89	$ 77,360.09	$ 44,951.75
7,755.73	202,429.58	9,000.00	9,000.00
36,713.77	95,426.61	99,317.58	99,419.91
1,000.00			
	1,000.00	1,000.00	
(33.519.10)	112,383.13	111,383.13	71,383.13
		104,000.00	117,200.00
5,052.53	2,956.11		
2,500.00	800.00		
14.75			
205.68			
2,800.00	1,914.59	998.36	
	5,711.48		
100.00	100.00	100.00	100.00
	20,000.00		
(375.00)		15.00	50.00
544.50	842.72	842.72	1,368.46
			35.00
			14,500.00
$ 45,399.35	$517,842.11	$404,016.88	$358,008.25
		2,790.00	1,716.72
			3,000.00
		2,790.00	4,716.72
45,399.35	517,842.11	401,226.88	353,291.53
$ 45,399.35	$517,842.11	$404,016.88	$358,008.25

Appendix D

RADIO LEAGUE OF THE LITTLE FLOWER, INCORPORATED
CASH RECEIPTS AND DISBURSEMENTS
FOR THE YEARS ENDED SEPTEMBER 30, 1936–1940

	1936		1937	
Cash Receipts				
Revenue				
Enrollments	$ 21,419.45		$ 32,016.11	
Donations	184,497.41		86,677.47	
God's Poor Society				
Rents	17,950.00		4,100.00	
Investment income	1,091.14		20,760.07	
Entertainments				
Knowledge			62,889.75	
Carter book				
Bulk sales–Social Justice				
Pub. Co.			198,026.58	
Commissions–Social Justice				
Pub. Co.				
Sale of Social Justice				
Pub. Stock	——		——	
		$225,399.47		$404,469.9█
Liquidations				
Investments			46,650.91	
Nat. Union for Social Justice	4,500.00			
Social Justice Pub. Co.	116,526.88			
Social Justice Poor Society				
Chas. E. Coughlin				
Choir	1,277.50			
C. Guthvere	110.00			
A. Matthews	125.00			
H. Roll				
R. Moynahan				
Condon Printing Co.				
Cuneo Press				
St. Therese Parish	——		——	
		122,339.38		46,650.9█
Deposits (Mass account)		110.00		305.0█
Total		$347,848.85		$451,425.8█

1938	1939	1940

1938		1939		1940
$ 14,607.02		$ 13,056.75		$ 19,031.00
88,561.48		76,803.75		15,344.44
144,126.66				
3,915.00		6,831.00		12,707.56
587,79		5,563.42		2,444.57
36,291.20				
				23,755.98
143,851.01				
142,475.50				
				9,000.00
	$574,415.66		$102,254.92	$ 82,283.55
3,198.24		193,429.58		
		1,000.00		40,000.00
				1,000.00
		2,956.11		
205.68				
14.75				
1,700.00		800.00		
885.41		916.23		998.36
		5,711.48		
		20,000.00		
	6,004.08		224,813.40	41,998.36
	$580,419.74		$327,068.32	$124,281.91

(continued next pages)

	1936	1937
Cash Disbursements		
Cost of Carter book	$	$
Cost of souvenir book		
Office salaries	17,705.12	17,477.65
Stationery & printing	10,357.79	12,597.16
Postage	4,667.50	7.156.55
Freight and express		363.41
Insurance	975.98	271.15
Janitor supplies		655.49
Telephone & telegraph	1,296.98	1,277.10
Interest payments	995.50	279.90
Taxes		342.09
Miscellaneous office expense	1,698:28	1,493.95
Light, gas & heat	3,767.61	2,578.21
Bank service charge		
Decorating & small repairs		
Legal expense		79.00
Books		
Expenses Young property		
Advertising		
Premiums		
Contest #4		
President's salary	2,600.00	2,600.00
Choir	1,089.50	44.00
Traveling		3,519.88
Mich. sales tax		459.69
Broadcasting services		105,984.11
St. Therese Parish		
Building church	260,766.66	
Construction salaries	6,227.91	3,046.27
Reliquary & grotto	11,540.17	1,158.75
Donations	15,998.00	168,602.94
Misc. expense	21.25	346.85
Church goods		2,814.21
Rectory upkeep		1,044.99
Garage annex		
School expense		
Miscellaneous donations		1,360.80
Gertrude H. Coogan–		
Collaborating fee		
Purchases, advances & loans		
Social Justice Pub. Co.	1,000.00	83,009.78
Nat'l. Union for Social		
Justice		86.78
Chas. E. Coughlin	2,988.12	2,506.68
H. Roll	14.75	
Loan–R. Moynahan		2,500.00
Cuneo Press		
Printing contract advance		2,800.00
Checks returned		
Employees		170.68
St. Therese Parish		
Notes receivable		
Bondy Library		
Mass account		
Real estate	1,104.50	36,497.62
Investments		
Office furniture & fixtures		544.50
	$344,815.62	$463,670.19

1938	1939	1940
$	$	$ 56,191.75
		7,268.40
20,705.93	28,767.30	15,748.00
9,926.02	1,603.12	2,072.17
5,503.96	737.50	1,631.00
212.37	256.05	416.77
441.10	297.47	1,246.31
243.23	373.59	44.93
833.74	1,277.35	2,789.79
238.27	184.03	196.76
825.20	1,633.45	3,153.09
706.94	677.98	501.03
1,618.75	2,111.63	2,204.85
	21.27	64.33
	62.95	102.50
90.05	12.53	339.18
	31.20	11.74
723.31	689.89	1,507.00
811.21	331.31	
12,198.33	485.14	
	831.51	
2,000.00	2,100.00	
150.00		
22,551.56	167,760.00	15,000.00
215.47		
3,222.66		
3,886.56	2,899.05	
3,707.38		
9.49		
1,168.48	2,936.83	19,729.30
9,982.89		
145,902.23		
5,711.48		
		35.00
20,000.00		
	104,000.00	13,200.00
		11,500.00
375.00	15.00	35.00
58,712.84	3,890.97	1,175.61
197,872.09		
298.22		525.74
$530,844.76	**$323,986.12**	**$156,690.25**

Appendix E

NATIONAL UNION FOR SOCIAL JUSTICE
ANNUAL REPORTS, 1935–1943
(AS OF DECEMBER 31 OF PRECEDING YEAR)

	1935	1936	1937	1938–1943
Assets				
Cash on hand	None	$ 8,621.79	$37,628.27	
Value of credits owing to the corporation		26,800.00		
	None	$35,121.79	$37,628.27	None
Liabilities				
Liability on all unsecured indebtedness	$8,945.69			
Total	$8,945.69	None	None	None

Appendix F

SOCIAL JUSTICE PUBLISHING COMPANY
BALANCE SHEETS, 1937–1943 (AS OF DECEMBER 31 OF PRECEDING YEAR)

	1937	1938	1939	1940	1941	1942	1943
Assets							
Cash	$ 65,711.02	$ 43,567.50	$ 65,786.30	$ 93,272.89	$ 89,299.41	$ 64,219.88	$ 846.72
Notes & accounts receivable			5,048.40	1,004.70	1,000.00	1,000.00	71,258.43
Investments							
Defense bonds						25,000.00	
Deferred charges							
Repairs		705.88					
Capital assets							
Land	13,711.59	14,163.45	14,222.16			3,849.60	3,330.80
Furniture & fixtures	13.91	96.26	1,852.74	1,961.12	2,510.24	806.05	1,125.07
Less reserve for depreciation		5.51		304.49	528.06	566.81	
Deferred broadcasting expenses					35,209.10	598.86	
Leasehold improvements							
Total	$ 89,436.52	$120,870.33	$ 86,909.60	$ 95,934.22	$127,490.69	$ 93,629.10	$227,225.01
Liabilities							
Notes & accounts payable	121,480.90	158,209.51	130,734.06	115,413.26	80,742.67	7,489.83	82,225.00
Accrued expenses	438.47	212.44	235.39	732.52	290.95		
Other liabilities							
Subscriptions paid in advance	103,588.89	37,406.80	85,098.29	115,190.62	73,172.61	72,992.06	84,440.58
Federal income taxes					20,898.99	32,335.54	1,588.42
Capital stock							
Common stock	1,000.00	1,000.00	1,000.00	1,000.00	1,000.00	1,000.00	1,000.00
Total	226,508.26	196,828.75	217,567.74	232,336.40	176,105.22	113,817.43	169,254.00
Deficit	571.74	75,958.42	130,658.14	136,402.18	48,614.53	20,188.33	
Profit							57,971.01
Total liabilities	$225,936.52	$120,870.33	$ 86,909.60	$ 95,934.22	$127,490.69	$ 93,629.10	$227,225.01

Appendix G

SOCIAL JUSTICE POOR SOCIETY
ANNUAL REPORTS, 1938 and 1939
(AS OF DECEMBER 31 OF PRECEDING YEAR)

	1938	Amended 1938	1939
Assets			
All other property (specify)			
One hundred shares in Social Justice Publishing Company		$1,000.00	
Ten shares in Social Justice Publishing Company		_____	$1,000.00
Total		$1,000.00	$1,000.00
Liabilities			
Surplus	_____	$1,000.00	$1,000.00
Total	None	$1,000.00	$1,000.00

Appendix H

CONTRIBUTORS OF ARTICLES TO *SOCIAL JUSTICE*

Politicians

Senator Homer Bone of Washington was a consistent and conscientious liberal. Yet, in an era when many well-meaning Americans believed in and promoted isolationism, Bone wrote an article for *Social Justice* urging the United States to place a prompt ban on arms to belligerent nations (*Social Justice*, September 27, 1937).

Senator William E. Borah of Idaho, in a Senate career lasting from 1907 to 1940, came to be regarded as one of the giants of Congress. He believed that war was always the eternal enemy of democracy, the friend of communism and the father of fascism. Borah's isolationist views were in harmony with the editorial views of *Social Justice* and in articles appearing in the journal he stressed the importance of the United States' avoiding involvement in a war (*Social Justice*, January 11, 1938; February 27, 1939).

Congressman Fred Crawford of Michigan was a foe of Roosevelt's fiscal policies, who also attacked the President for limiting freedom of the press. His one article in *Social Justice* typified his antipathy to President Roosevelt (*Social Justice*, April 25, 1938).

Congressman George Dondero of Michigan represented the congressional district in which Father Coughlin resided and was a close friend of the Royal Oak priest. Dondero represented the know-nothing congressmen who all too frequently got elected to office. Dondero was lauded by *Social Justice* and Gerald L. K.

Smith's *Cross and Flag*. He labeled Albert Einstein a communist, and made anti-Semitic remarks in Congress (Anti-Defamation League File on Dondero). In *Social Justice*, Dondero criticized the New Deal for being communist-oriented (*Social Justice*, February 5, 1940).

Senator Lynn Frazier of North Dakota was another anti–New Dealer, who favored an inflationary fiscal policy as a means of helping small, poor farmers. This was reflected in one article Frazier wrote for *Social Justice* (March 11, 1940).

Democratic Congressman Arthur Lamneck of Ohio was an extreme isolationist who wished to impose an embargo on all loans, credits and exports to any nation involved in war. Lamneck also voted against the Wages and Hours bill in 1936 and, on the whole, was a vigorous opponent of the New Deal (*New York Times*, January 14, 1938; July 16, 1936). The one article he wrote for *Social Justice* was typical of the views he expressed in Congress (*Social Justice*, May 10, 1938).

Congressman William Lemke of North Dakota was the presidential candidate on Father Coughlin's Union party ticket in the 1936 presidential election. Lemke was a spokesman for the small farmer and favored a cheap money fiscal policy. Along with Senator William Frazier, he was co-author of a bill which would have placed a moratorium on debts of farmers (*Social Justice*, May 3, 1937).

Senator Ernest Lundeen of Minnesota emulated Shipstead in his isolationist position. He once was described as a "stooge" of George Sylvester Viereck. Some of Lundeen's speeches were written by Viereck and he was active in placing material published by Viereck in the *Congressional Record*. Lundeen, like Shipstead, also used his office to mail at taxpayers' expense, under the franking privilege for members of Congress, reprints of material issued by Viereck (O. John Rogge, *The Official German Report*, pp. 266–267, 152–153, 163, 166, 171). In an article for *Social Justice*, Lundeen urged that European nations pay their remaining World War I debts owed this country before the United States should even consider any involvement in European affairs (*Social Justice*, April 29, 1940).

Congressman John J. O'Connor of New York was chairman of the House Rules Committee. At one time Father Coughlin and O'Connor were enemies; Father Coughlin protested his renomination for office in 1936 and then advocated his defeat for reelection. But on the eve of the 1938 elections, President Roosevelt was attempting to purge O'Connor from his House seat because of his consistent opposition to New Deal policies and legislation. *Social Justice* then called for the reelection of O'Connor, and printed an article by him in which he outlined his reasons for opposing Roosevelt's political views (*Social Justice*, July 11, 1938; September 12, 1938).

Robert Owen was a former senator from Oklahoma when he wrote for *Social Justice*. As a senator, Owen had served as chairman of the United States Senate Committee on Banking and Currency. In this capacity he worked closely with Father Coughlin in an effort to create a central bank and to remonetize silver. He also worked closely with Robert Hemphill and Father Coughlin to carry out this program. Owen's articles in *Social Justice* stressed the necessity of a central bank and were critical of New Deal fiscal policies (*Social Justice*, May 31, 1937; June 7, 1937; June 14, 1937).

Congressman Wright Patman of Texas is chairman of the House Banking Committee. Patman has been a consistent critic of the Federal Reserve Board, which, he believes, is controlled by the great eastern banking houses. In earlier years Patman desired to curb the activities of large chain stores and favored policies which would aid small banks to be more competitive against larger banks. His writings in *Social Justice* favored a generally inflationary policy (*Social Justice*, April 26, 1937).

Senator Henrik Shipstead of Minnesota was an ardent isolationist, elected to the Senate three times on the Farmer-Labor party ticket, and once on the Republican party ticket, in the period from 1922 to 1946. He and Senator Langer were the only senators to vote against United States entry into the United Nations. He opposed passage of the Selective Service Act and any aid to England prior to United States entry into World War II. Shipstead used his senatorial franking privileges to mail a great deal of material written by George Sylvester Viereck, and also inserted pro-Axis material into the *Congressional Record*. In an article for *Social Justice*, Shipstead advised homeowners and farmowners on how to keep their mortgages from being foreclosed (*Social Justice*, August 21, 1939).

Senator Elmer Thomas, Democrat from Oklahoma, opposed all immigration into the United States. He was lauded by Gerald L. K. Smith's *Cross and Flag*, and was a warm personal friend of Father Coughlin. In *Social Justice* Thomas criticized United States efforts to remain on the gold standard (*Social Justice*, February 19, 1939).

Spokesmen for the Far Right

Major James Strachey Barnes was an Englishman from a prominent family who was personally decorated by Mussolini. He wrote many articles for *Social Justice* that indicated his pro-fascist sympathies. Barnes was very strong in his praise for Mussolini, favored Germany in the Czech crisis, and justified the German invasion of Norway. He advocated a Jewish solution which would lead to the establishment of a Jewish national homeland. Barnes denied being anti-Jewish, claiming "that some of my best friends are Jewish." He also chastised Germans for believing that they were racially superior (*Social Justice*, June 27, 1938; June 3, 1940; October 10, 1938; December 5, 1938; June 3, 1940; February 27, 1939).

Merwin Hart, who was president of the New York Economic Council, vehemently opposed Roosevelt and the New Deal because he believed that the President and his supporters were communists. Secretary of the Interior Ickes once described Hart as being fascist-minded (*New York Times*, December 18, 1940). Hart opposed legislation establishing the New York State Commission Against Discrimination. In the 1950s Hart was a strong supporter of Nasser against Israel. In an article he wrote for *Social Justice*, Hart commended Franco and his cause and labeled all Loyalists communists (*Social Justice*, January 30, 1939).

J. B. Matthews, who supposedly wrote an article which appeared in the June 5, 1939 issue of *Social Justice* on the threat of communism to the United States, was a former communist who eventually became a supporter of Senator Joseph McCarthy. He was director of research for the Dies committee in the late 1930s, and later became research director for the McCarthy committee. He was dismissed from the latter position after stating that seven thousand American Protestant clergymen served the Kremlin.

Matthews denied that he had ever written the article which appeared in *Social Justice*. On August 10, 1939, Matthews wrote to Father Coughlin, protesting the appearance of the article in *Social Justice*. Matthews charged Coughlin with misrepresentation and pointed out that the article was actually a reprint of testimony he had given before the Special Committee on Un-American Activities in August, 1938.

The letter from J. B. Matthews to Father Coughlin indicates the possibility that other articles appearing in the journal may have been used without the authorization of those to whom they were attributed. Matthews' letter, however, was the only item discovered by this author which casts doubt on the reliability of the contents of the articles written for *Social Justice* by the individuals discussed above.

Amos Pinchot, one of the founders of the America First Committee, was a strong supporter of Colonel Charles Lindbergh. He was the brother of Gifford Pinchot and, along with him, had been a prime mover in organization of the Bull Moose party. He defended pacifists during World War I and was active in the defense of Sacco and Vanzetti. Pinchot intensely disliked Roosevelt because of his fear that the President wanted to make himself a dictator and lead the country into war. In articles Pinchot wrote for *Social Justice* he accused Roosevelt of moving the government towards autocracy (*Social Justice*, January 3, 1938).

Patrick Scanlan, as mentioned in the text, was one of Father Coughlin's staunchest supporters and a regular contributor to *Social Justice*. Scanlan usually attacked the communist menace in the United States (*Social Justice*, November 22, 1937; January 24, 1938). Scanlan was managing editor of the *Brooklyn Tablet*, which frequently featured the transcripts of Father Coughlin's radio speeches on page one. Scanlan was an enthusiastic supporter of

Franco and was associated with Merwin K. Hart and Joseph Kamp in the American Union for Nationalist Spain. The *Tablet* printed material directly or indirectly attacking opponents of anti-Semitism, and Jewish as well as nonsectarian human relations agencies. Scanlan holds LL.D. degrees from St. Francis College of Brooklyn and from Villanova and Fordham universities.

Kenneth Scott, in an article for *Social Justice*, outlined the importance of the United States' remaining aloof from European affairs (*Social Justice*, January 30, 1939). Scott was a member of the faculty of Western Reserve University and was in Germany at the outbreak of World War II. He was a close friend of Richard Sallet, attaché and representative of the Ministry of Propaganda of the German Embassy in Washington. He was closely linked to political extremists such as Joseph P. Kamp and Reverend Gerald Winrod and was indicted for sedition during World War II.

Roland Strunk was a correspondent for the *Volkischer Beobachter*, which was the official organ of the German-American Bund. Most of its stories were released through the World Service, which was the Nazi propaganda agency in the Western Hemisphere. *Social Justice* printed a portion of a story filed by Strunk through the World Service, which stressed that the war in Spain was being fought between Christians, on the one side, and atheistic communists on the other (*Social Justice*, March 15, 1937).

George Edward Sullivan, a Washington, D.C., attorney, represented General George Van Horn Moseley, the pro-fascist, former Assistant Chief of Staff of the United States Army, when that individual testified before the President's committee. Sullivan was also a friend of Elizabeth Dilling, William Dudley Pelley and Reverend Gerald Winrod, all sympathizers with fascist ideology. *Social Justice* printed excerpts from Sullivan's pamphlet *Wolves in Sheep's Clothing*, which associates Judaism with the worldwide communist conspiracy (*Social Justice*, November 29, 1937; George E. Sullivan, *Wolves in Sheep's Clothing* [Washington, D.C.: The Sodality Union, 1937]).

Jennings C. Wise's articles emphasized that Roosevelt had dictatorial ambitions and that he was instituting communist reforms in the United States (*Social Justice*, August 29, 1938). Wise, the son of a former governor of Virginia, was an associate of Upton Close, George Deatherage and Gerald Winrod, and at times spoke at the same meetings as the above-mentioned gentlemen. Wise, speaking of the Western world, said that "Jewry has weakened its mentality" (Letter from Jennings C. Wise to a Mr. Thompson, November 28, 1955, in Anti-Defamation League file).

Clergymen

Reverend Edward Lodge Curran, a Brooklyn priest, was president of the International Catholic Truth Society. He was Father Coughlin's friend and had a powerful voice in shaping the policies of the Brooklyn archdiocese. Curran was known to have made many anti-Semitic utterances (Anti-Defamation League file on Curran). But although viewed by many as an anti-Semite, he did criticize Charles Lindbergh after the aviator said that the entire Jewish race was seeking to get America involved in war. On the other hand, Father Curran was a long-time contributor to *Common Sense*, which *The Legionnaire*, the official publication of the American Legion's Department of New York, described as violently anti-Semitic. Father Curran's articles in *Social Justice* urged that America remain aloof from European affairs, criticized Jews for not condemning communism, sang the praises of Franco, and criticized President and Mrs. Roosevelt (*Social Justice*, February 7, 1938; April 4, 1938; April 18, 1938; May 6, 1938; June 20, 1938; July 4, 1938; July 11, 1938; August 1, 1938; August 15, 1938; November 7, 1938; December 19, 1938; July 31, 1939).

Reverend Joseph Deisz, a Queens, New York, priest and a friend of Father Edward Lodge Curran and Patrick Scanlan, was known for his anti-Semitic views. In *Social Justice*, Reverend Deisz wrote about the power of the big banking houses in moving Europe into war (*Social Justice*, November 27, 1939).

Reverend Urban Freundt, the dean and rector of St. Francis Seminary, Cincinnati, Ohio, was considered one of the outstanding Church educators of his time. In an article for *Social Justice*,

Freundt wrote about the social contributions of the Church under Pope Pius XII (*Social Justice*, March 13, 1939).

Reverend John F. Noll, bishop of Fort Wayne, Indiana, supported Coughlin's formation of a Christian Front to oppose what he called the anti-Christian Front which was propagating communism in the United States (*Social Justice*, August 8, 1938). In one article for *Social Justice* Bishop Noll cited Father Coughlin as being one of the great leaders in the fight against communism.

Reverend John A. O'Brien, Ph.D., LL.D., was a member of the faculty of Notre Dame University, the former head of the Newman Foundation at Illinois University and a teacher at Oxford. He was a prominent isolationist, whose articles in *Social Justice* were concerned with exhortation of readers to keep America out of war (*Social Justice*, December 4, 1939; January 28, 1940; March 25, 1940; January 27, 1941).

Other Contributors

Francis Donohue, a noted educator, served as director of academic planning for the State University of New York. He also was a faculty member at the University of Detroit, Gannon College, Villanova and St. Bonaventure. He married Jean Perrin Schwartz, the daughter of E. Perrin Schwartz, who was herself a frequent contributor to *Social Justice*. Donohue, in one article, and Jean Perrin Schwartz, in several articles, wrote about the evils of communism and criticized the New Deal (*Social Justice*, May 9, 1938; July 4, 1938; April 8, 1940).

Mrs. Donohue told of her many recollections of Father Coughlin in an interview with this author. Most vivid is her remembrance of the close control Father Coughlin exercised over the contents of *Social Justice*. "He was an amazing man. He knew everything about every subject imaginable."

Horace Frommelt, professor and chairman of the Mechanical Engineering Department at Marquette University, was a prominent Catholic educator. Frommelt was very concerned with the scarcity of jobs and the fact that high school students were following courses of study that would not train them for decent jobs.

His articles for *Social Justice* focused on giving vocational guidance to young readers of the journal (*Social Justice*, October 11, 1937; October 18, 1937).

Judge Joseph Gillis, a Detroit Recorders Court judge, wrote a series of articles warning consumers of what to look for when making purchases and warning *Social Justice*'s readers of the dangers of installment buying (May 23, 1938).

Robert Hemphill, a frequent author of articles dealing with the money crisis facing Americans, consistently attacked Roosevelt and the New Deal (*Social Justice*, April 18, 1938). Hemphill was regarded as well informed on financial questions and was an adviser to Father Coughlin on monetary matters. On occasion, the priest even used Hemphill to present his monetary views to congressional legislators.

Edward Kennedy was the national secretary of the National Farmers Union and a close friend of Father Coughlin. His articles in *Social Justice* were quite critical of New Deal agricultural policies (*Social Justice*, December 31, 1936).

Lawrence Lucey, a Brooklyn lawyer, was considered one of the most prominent Catholic laymen in the United States. He was a frequent contributor to such journals as *Catholic World, Commonweal* and *Forum*. His writings in these magazines and in *Social Justice* reflected a basically anti–New Deal point of view (*Social Justice*, March 28, 1938).

Frederick Soddy was a noted English chemist and economist who was awarded a Nobel Prize in Chemistry in 1921. He opposed the large international bankers and urged monetary reform that would result in greater equity in the distribution of wealth. His material for *Social Justice* discussed methods of redistributing wealth (Frederick Soddy, *Wealth, Virtual Wealth and Debt* [London: Allen and Unwin, 1926]. See *Social Justice*, May 24, 1937).

Louis Ward, who wrote an authorized biography of the priest in 1933, was the Union party senatorial candidate in Michigan in the 1936 election. Ward's articles in *Social Justice* usually were concerned with domestic affairs and reflected the standard anti–New Deal views which were constantly repeated in *Social Justice* (May

24, 1937; June 14, 1937; November 1, 1937; December 25, 1939; January 15, 1940).

Spokesmen with Opposing Views

Social Justice allowed two spokesmen who differed from its usual editorial stance to use the pages of the magazine to promulgate their point of view. One article, written by Philip Slomovitz on the "Protocols of the Elders of Zion," was discussed in an earlier chapter. The second article was written by the Reverend Wenceslaus Michalicka, chaplain of the National Alliance of Bohemian Catholics, a pro-Czechoslovakian organization. This article states Czechoslovakia's position in the confrontation with Germany, praises Thomas Masaryk as a fighter for freedom, and emphasizes that Czechoslovakia in the twenty years of its existence had advanced the cause of justice and democracy. The article probably appeared in *Social Justice* (November 28, 1938) as the result of the protests made by many American Catholics of Bohemian background who opposed the position of *Social Justice* during the Munich crisis.

Appendix I

A Comparison of the *Social Justice* Article, "An Explanation of the Czech Myth" from the September 19, 1938, Issue with Fichte Bund Pamphlet 1102 (in English), "What Do You Know About Czechoslovakia?"

"AN EXPLANATION OF THE 'CZECH MYTH'"	"WHAT DO YOU KNOW ABOUT CZECHOSLOVAKIA?"
SOCIAL JUSTICE September 19, 1938	FICHTE BUND Hamburg, Germany

(1)

The original government of Czechoslovakia was set up in Paris, under instructions from the French Foreign Minister M. Pichon, to Dr. Edouard Benes.

(1)

A letter dated June 29, 1918, addressed by M. Pichon, the former French Foreign Minister, to Dr. Benes, contained the reference to a Czechoslovakian National Council. . . . The Government of this State was compelled to have its seat in Paris as it had no country to call its own.

(2)

Germany was obliged to cede large tracts of land in the Ratibor district. Austria had to part with Bohemia and Moravia and a part of Silesia. Hungary lost the Carpathian-Russia region, as well as Slovakia and the Pressburg part of Burgenland.

(2)

Germany was called upon to give up great tracts of land in the Ratibor district. Austria had to part with Bohemia and Moravia, and a part of Silesia. Hungary was to lose Carpathian-Russia; Slovakia, and the Pressburg part of Burgenland. The struggle for the Czech Duchy led to a fight with Poland.

(3)

Already in 1919, the antagonism was so pronounced that Father Hlinka, who died only last month and who was the Slovak leader, left with a deputation for Paris to make a plebiscite for the Slovaks inasmuch as the contemporary popular catchphrase was "self-determination for all peoples." He was not even given a hearing in France, and on returning home the group was arrested and thrown into prison.

(4)

In 1918, President Masaryk had come to America and concluded the "Pittsburgh Agreement" dated May 30, 1919, guaranteeing to the Slovaks their own administration, parliament, and judiciary.

(5)

Following the setting up of Czechoslovakia, the Sudeten Germans demanded fair representation as guaranteed in Section IV of a report known as "Memoire III," which says: "The Czechoslovakia Republic is prepared to acknowledge the international laws enacted on behalf of minorities; it is prepared to go beyond the prescribed limits. Official positions should be open to all citizens. The language of the minorities should avail, be admissable, and the rights of minorities to possess their own schools, judges, courts, would never be disputed. German would be the second official language and

(3)

But already in 1919 the antagonism was so marked that Father Hlinka, the Slovak leader, left with a deputation for Paris to demand a plebiscite for the Slovaks. Without attempting to get in touch with Father Hlinka, the Czechs were able to have him summarily deported from France. When the deputation returned home, its members were arrested and thrown into prison.

(4)

In 1918 Prof. Masaryk, who was then living in Paris, travelled to the United States for the purpose of negotiating with innumerable Slovaks who had emigrated. He succeeded in concluding an Agreement with them at Pittsburgh on May 30, 1918, which, in the event of a common State, guaranteed the Slovaks their own administration, their own parliament, and their own judicature.

(5)

In order to pacify the originators of the Versailles Peace Treaty, they were given a Report known as "Memoire III." Section IV of this Report promises inter alia: "The Czechoslovakian Republic is prepared to acknowledge the international laws enacted in behalf of minorities; it is even prepared to go beyond the limits. Official positions should be open to all citizens. The language of the minorities should avail, be admissable, and the rights of minorities to possess their own schools, judges, and courts would never be disputed. German would be the second official language of no discrimination would ever be shown against the German section of the population. The country would be governed in a similar way as Switzerland with Canton."

(6)

On February 12, 1937, Lord Rothermere published an article in *The Daily Mail* under the heading "Prisoners in Czechoslovakia." In this article, Lord Rothermere referred to the hypocritical conduct of the Czech representatives in Paris, and maintained that they duped the Peace Conference representatives into creating Czechoslovakia, and that the gigantic swindle has lasted many years and that it was now time for revealing the facts.

the country, and no discrimination would ever be shown against the German section of the population. The country would be governed in a similar way as Switzerland."

(6)

On February 12, 1937 Lord Rothermere published an article in *The Daily Mail* under the heading "Prisoners in Czechoslovakia." In this article Lord Rothermere, referring to the conduct of the Czechs in Paris, stated that the Peace Conference was bluffed into creating Czechoslovakia, that this swindle has lasted many years, and that it was now time for revealing the true facts.

Appendix J

1. Liberty of conscience and education.
2. Just, living, annual wage.
3. Nationalization of important public resources.
4. Private ownership of all other property.
5. Control of private property for public good.
6. Abolition of Federal Reserve Banking System and establishment of a government-owned Central Bank.
7. Restoration to Congress of its sole right to coin and regulate the value of money.
8. Maintain cost of living on an even keel.
9. Cost of production plus a fair profit for the farmer.
10. Labor's right to organize.
11. Recall of non-productive bonds.
12. Abolition of tax-exempt bonds.
13. Broadened base of taxation on basis of ownership and capacity to pay.
14. Simplification of government and lower taxes.
15. Conscription of wealth as well as men in event of war.
16. Sanctity of human rights preferred to sanctity of property; with government's chief concern for the poor.

INDEX